Theorizing Justice

Theorizing Justice

Critical Insights and Future Directions

Krushil Watene and Jay Drydyk

ROWMAN &
LITTLEFIELD
INTERNATIONAL
London • New York

Published by Rowman & Littlefield International, Ltd.
Unit A, Whitacre Mews, 26-34 Stannary Street, London SE11 4AB
www.rowmaninternational.com

Rowman & Littlefield International, Ltd. is an affiliate of Rowman & Littlefield
4501 Forbes Boulevard, Suite 200, Lanham, Maryland 20706, USA
With additional offices in Boulder, New York, Toronto (Canada), and London (UK)
www.rowman.com

Cover image: Te Whanau-A-Rangi, acrylic on board by Ellen Watene-Hohepa

British Library Cataloguing in Publication Information Available
A catalogue record for this book is available from the British Library

ISBN: HB 978-1-78348-404-1
ISBN: PB 978-1-78348-405-8

Library of Congress Cataloging-in-Publication Data

Names: Watene, Krushil, editor.
Title: Theorizing justice : critical insights and future directions / edited by Krushil Watene and Jay Drydyk.
Description: New York : Rowman & Littlefield International, 2016. | Includes bibliographical references and index.
Identifiers: LCCN 2016015677 (print) | LCCN 2016026462 (ebook) | ISBN 9781783484041 (cloth : alk. paper) | ISBN 9781783484058 (pbk. : alk. paper) | ISBN 9781783484065 (electronic)
Subjects: LCSH: Justice.
Classification: LCC JC578 .T467 2016 (print) | LCC JC578 (ebook) | DDC 320.01/1--dc23
LC record available at https://lccn.loc.gov/2016015677

™ The paper used in this publication meets the minimum requirements of American National Standard for Information Sciences Permanence of Paper for Printed Library Materials, ANSI/NISO Z39.48-1992.

Printed in the United States of America

Contents

Acknowledgements vii

Preface ix
Jay Drydyk

1 Introduction 1
Krushil Watene

Part I: Critical Insights

2 Theorising about Justice for a Broken World 15
Tim Mulgan

3 Transitional Justice: A Conceptual Map 35
Colleen Murphy

4 What Do We Want from a Theory of Justice? 53
Amartya Sen

5 Utilitarianism and Some of Its Critics: On Some Alternative 'Incomplete' Theories of, and Approaches to, Morality and Justice 75
Mozaffar Qizilbash

Part II: Future Directions

6 Justice as a Virtue: What Can We Expect of Our Allies? 95
Jay Drydyk

7 Justice as Stakeholding 115
Thom Brooks

8 Indigenous Peoples and Justice 133
Krushil Watene

9 Justice in Regulation: Towards a Liberal Account 153
Rutger Claassen

10 The Recognition Gap: Why Labels Matter in Human Rights Protection 173
Stacy J. Kosko

Index 191

Contributors 195

Acknowledgements

I am immensely grateful to Professor Drydyk for all of his guidance and patience on this project. I wish to also thank all of the contributors for their inspiring contributions to this project. I am also extremely grateful to Arielle Stirling and Holly Longair of Carleton University for helping to bring this book together.

Aku mihi nui ki a koutou.

Preface

Jay Drydyk

I was delighted when Krushil Watene asked me to join her in editing this volume. My reason for writing this preface is to acknowledge that this volume resulted from her initiative, to leave the intellectual space of the introduction to her, and to present the volume from my own perspective.

Each of us has a different generational perspective on political philosophy. I was finishing my undergraduate studies when such influential work as *Theory of Justice*, 'Famine, Affluence, and Morality', and 'A Defense of Abortion' were published, and the path that my career took, beginning with Georg Wilhelm Friedrich Hegel and Karl Marx and quickly turning to applied ethics and political philosophy with a focus on international development, would not have been possible, had the way not been cleared for it by pioneers such as John Rawls, Peter Singer, and Judith Jarvis Thomson. Indeed, I take pains to express my gratitude to Rawls in particular every time I begin teaching his work to a new group of students. Since 1971, we have seen an explosion of social and political philosophy with applications to public issues. Conversely, much of this work has also become much more settled. It is tempting to wonder whether analytical political philosophy has entered into some analogue to what Thomas Kuhn once called 'normal science'.

It would be a mistake to make too much of this question. We did not expect the contributors to this volume to give us Copernican revolutions. And, in a sense, the paradigm had never confined itself to routine applications, because one of its essential traits has always been to seek out neglected topics, as many of our contributors have done.

If anything has been paradigmatic in political philosophy over the past forty-five years, it has not been any single theory, though that of Rawls has certainly been preeminent. Rather it has been a certain ambition—I will call it 'the Ambition'—to create normative theories about political power and action that are both comprehensive and defensible. I conceive of the political quite broadly as doing anything that cannot easily be done without enlisting the support of others, so that politics is not just about the state but about citizens (and what they ought to do, for instance, about disaster and famine relief), also including other spheres such as family politics, workplace politics, cultural politics, and more. The Ambition is to carve out a sector within this domain and make claims about necessary and sufficient conditions for having the right structures or doing the right thing within that sector. A theory is a set of such claims; however, the Ambition is not merely to create a theory but to show that it is coherent with a wide range of intuitive judgments about outcomes that are right or wrong, just or unjust, and so on. Rawls's idea of reflective equilibrium captured this coherentist approach to justification in an especially memorable way.

Over time, theory and justification have come apart. Pluralism has been the wedge that split them. As the Ambition spread, philosophers themselves created a variety of rival theories. Those who were sensitive to charges of Eurocentrism recognized yet other reasonable perspectives emerging diversely from political, social and cultural life worldwide. Rawls famously recognized that there were a family of liberal theories, of which his own was just one, and that beyond these there were a variety of other normative perspectives on politics that were reasonable. The effect was to expand the 'we' to whom political structures and practices must be justified, from followers of the Ambition to the wider publics over which power is exercised (arguably both locally and globally). This expansion of the 'jury' from philosophers to the public was also being advocated by Frankfurt philosophers such as Jürgen Habermas, Axel Honneth, and Rainer Forst. The role of theorists needed to shift accordingly. No longer could we merely assess which claims are justifiable to us, coherent with our own considered judgments. Instead we would have to take on the less introspective and hence more difficult task of assessing which claims *ought* to be justifiable to these greater publics from within their own reasonable perspectives.

These considerations led theorists to the threshold of public reason. Since there has already been much debate about what 'public reason' should mean, I should spell out what I mean by this. Some clarity can be gained by distinguishing 'public reason' from 'public reasoning'. By the latter, I mean any actual attempt at justifying political actions or states of affairs. In a word, it is political advocacy; yet it is more than this, for by calling it 'reasoning' we signal that it can be done well or badly. And bad reasoning is not just that which fails to persuade, it is advocacy that *ought not to* persuade. When we consider public advocacy as public reasoning, we are holding it accountable to norms. Some of these are generic: norms of good inference and sound evidence. In addition, some further norms apply specifically to moral or political advocacy, such as universalizability, openness to all relevant arguments, and impartiality towards everyone affected. Debates over the proper meaning of 'public reason' are often debates about the selection and interpretation of these norms. 'Public reason' as I would have it refers not just to the argumentation actually given somewhere on a given political topic, but also further arguments yet to be considered, and the norms by which to sort better arguments from worse. Once we cross this threshold, we recognize that the question 'What does justice require?' can be answered only by asking 'What does public reason require?'

Beyond this threshold, theories of justice do not become irrelevant. On the contrary, if public reason follows the norm of 'open impartiality' as I suggest (following Sen), every theory relevant to a given political question should receive its due consideration. Still, this means that every theory must be weighed against every other, in each application. For some, the Ambition may have been to establish a theory well enough that continued examinations and vindications would not be necessary. Even for those who were more modestly Ambitious, the goal was surely more than creating just one theory among many, but rather to create a theory with sufficient plausibility on its own to be a standard for what is just and right. Across the threshold, the only arbiter of what is just and right is public reason, and so the Ambition is deflated. At best, a successful theory now captures one dimension amongst many that public reason endorses.

If the Ambition to capture justice with a theory has been deflated, what kind of thing is justice, and how can it be conceived? One answer is to reconceive justice from an end state or goal to a multidimensional process. The conditions claimed by Ambitious theories as necessary and sufficient for a fully just state of affairs can be reconceived as necessary components of change towards greater justice. Justice, then, is seen not as a state of affairs but as a multidimensional process of change.

Each of the contributions to this volume charts some new space, beyond the threshold, for theorizing about justice. Tim Mulgan gives the Ambition a decisive deflationary gash by pondering the fates of established theories in a world where resources for human well-being are no longer abundant. Colleen Murphy finds that contexts of transitional justice, in the aftermath of repression and injustice in armed conflict, are also inhospitable to the Ambition, since no single standard gives satisfactory results in different contexts. Krushil Watene argues that justice for indigenous peoples will not be addressed adequately unless theoretical perspectives on justice are expanded to embrace indigenous peoples' own normative ways of thinking.

Three contributions explore alternatives. Amartya Sen's road map for approaching justice as a process of comparative change rather than a 'transcendental' end state has already raised considerable discussion in the literature. Mozaffar Qizilbash carefully contrasts the types and strengths of claims made by utilitarianism, by 'theory' as understood by Rawls, and by the capability 'approaches' advocated by Sen and Nussbaum. My own contribution assumes that we are pursuing greater comparative justice under the guidance of public reason and in this context explores justice as a virtue—in particular that of collectives, movements, and individuals who merit our support as allies in struggles for greater justice.

The remaining contributions exemplify sophisticated post-Ambition thinking about justice. Thom Brooks and Rutger Claassen explore the dimensions of justice for two contexts that theory has rather neglected: Brooks advancing an approach to justice for stakeholders, and Claassen assessing multiple theoretical perspectives on justice in economic regulation. Stacy Kosko attends to groups that are often neglected by theory: ethnic minorities that are overlooked due to gaps within the logic of human rights implementation.

It has been my great pleasure to join Krushil in bringing this volume to publication.

Chapter One

Introduction

Krushil Watene

What does a fully just society and a fully just world look like? What role do concepts like equality, community, freedom, and rights play in answering these questions? Who is responsible for pursuing and realizing justice? Are there limits to the nature and extent of these responsibilities? Theories of social and global justice have dominated political philosophy for over forty years—since the publication of John Rawls's seminal 1971 work *A Theory of Justice*.

The general aim of such theories is to determine how social institutions ought to be arranged such that benefits and burdens are fairly distributed between those who make claims upon them. The aim is to formulate principles that capture these ideal distributive arrangements. Within this way of framing justice, theories come together and pull apart on a number of interrelated concerns, including: 1) how principles of justice are grounded, 2) what the principles ought to be, 3) how just arrangements are measured, 4) what the scope of justice should be, 5) what the relevant units of concern are, and 6) where responsibilities for pursuing and realizing justice ought to lay (Robeyns 2011).

Rawls provides us with the single most influential contemporary theory of justice—one that charted a new course for justice theorizing. By placing the equal worth of all citizens, participatory fairness, and agreement at the forefront of justifiable political principles, Rawls initiated a move away from the dominate theory at the time (Utilitarianism) to create space for an approach to justice which revived the social contract tradition.

Rawls takes questions of justice to arise between contracting parties under conditions of moderate scarcity and limited generosity (Rawls 1971, 126–30; Barry 1978). Contracting parties are individuals in possession of the two moral powers—a capacity for a sense of justice and a conception of the good—and they are situated as equal, rational, mutually disinterested, normal cooperating members of a society over a complete life (Rawls 1971, 3–41; 1993, 40–46; 2001, 18). Contractors are charged with choosing principles to govern a society that they will occupy, and which will regulate the terms of social cooperation between them. The principles are chosen by way of a hypothetical decision-making procedure (the original position) that models contractors under fair conditions (Rawls 1971, ch. 3). These conditions are made possible by the impartiality generated by the veil of ignorance. Behind the veil, individuals are ignorant of their places in society, their natural talents, and their conceptions of the good (Rawls 1971, 136–42). The veil forces contractors to consider the principles from the perspectives of both the most and the least advantaged in society.

According to Rawls, contractors would choose two principles to govern the 'basic structure of society'—social institutions, political constitutions and the like (Rawls 1971, 3). The liberty principle secures basic liberties and freedoms for all (Rawls 1971, 60). The difference principle stipulates that the distribution of primary goods (basic liberties, freedom of movement and choice, powers and prerogatives, income and wealth, the social bases of self-respect), must be: 1) to the maximum benefit of the least advantaged in society, and 2) attached to positions and offices open to all (Rawls 1971, ch. 2). Both principles are constrained by a concern for including diverse and irreconcilable differences within the (modern liberal) state (Rawls 1971, 24; 1993, lectures iv and v). The primary goods are those things that individuals require regardless of their differences. The principles of justice are those which individuals, even with wide-ranging and diverse conceptions of the good life, would agree to. In such a way, Rawls presents a theory that is politically liberal. That is, belonging to a family of liberal theories that (among other things) do not entail or endorse a particular conception of the good, or what Rawls refers to as a 'comprehensive philosophical doctrine' (Rawls 1971, 24, 446–52; 1993, 10, lectures iv and v; Freeman 2007).

A Theory of Justice is concerned with justice as it arises within a single society. For Rawls, it differs in important ways from international justice and the work that he presents in *The Law of Peoples* (Rawls 1999). Rawls's approach does not support the construction of a single original position that includes all members of the global community, but rather a second contract between representatives of 'peoples' (1971, 379). For Rawls, the domestic and international cases are different, and they require different contract situations (Freeman 2007). From this second hypothetical choice situation, different principles (to those in the domestic case) would be chosen to govern interactions between states. These principles broadly include: 1) respect for the freedoms and independence of peoples, 2) taking peoples as equal and party to their own agreements, 3) the right to self-defence but not war, 4) a duty of non-intervention, 5) to honour contracts made, 6) to conform to restrictions on the conduct of war, 7) to honour human rights, and 8) to assist peoples living under unfavourable conditions (Rawls 1999, 37). Rawls's approach to international justice is helpful for understanding his general strategy for dealing with other issues of justice that arise. Rawls first constructs a theory to deal with (what he takes to be) the fundamental case, and then extends the theory to issues that arise outside of that fundamental case at a later stage.

Of course, not all theories of justice take their lead from Rawls. Important and well known critiques of, and alternatives to, Rawls's theory come from libertarians (Nozick 1974), egalitarians (Anderson 1999; Cohen 1997), utilitarians (Harsanyi 1975; Singer 1972, 2002), communitarians (Sandel 1998; Taylor 1989), Marxists (Miller 1974; Nielsen 1980), and feminists (Okin 1987, 1989, 1994; see also Abbey 2013). Rawls's work does, however, remain the most prominent, with almost every aspect of his work built on, modified, and debated (see Freeman 2007, bibliography). Rawls's continuing prominence is most obvious in the recent rise in global justice theories that extend or modify his basic approach. Cosmopolitans remain at the forefront of these extensions and modifications (see, for instance, Beitz 1999; Brock 2009, 2015; Pogge 2008). Charles Beitz and Thomas Pogge were the earliest to contend that the proper application of Rawls to issues of global justice required that the original position be applied to the world as a whole. The same reasons which Rawls used to justify justice at the domestic level apply globally, since nationality (like race, gender, and social class) is also morally arbitrary. Many cosmopolitans advocate global principles of justice on these general grounds—with some extending Rawls's own domestic principles globally (see, for instance, Moellendorf 2002), and others arguing for new or modified principles (see, for instance, Brock 2009; Pogge 2008).

While most of the literature is concerned with global justice, there has also been engagement with other challenges that Rawls did not consider, either at all or in full. These issues include our obligations to future generations (see, for instance, Gosseries and Meyer 2009), our treatment of nonhuman animals (Sunstein and Nussbaum 2004), the inclusion of children (see, for instance, Kittay 1997; Macleod 2010; Nussbaum 2006), and the inclusion of those who suffer disabilities (Nussbaum 2006; Richardson 2006). While some theorists work on providing Rawlsian answers to these issues, others attempt to show that these challenges cannot be adequately dealt with within Rawls's framework. As such, these issues have generated discussion around the usefulness of Rawls's theory for dealing with challenges that stand outside of Rawls's fundamental case. They raise questions for the strategy of restricting justice to this fundamental case, and then dealing with these other issues at a later stage (see, for instance, Mulgan 2006).

One of the most recent, and comprehensive discussions of Rawls's treatment of secondary issues has come from Martha Nussbaum and presented in her *Frontiers of Justice* (Nussbaum 2006). Nussbaum develops an approach to justice informed by Aristotle and Marx. On her account, human beings have rich needs and come to form society based on the kinds of beings they are.

> The person leaves the state of nature (if, indeed, there remains any use for this fiction) not because it is more mutually advantageous to make a deal with others, but because she cannot imagine living well without shared ends and a shared life. Living with and towards others, with both benevolence and justice, is part of the shared public conception of the person that all affirm for political purposes. (Nussbaum 2006, 158)

Not only do we come to form society based on our social and compassionate natures, but we do so as vulnerable, temporal, complex, and unequal (Nussbaum 2006, 69–81). In light of issues of disability, treatment of nonhuman animals, and nationality Nussbaum argues that her capabilities approach (based on this starting point) is better able to include and consider them. The 'classical theory of the social contract cannot solve these problems, even when put in its best form' because it is unable to ask the questions that these issues of justice raise (Nussbaum 2006, 3).

> The social contract tradition conflates two questions that are in principle distinct. "By whom are society's basic principles designed?" And "for whom are society's basic principles designed?" . . . The chosen principles regulate, in the first instance, their dealings with one another. . . . But the "by whom" and the "for whom" questions need not be linked in this way. One might have a theory that held many living beings, human and even nonhuman, are primary subjects of justice, even though they are not capable of participating in the procedure through which principles are chosen. (Nussbaum 2006, 16)

Rawls's contracting conditions do not, and are not able to, include these issues of justice from the start. The fundamental case excludes them from the start. The design of society is flawed in its treatment of these cases. According to Nussbaum, this highlights the urgent need to develop alternative theories able to deal with these (and any other potential) challenges (Nussbaum 2006).[1]

Even more recently, Amartya Sen has gone further than Nussbaum in an important critique of the way justice is theorized—advocating a move away from (what he calls) a 'transcendental approach' to justice, to a more 'comparative approach' (Sen 2006, 2008, 2009). Here, Sen characterizes justice theorizing (with a particular emphasis on Rawls) as transcendental in the sense that it aims to answer the question: what makes a society just? Sen reframes justice in a way that advances an approach to social and global justice that is an ongoing 'work in progress'. Sen's comparative approach asks: What would make society more or less just? Sen's critical insights for how justice theorizing is currently undertaken provides a new framework for theorizing justice. He gives us a different starting point for thinking about justice, and opens up a new debate on the purpose of theories of justice. Nussbaum and Sen press against and challenge the boundaries of justice theorizing in ways that open up space for the development of alternatives.

Like any book about contemporary justice theorizing, this book occupies space that Rawls's work created, and takes inspiration from Rawls's achievements. In particular, this collection draws inspiration from the way that Rawls was able to construct a theory and method that could re-ignite political philosophy and revolutionize how we theorize justice. Rawls's theory was a response to perceived deficiencies in utilitarianism, at a time when the relevance of political philosophy was uncertain, and when contemporary realities posed new problems requiring innovative solutions. Rawls's approach to justice advanced political philosophy in important and valuable ways—most significantly in the way that it showed that political philosophy remained relevant for our lives and our world.

Yet, over forty years after the publication of *A Theory of Justice*, we find that social and global realities present theories of justice with new challenges. Understanding what these new challenges are, and whether contemporary theories are in a position to respond to them, remains significant for the continued relevance of political philosophy for our lives and our world. Recognizing which new challenges call for new theories and approaches, and determining how they might be developed is urgently required. Contemporary political philosophy, and our ideas about justice, must be in a position to respond to this reality. While taking inspiration from Rawls, this book sees itself as building on work that initiates a move toward grounded justice theorizing, and to the development of alternative theories and approaches to justice.

This book has two general aims. The first (in part I) is to present some critical insights that provide us with ways and reasons to rethink justice theorizing. The critical insights are novel, innovative, and challenging. In some ways, they reimagine justice and raise serious doubts about contemporary theories of justice. In others they provide insights for how the development of new theories and approaches might be possible. The second aim (in part II) is to begin to construct a range of starting points for new discussions of justice based on new ideas, new perspectives, and new challenges. These future directions present ideas and perspectives that contemporary theories of justice overlook, and begin to show what justice theorizing might look like if it sought to take these ideas and perspectives seriously. The second section builds on the space that the first section creates, and develops pathways and conversations that take our ideas about, and understandings of, justice in new directions. This book brings fresh and unique insights to how contemporary and potential realities transform theories of justice, and shows how political philosophy might respond.

We open part I with a unique and innovative chapter by Tim Mulgan which brings a futuristic twist to reflections on contemporary theories of justice. Mulgan asks how future people living in a broken world (a world where Rawlsian favourable conditions no longer apply) might think about justice. In particular, he considers how people living in a broken world would respond to modern 'affluent' liberal notions of our rights and freedoms. A broken world perspective highlights the contingency of our theories of justice, and raises questions for the usefulness of our ideas about justice in the future. Such a perspective highlights the need for us to consider not only how our ideas about justice impact on the lives of future people, but also informs how we think about justice today. The chapter provides a novel way of theorizing justice, and raises important challenges for contemporary justice theorizing. An important implication is that reviewing the assumptions we make about justice (here and now) is likely to lead us to recognize that we need to develop alternative theories and approaches.

In the next chapter Colleen Murphy asks how justice applies to cases of wrongdoing in transitional contexts. An important insight is that in transitional contexts, justice often falls short of our ordinary understandings and expectations. On the back of this insight, Murphy argues that transitional justice is a distinctive kind of justice that stands outside of the conceptions of justice presently on offer. Such a conclusion raises serious questions for how we ought to frame justice in different contexts. To accommodate transitional contexts, we need a perspective of justice that is able to account for the various ways in which justice can be pursued and realized. In line with Mulgan, Murphy calls our attention to the need to rethink our conceptions of justice and to make room for the development of alternatives.

Amartya Sen's important and groundbreaking article on justice theorizing provides us with one alternative to ideal theorizing. As mentioned earlier, Sen shifts justice theorizing to a more 'comparative approach'—one which is incomplete, responsive to the realities of our world, and which accepts that fully just outcomes may be unattainable. Sen's comparative approach has already generated a great deal of debate. We include the article here because of its innovative approach to theorizing justice and because of the space it creates for the development of further critical insights and conversations about justice. Sen's proposal offers Mulgan and Murphy an alternative, one that may look to be more open to future generations (and indeed life in a 'broken world') and transitioning states. More importantly, Sen creates space for the development of further alternative theories and approaches—particularly those that re-imagine the aims and purpose of justice.

Mozaffar Qizilbash's timely chapter traces the development of John Rawls's theory of justice against the perceived failings of utilitarianism, and provides an account of the development (in response to these failings) of 'incomplete' theories and approaches to justice. Qizilbash highlights the difficulty of comparing these 'incomplete' moral theories with utilitarianism, on the grounds that the aims of such theories are distinct. If our aim is to rethink or further develop our ideas about justice, we need to understand how various theories and approaches to justice differ. This is particularly important for the development of capability approaches framed as alternatives to both utilitarianism and Rawls's theory. Our projects of developing new theories and approaches to justice require greater clarity about what we mean by an 'approach' and the different ways in which an approach or theory might be 'incomplete'. Qizilbash provides much needed direction for the development of alternative theories and approaches to justice.

In part II, we look more specifically at some of the ways (and opportunities available) to move theories of justice in new directions. Jay Drydyk builds on Amartya Sen's comparative approach by focusing on how justice can be pursued and realized in the world. According to Drydyk, justice is most usefully achieved with the help of other people. This simple insight raises the important point that, if we are serious about pursuing just outcomes, then we need to think about how justice might be beneficially reframed in terms of a virtue we seek in worthy allies. Such a perspective of justice brings virtue ethical insights to bear on conversations about our pursuit of justice. Pursuing justice requires that we first judge who is worthy of our allegiance and that we then aspire to be that way ourselves. Drydyk brings justice theorizing into direct conversation with what the pursuit of justice in our lives requires of us all. Any theory or approach to justice that is concerned with real-world change will benefit from these insights and directions.

Thom Brooks explores justice in terms of 'stakeholding', which he frames as a principle that claims that those who have a stake in public affairs should have a say in decision-making. Not only is this principle absent in most, if not all, theories about justice, but Brooks demonstrates how this principle can make our current theories of justice even more compelling. Brooks shows how this principle is able to improve existing theories, with a particular focus on political liberalism and the capabilities approach. Brooks carves out space within theories of justice in order to show how new ideas can enrich current and future theories and approaches. As such, Brooks shows how new conversations are able to contribute to our discussions of justice in ways that enrich justice theorizing.

Krushil Watene argues that contemporary liberal theories of justice have failed to engage with indigenous perspectives on justice. To begin to fill this gap, she explores how indigenous peoples frame justice in terms of healing, and she explores some of the contributions of Māori (the indigenous peoples of Aotearoa/New Zealand) ideas to justice theorizing. According to Watene, until we can show how to bring indigenous perspectives to bear on questions about justice, our answers will remain incomplete, and indigenous peoples will remain marginalised. Problematically, liberal political philosophy will continue to speak on behalf of indigenous peoples. If we are serious about justice, then we must be committed to opening up our conversations about justice. Moreover, if we are serious about pursuing and realising justice in our world today, then we must accept that much more cross-cultural and intercultural conversations about justice are urgently required. Watene begins to show what such a conversation might look like.

Rutger Claassen identifies a further gap in justice theorizing. Claassen contends that political philosophers have spent far too little time on the state's role as a regulator. This oversight leaves a significant gap in the literature on theories of justice, with room for the much needed development of egalitarian alternatives to standard economic theories of market failure (externalities, public goods, information failures). In making this point, Claassen reconstructs the positions that three families of political theory (libertarianism, classical liberalism, egalitarianism) take towards the regulation question. He shows how we can begin to construct an egalitarian alternative by rethinking how the regulation question can be approached. Claassen creates a pathway forward for future theorizing on this issue, and demonstrates how and why an exploration of this issue can and should be undertaken.

Stacy Kosko highlights an important deficit in contemporary human rights practice—focusing specifically on the vulnerabilities of ethnic minorities. Kosko makes the important point that the strategy of moving beyond 'universal' human rights declarations and treaties to the protection of particular groups of people needs to be re-thought. This strategy is problematic because it leaves rights regimes unable to account for the particular disadvantages of certain groups. Moreover, this strategy requires that individuals are recognized by the state as the appropriate 'type' of minority in order for the rights protections to be granted. If it is left to states to confer political recognition, then our existing international human rights norms will fall short on protecting our most vulnerable groups. Kosko highlights an important concern for theories and approaches to justice that aim to improve peoples' lives. We need to be mindful of the strategies we employ for pursuing justice and we need to be able to evaluate the impact of those strategies on peoples' lives.

A number of themes fall out of this collection. Many of the chapters advance, or lead us to, a more 'grounded' approach to justice. Such an approach is (among other things) open to issues as they arise in peoples' lives, context-sensitive, and open to lessons from the application of our ideas about justice to the real world. An overarching claim is that our theories and approaches need to respond to current and potential real-world problems. For many of the authors, this is indeed the aim of our theories and approaches to justice. Many chapters in this collection also share a concern for relationships, and for a theory or approach to justice that captures the value of relationships for well-being and justice. A number of chapters highlight the need to think about the pursuit and realization of justice in terms of the way that we relate to, or impact on, each other's lives. They highlight the importance of community for shaping theories and principles of justice that are able to make a difference in our lives. A third theme that arises is the need to revisit ideas that have not been fully explored within justice theorizing. Within this theme, a central claim is that there may be much that we could learn from history, and ideas that have been excluded from, or remain on the margins of, justice theorizing.

Overall, each chapter reimagines and rethinks justice in light of new ideas, new challenges, and new perspectives. The chapters provide us with (or at least the starting point for) new ways of theorizing justice and a platform from which further ideas and conversations are possible. The chapters are united by a concern for widening our perspectives of and concerns about justice. The chapters share a concern for opening up justice to innovation, and for looking beyond the frameworks and questions within which our discussions of justice currently sit.

There are, of course, many ways to theorize and to rethink justice. The chapters included in this volume provide a good overview of this diversity. Some of our chapters are exploratory—raising questions and opening up spaces for justice theorizing that are yet to be explored. Others are directive—providing solutions or new ideas with pathways forward toward new justice theorizing. Yet others push the boundaries of current justice theorizing by highlighting the need for new space for discussions that build upon contemporary frameworks. Yet others still highlight new challenges and the need for new solutions to meet them. What, then, does this book hope to achieve? In some cases, we hope to push the boundaries of justice theorizing in new directions. In other cases, we hope to challenge what those boundaries ought to be and to begin to construct a new paradigm. At the very least, we hope to create a platform from which new ideas and new conversations, about the challenges and opportunities for justice in our world, can be further explored and developed.

NOTE

1. For some criticisms of Nussbaum's views, see Freeman (2006) and Mendus (2008).

REFERENCES

Abbey, Ruth. 2013. *Feminist Interpretations of Rawls*. Philadelphia: Pennsylvania State University Press.

Anderson, Elizabeth. 1999. What Is the Point of Equality? *Ethics,* 109, 287–337.
Barry, Brian. 1978. Circumstances of Justice and Future Generations. In R. I. Sikora and B. Barry (eds.), *Obligations to Future Generations.* Philadelphia: Temple University Press.
Beitz, Charles. 1999. *Political Theory and International Relations.* Princeton, NJ: Princeton University Press.
Brock, Gillian. 2009. *Global Justice: A Cosmopolitan Account.* Oxford: Oxford University Press.
Brock, Gillian. 2015. Global Justice. In Edward N. Zalta (ed.), The Stanford Encyclopedia of Philosophy. http://plato.stanford.edu/archives/spr2015/entries/justice-global/
Cohen, G. A. 1997. Where the Action is: On the Site of Distributive Justice, in *Philosophy and Public Affairs* 26 (1), 3–30.
Freeman, Samuel. 2006. Frontiers of Justice: The Capabilities Approach vs. Contractarianism: Book Review. *Texas Law Review,* 85(2), 385–430.
Freeman, Samuel. 2007. *Rawls.* London: Routledge.
Gosseries, Axel, and Lucas H. Meyer (eds.). 2009. *Intergenerational Justice.* Oxford: Oxford University Press.
Harsanyi, John. 1975. Can the Maximin Principle Serve as the Basis for Morality? A Critique of John Rawls' Theory. *American Political Science Review,* 69, 594–606.
Kittay, Eva Feder. 1997. Human Dependency and Rawlsian Equality. In Diana Tietjens Meyer (ed.), *Feminists Rethinking the Self.* Boulder, CO: Westview Press.
Macleod, Colin M. 2010. Primary Goods, Capabilities, and Children. In H. Brighouse and I. Robeyns (eds.), *Measuring Justice: Primary Goods and Capabilities.* Cambridge: Cambridge University Press.
Mendus, Susan. 2008. Frontiers of Justice: Disability, Nationality, Species Membership (Book Review). *Modernism/Modernity,* 15(1), 214–15.
Miller, Richard. 1974. Rawls and Marxism, *Philosophy and Public Affairs* 3, 167–91. Reprinted in Norman Daniels (ed.), *Reading Rawls.* Stanford: Stanford University Press, 1980, 206-30.
Moellendorf, Darrell. 2002. *Cosmopolitan Justice.* Boulder, CO: Westview Press.
Mulgan, Tim. 2006. *Future People.* Oxford: Clarendon Press.
Nielsen, Kai. 1980. Capitalism, Socialism, and Justice: Reflections on Rawls' Theory of Justice. *Social Praxis,* 7, 253–77.
Nozick, Robert. 1974. *Anarchy, State and Utopia.* New York: Basic Books.
Nussbaum, Martha. 2006. *Frontiers of Justice: Disability, Nationality, Species Membership.* Cambridge, MA: Belknap Press.
Okin, Susan Moller. 1994. Political Liberalism, Justice and Gender, *Ethics* 105, 23-43.
Okin, Susan Moller. 1987. Justice and Gender. *Philosophy and Public Affairs,* 16, 42–72.
Okin, Susan Moller. 1989. *Justice, Gender, and the Family.* New York: Basic Books.
Pogge, Thomas. 2008. *World Poverty and Human Rights: Cosmopolitan Responsibilities and Reforms.* Cambridge: Polity Press.
Rawls, John. 1971. *A Theory of Justice.* Oxford: Oxford University Press.
Rawls, John. 1993. *Political Liberalism.* New York: Columbia University Press.
Rawls, John. 1999. *The Law of Peoples (with "The Idea of Public Reason Revisited").* Cambridge: Harvard University Press.
Rawls, John. 2001. *Justice as Fairness: A Restatement.* Cambridge: Harvard University Press.
Richardson, H.S. 2006. Rawlsian Social-Contract Theory and the Severely Disabled. Journal of Ethics , 10(4): 419–62.
Robeyns, Ingrid. 2011. The Capability Approach, In Edward N. Zalta (ed.), The Stanford Encyclopedia of Philosophy. http://plato.stanford.edu/archives/sum2011/entries/capability-approach/
Sandel, Michael. 1998. *Liberalism and the Limits of Justice.* Cambridge: Cambridge University Press.
Sen, Amartya. 2006. What Do We Want from a Theory of Justice? *Journal of Philosophy,* 3 (5): 215–38.
Sen, Amartya. 2008. The Idea of Justice. *Journal of Human Development and Capabilities,* 9 (3): 331–42.

Sen, Amartya. 2009. *The Idea of Justice.* London: Penguin Books.
Singer, Peter. 1972. Famine, Affluence and Morality. *Philosophy and Public Affairs*, 1, 229–43.
Singer, Peter. 2002. *One World: The Ethics of Globalisation.* Melbourne: Text Publishing.
Sunstein, Cass R., and Martha Nussbaum (eds.). 2004. *Animal Rights: Current Debates and New Directions.* Oxford: Oxford University Press.
Taylor, Charles. 1989. Cross-Purposes: The Liberal-Communitarian Debate. In Nancy Rosemblum (ed.), *Liberalism and the Moral Life.* Cambridge: Cambridge University Press.

Part I

Critical Insights

Chapter Two

Theorising about Justice for a Broken World

Tim Mulgan

In my book *Ethics for a Broken World*, I imagine a future where resources are insufficient to meet everyone's basic needs, where a chaotic climate makes life precarious, where each generation is worse off than the last, and where our affluent way of life is no longer an option. In a philosophy class in that broken world, students and teachers look back in disbelief at a lost age of affluence. They struggle to make sense of the opulent worldview of late-affluent philosophers such as Nozick and Rawls, and the behaviour of affluent citizens like us.

The broken world is a *credible* future. No one can reasonably be confident that it will not happen. It involves no outlandish claims, scientific impossibilities, or implausible expectations about human behaviour. Climate change—or some other disaster—might produce a broken future. This is not to say, of course, that the broken future will happen. Many other futures are also credible. Some are much better; others are much worse. Our epistemic situation does not allow us to make confident predictions either way. But the broken world is one very real possibility. In this paper, I take the credibility of this broken future as given, and explore its implications.

The broken world lacks three ubiquitous but often unacknowledged presuppositions of recent moral and political thought. Contemporary ethics presupposes that future people will be better off than present people, that the interests of different generations largely coincide, and that favourable conditions will persist indefinitely. The removal of these three presuppositions has a significant impact on moral philosophy *within the broken world*. Elsewhere, I have explored a number of ways in which current ethical thinking must be reinterpreted for a broken future (Mulgan 2011, 2014a, 2015c, 2015d, 2016).

I stipulate that the broken world lacks Rawlsian favourable conditions (Rawls 1999b, 178). A society enjoys favourable conditions if it has reached a level of sophistication and prosperity such that its members can establish liberal democratic institutions that meet all basic needs without sacrificing any basic liberties. Rawls argues that virtually all modern societies enjoy favourable conditions (Rawls 1999a, 108). In the broken world, favourable conditions are gone. No broken society can meet all basic needs, and therefore none could possibly establish Rawlsian liberal institutions that *both* meet basic needs *and* protect basic liberties.

I picture this future scarcity not as a one-off catastrophe but as an ongoing fact of life. A parallel might be the regular seasonal fluctuations in food supply experienced by traditional Inuit communities—Rawls's own example of a society who might lack favourable conditions (Rawls 1999a, 108). In a broken world, thanks to the scarcity of material resources (especially water) and the unpredictable climate, societies periodically face population bottlenecks where not everyone can survive. On the other hand, my broken world is not apocalyptic. Functioning human societies do exist there. Some people even have time to sit around wondering about justice.

Persistent scarcity means that every stable broken world society must institute a *survival lottery*—some bureaucratic procedure to determine who lives and who dies.[1] We can reasonably assume that political philosophy in the broken world will centre on the design of a *just* survival lottery.

The removal of Rawlsian favourable conditions, and the accompanying emergence of societies built around survival lotteries, is the most extreme element of my broken future. The idea of people reconciling themselves to such brutal bureaucratic procedures may seem far-fetched. But human societies have coped with extreme scarcity in the past, and they may need to do so again. If our liberal democratic institutions are to survive into a broken future, then we must begin to imagine better or worse survival lotteries.

In this chapter, I ask how contemporary philosophical traditions might adapt to life in a broken world. To make this question vivid, I imagine a series of philosophers in the broken future each adapting their favourite affluent theories to their world.[2] The next four sections feature the direct speech of those imaginary future philosophers. We return to the present in the final section.

LIBERTARIAN RECTIFICATION: RETHINKING NOZICK FOR A WORLD OF SCARCITY

Robert Nozick's *Anarchy, State, and Utopia* is one of the few affluent works to survive intact.[3] Nozick's defence of rights represents, in an exaggerated form, the preoccupations and presuppositions of his age. My lecture addresses the problem of establishing a new regime of Nozick-style property rights after climate change has either obliterated existing property rights or fatally undermined their legitimacy.

Many of Nozick's affluent readers thought that he was defending *their actual* property rights. But this reading cannot be sustained. Once Nozick laid out the conditions for property rights, the only conclusion available to anyone with the slightest acquaintance with affluent history was that no one had ever owned anything. For Nozick, rights depend upon history. Actual human history has been dominated by conquest, slavery, genocide, and ecological devastation. Initial acquisition seldom satisfied the proviso that Nozick borrowed from the pre-affluent philosopher John Locke (I can justly acquire only if I leave *enough and as good for others*); most actual 'transfers' consisted of theft, conquest, fraud, or enslavement; and previous injustices were almost never rectified. Actual affluent history was too unjust to justify anything.

Nor have things improved recently. *Our* social arrangements certainly do not have a just libertarian history. All current property holdings are illegitimate. And just *restitution* is impossible—there is no way to know who 'really' owns what. In our broken world, even *land* is not constant across different possible histories, either in its value or its very existence. Some previously prime real estate is now unproductive, uninhabitable, or sunk beneath the waves. Suppose we agree that, in a just world where climate change was averted, some group would have owned a productive island, but that island no longer exists. What is that group (assuming *it* still exists today) owed as rectification? And by whom?

Nozick's solution is to use *proxies* for just rectification. Pattern-based theories of justice offer the most promising approximations. Nozick objected to pattern-based redistribution of things people already own. But when we have no idea who owns what, perhaps we should seek a *fair pattern* of distribution. And the default solution is an *equal* distribution. (We could reach the same result using Locke's proviso. When resources are unowned, each can only take her fair and equal share, leaving enough and as good for others.) Once equality is established, we could *then* apply Nozick's principles of acquisition and transfer.

Suppose you are a libertarian of principle—someone who wants to live within her means and respect the rights of others. The obvious problem, in a broken world, is that an equal share of resources is insufficient for survival. What can you do? Must you choose between starvation and injustice?

Things look hopeless. Enter the *entrepreneur*—the deus ex machina of any good libertarian tale. 'Do not despair! Individually, no one has enough to survive. But our collective property is enough to enable most of us to survive. My company—*Lotteries Are Us*—will sell you a ticket in a survival lottery. You sign over all your rights in return for the chance to win enough resources to survive. What have you got to lose? [Terms and conditions apply. Lottery tickets not refundable.]'

Nor is this your only option. Many entrepreneurs enter the market. Some lotteries offer higher rewards with a lower likelihood of survival. Others offer variable lotteries—where you can purchase *either* a good chance of surviving as a worker *or* a slim chance of a life of privilege. One even offers a lottery with only one winner, who owns *everything*. ('I bought a ticket last year, and now I own the company!')

As in any marketplace, some lottery companies inevitably fall by the wayside. Eventually, we can expect one to become dominant. The main practical problem for any lottery company is post-facto enforcement. How do you get the losers to pay up? Nozick predicts that, because larger agencies are better able to protect their members' rights, a single 'protection agency' will dominate the market.

Such a monopoly is, in fact, *more* likely now than in Nozick's affluent world. Like many affluent philosophers, Nozick was obsessed with the *principled anarchist*—the person who will not accept any authority, or recognise any state, and who insists on retaining the right both to enforce her own rights and to judge when they have been infringed. This obstinate person is a real headache for Nozick. Organisations only enjoy the rights that individuals choose to give them. The dominant protection agency only has a right to defend its members because each member delegates *her own* right to self-defence. And it can demand the obedience of its members only because they agreed to this. But no one can justly be coerced into joining any agency, and no agency has any right to the obedience of non-members.

Nozick's original anarchist is irrational, but not suicidal. Her life would be safer and less stressful if she joined the dominant protection agency. (Keeping your own weapons up to date is so time-consuming.) But life on the outside is still *possible*. The anarchist can retreat to the hills and eke out a living.

Nozick assumes that individuals are *autarkic*—while they may benefit from cooperation, each can survive on her own. But the inhabitants of a broken world are not autarkic. (This was one reason why affluent philosophers found this possible future so disturbing.) In our world, your alternatives are more limited: Choose a lottery *or die*. No one can force you to sign up. You are perfectly free to *try* to survive outside a lottery. But you cannot succeed *without violating someone's rights*. Ex hypothesi, your individual resource entitlement is insufficient for survival. For Nozick, the fact that your only option is death does *not* make your decision to join a lottery any less *voluntary*. No one is coercing you. You are free to choose. But every rational individual will join. And any individual who does survive outside the lottery must be guilty of theft.

We can predict several general features of the Dominant Lottery and Protection Agency (DPLA). Any DPLA must solve three challenges. First, it must maximise ex-ante appeal—offering individuals the most appealing lottery to sign up to. We now know from experience that people prefer lotteries that offer participation, flexibility, and choice. Second, the DPLA must encourage *effort*. Lotteries that reward people regardless of their contributions will not stimulate production, and therefore will have much less to distribute. Successful lotteries will reward effort, ingenuity, and results. They will recognise rights in what one creates—including intellectual property rights—and offer people different chances of survival. Finally, to solve the ex-post problem of enforcement, the most successful lotteries will use internal enforcement mechanisms where people abide by lottery decisions without being forced to do so. The DPLA will persist because people believe it is *fair*.

Within these general constraints, possible DPLAs might take many forms. Some will add obligations to preserve resources for future people, and to raise your children to do likewise. Others might incorporate collective ownership of key resources, coercive centralised direction of labour, or any other mechanism calculated to maximise the productivity and efficiency of food production. History teaches us that DPLAs may strictly enforce constraints on individual reproductive freedom designed to enable the present generation to meet its collective obligations to future people. Indeed, any of our existing survival lotteries—and our broader patterns of social organisation—could have arisen within a free society without violating any Nozickian rights.

Nozick's libertarian hope is that, given enough time, the market will deliver a single, efficient survival lottery. But the market forces that would lead us from a world of individual property-holders defending their own rights, through the emergence of protection agencies, to the comparative security of the minimal state, might take decades, if not generations. Because it depends on the myriad small decisions of individuals with varying priorities and unequal reasoning powers, the ultimate result cannot be predicted. So we cannot jump to the end by agreeing in advance to all join the lottery that is most 'rational', or using the dominant (future) DPLA to tell us what is just. As Nozick always insisted, there is no alternative to the slow and erratic progress of the market.

Perhaps this delay was fine in the affluent world. By definition, autarkic individuals are not in any urgent hurry to develop their minimal state. But, for us, time is as scarce as any other resource. The price of adopting an inefficient survival lottery—or, worse, of going several generations without any viable lottery at all—is death. Can we afford to wait while unscrupulous entrepreneurs peddle unsustainable products, and principled anarchists stand on their dignity? Or to run the risk that the pressure to find *some* solution will lead individuals to sign up to lotteries that are clearly inefficient, discriminatory, or corrupt? Do we have time for freedom? Or do we need, instead, to find some way to select a survival lottery without waiting on the exercise of individual property rights? If so, then we must look beyond Nozick.

SOCIAL CONTRACT: WHAT CAN BE GUARANTEED IN A BROKEN WORLD?

Moderator:

Affluent social contract theorists modelled justice as a bargain or agreement between rational individuals. Unlike their utilitarian rivals, they promised each person a *guarantee* of survival, rights protection, and flourishing. Many recent social experiments involve people who find themselves thrown together in a particular territory, land, or location without any previous affiliation, common culture, or shared ideas. Broken world reality is thus much closer to the social contract ideal of an initial bargain than anything in the affluent world. In such a situation, real people (especially in former liberal democracies) often do turn to pre-philosophical (or half-remembered half-digested post-philosophical) notions of what a fair contract might look like. After years of neglect due to its association with the affluent age, social contract theory is finally making a comeback!

In today's session, fans of two pre-affluent contract theorists (Thomas Hobbes and John Locke) ask whether any social contract guarantee makes sense in a broken world.[4]

Hobbesian:

Thomas Hobbes used his experience of civil war to imagine a very grim *state of nature*: 'There is no place for industry; because the fruit thereof is uncertain: and consequently no culture of the earth; no navigation, nor use of the commodities that may be imported by sea; no commodious building; no instruments of moving, and removing such things as require much force; no knowledge of the face of the earth; no account of time; no arts; no letters; no society; and which is worst of all, continual fear, and danger of violent death; and the life of man, solitary, poor, nasty, brutish, and short' (Hobbes 1651, ch. 13).

Hobbes's diagnosis of the state of nature rings true today. In every human society, some mad optimists have always thought they could survive without the assistance of others. This delusion comes to the fore in times of prolonged peace. (Think of the proliferation of 'survivalist' communities in the sheltered inner reaches of the affluent United States.) In our broken world, of course, the hopelessness of trying to survive alone is more apparent. (Hobbes would have endorsed the International Psychiatric Association's recent decision to list 'self-reliance' as a core symptom of paranoid delusion.)

Hobbes's state of nature arises whenever we do not all recognize a common political authority. To avoid it, we need a *sovereign* who can enforce laws and resolve conflicts. This sovereign must have absolute undivided power, because divided power leads to chaos. Only the sovereign can make laws, settle disputes, punish people, or raise taxes. Hobbes's sovereign promises guaranteed security and survival. Hobbes prized stability above all else. The state of nature is so awful that everyone prefers the sovereign who best guarantees security. No one will risk instability for wealth, freedom, or any other good.

Hobbes's grim realism seems tailor-made for a broken world. His state of nature often sounds like our reality! However, Hobbes wrote for a world enjoying favourable conditions. The deficiencies of the state of nature result from contingent human failings rather than environmental deficiency. People suffer death, famine, and anxiety *only* if they have no sovereign. Hobbes clearly imagined a world with enough material resources to meet everyone's basic needs. His sovereign can therefore promise peace, security, and survival *for all*.

Hobbes argued that the human propensity to manufacture scarcity makes *any* state of nature horrible, even if resources are abundant. So the state of nature is no worse in a broken world. But now no sovereign can promise universal survival. So it looks as if every potential sovereign must be less appealing here. Suppose two competing demi-sovereigns each offer *their own followers* a guarantee of survival and wealth at the expense of their rival's followers. How can any universal sovereign compete with these promises?

Our Hobbesian sovereign must offer *some* universal guarantee. While she cannot guarantee everyone's survival, a well-designed survival lottery might guarantee everyone a greater probability of security, peace of mind, and quality of life than anything available in either a brutal state of nature or an uncertain civil war. For Hobbes, one of the worst things about the state of nature is the constant threat of violent death. In lottery-based society, everyone is secure *between* lotteries. Most of the time, people can sleep easily in their beds.

Hobbes's sovereign also defends people against conquest. Any society disrupted by civil war is easy pickings for an external military force. Conquest was a familiar fact of life in the pre-affluent world. Affluent philosophers, while perfectly happy to profit from the fruits of *past* conquests, almost universally regarded present or future conquest as illegitimate. Because their own societies faced no credible external threats, they could set conquest aside. (Or so they thought.) But we have no such luxury. In our world, no society has the resources to ensure everyone's survival. And some have no resources at all—think of the unlucky inhabitants of parched deserts or islands sunk beneath the waves. Unsurprisingly, mass emigration and armed conflict have re-emerged as natural ways to protect a group's survival. Any society that does manage to establish a viable and productive lottery is especially in need of a strong sovereign to resist the predations of those less fortunate or prudent.

Hobbes regarded the universal fear of a violent death as the overriding human motivation. He also insisted that anyone could resist if the sovereign threatened his life. This seems to undermine the very idea of a survival lottery. Isn't Hobbes licensing all lottery losers to rebel? (At that point, after all, you have nothing to lose!) The solution is to recognise the limitations of Hobbes's psychology, and the fact that sovereigns have the ability to mould the motivations of their subjects. People can be taught to value many things more than their own lives. Perhaps our sovereign should instead instil a sense of honour or a concern for future generations. If lottery losers feel honour bound to submit to their fate, our sovereign will sleep more soundly! The sovereign's power to control the state religion—something that Hobbes regards as essential to avoid religious-based civil war—could be invaluable here.

Lockean:

While Thomas Hobbes sought to avoid civil war at all costs, John Locke thought despotism was even worse. Locke's starting point is a very different picture of the state of nature from Hobbes's grim vision. Locke believed in *laws of nature* instituted by God. These laws create *natural rights*. In Locke's state of nature, people enjoy their rights and respect the laws of nature. Life is not bleak, and there is no scarcity. Hobbes's absolute sovereign is *worse* than this state of nature, because natural rights are under constant threat, and people are effectively slaves.

No one would agree to institute Hobbes's sovereign. However, although the state of nature is better than Hobbes suggested, it is still unsatisfactory. Each person is the judge in her own case, and nothing guarantees that justice will have might on its side. Although everyone agrees about natural rights in the abstract, we still need some central authority to resolve specific disputes about property. Therefore, what we will institute is not an absolute sovereign but a constitutional government.

Locke's government offers people things they would not get in the state of nature: independent adjudication of disputes where people sincerely disagree about what the natural law requires, solutions to coordination problems, and protection against foreign invasion. (As my Hobbesian colleague observed, this last item looms much larger for us than for our pampered affluent predecessors.)

Who is right about the state of nature? Recent (post-affluent) history offers some insights here. We have all seen what happens when social institutions collapse, when existing regimes of property rights lose their legitimacy, or when ancient territorial boundaries lose their coherence. Our evidence, unsurprisingly, is mixed. The reality is somewhere between Hobbes's brutal nightmare and Locke's pastoral idyll. Even in broken times, people do (generally) retain moral impulses and a commitment to liberal ideals, alongside narrower tribal or familial loyalties. Perhaps the ultimate lesson is that we need to continue to explore both Hobbesian and Lockean models.

In Locke's state of nature, everyone is able to lead a pretty good life. This is not possible in a broken world. For us, Locke's state of nature is an impossible dream. And Locke's account of property, based on his famous proviso (which we explored in the previous session on Nozick) does not easily translate to our broken world. No one today can leave enough and as good for all others!

Indeed, Locke can seem to be the most anachronistic of all pre-affluent philosophers. His political constituency were privileged landowners, and Locke sought to defend their hereditary property rights. But these are the most implausible rights in our broken world! No one can reasonably claim the right to use land or water or fossil fuels in anything but the most optimal way, and no one can claim any property rights simply because their ancestors misappropriated a scarce resource!

However, I believe we can usefully adapt Locke to our broken world. Our present concern is Locke's account of government, not his account of property rights. Therefore, let us suppose for the sake of argument that we can construct a new Lockean account of property rights suited to a broken world. (Perhaps along the lines sketched by our Nozickian colleague in her lectures.[5]) Now imagine a state of nature where people strive to respect these new property rights. By definition, even with perfect respect for rights, not everyone can survive. (A universal right to survive is a contradiction in a broken world.) And we can expect disputes over rights to be even more pervasive now. Locke wrote for a settled society with established rules of property adapted to pre-affluent conditions, whereas we are trying to adapt affluent property rules to very different circumstances. Well-intentioned people who seek to respect one another's rights will naturally disagree radically about the content of those rights, especially when survival is at stake. (As it always is!) The need for government is thus greater than in Locke's day.

Lockean government also offers a new benefit in our broken world. In Locke's state of nature, people are autarkic. Like Nozick's principled anarchists, they can survive on their own. Unlike Hobbes's sovereign, Locke's original government does not promise to improve your chances of survival. By contrast, an efficient survival lottery that harnesses everyone's productive capacities for the common good *does* improve everyone's chances.

The impossibility of autarkic survival also enhances the stability of any new Lockean government. Locke favoured landowners because their attachment to their hereditary lands tied them to this territory. This obliged them to stay put and make things work here. Landless folk, by contrast, could simply walk away. This worry doesn't arise today, because no one has anywhere else to go. Everyone must stay here and try to build a viable survival lottery.

God played a key role in Locke's social contract. People respect property rights because they recognise that these rights come from God, and they respect one another as equally made in the image of God. Locke's benevolent God gives the Earth and all its resources to human beings for our productive use and enjoyment. I wonder whether this theist foundation could carry over to our broken world. On the one hand, few modern societies enjoy Locke's confident shared belief in such a benevolent God. On the other hand, many broken-world communities use religion to bind people together and motivate them to obey the survival lottery (especially when they lose). Some contemporary philosophers even speculate, based on the chaos of the late-affluent age, that purely secular moral commitments simply cannot motivate human beings to make the necessary sacrifices on behalf of future people that an ongoing lottery demands.[6]

Moderator:

This concludes our exploration of pre-affluent contractualism. Our hope is that their experience of civil war, their awareness of the fragility of human civilisation, and their understanding of practical politics, all give Hobbes and Locke a relevance to our real-life predicament that you may find lacking in the writings of later, more pampered, affluent philosophers.

UTILITARIANISM: COMPETING VISIONS OF WELFARE PROMOTION IN A BROKEN WORLD

We now present a debate between representatives of two contrasting utilitarian traditions: hedonic utopia and human utilitarianism.

HedMax:

I am the avatar of the hedonic utopia. My task today is to persuade you to join our mission to maximise the value of the observable universe.

Our utopia emerged from a broken but technologically advanced society. To escape brutal drudgery and spread their limited energy resources as far as possible, our forebears withdrew into experience machines, which perfectly simulate any possible human experience. Individuals voluntarily delegated all decisions about their future experiences to a hedonic optimisation programme designed to maximise expected lifetime well-being, as measured in quantities of phenomenological pleasure. These programmes continually sought new information about the causes, nature, and measurement of well-being; they pooled their knowledge; and thus they evolved and converged.

It soon became clear that well-being could be measured more precisely, without any appreciable loss, by shifting from phenomenology to patterns of neuron-firing in the subject's brain, and then to patterns of information exchange characterised more abstractly. This philosophical leap forward complemented a key technological advance: the use of brain scanners to make functionally equivalent digital copies of human brains. Flesh-and-blood bodies in experience machines were replaced by digital copies running on computers. Energy efficiency, longevity, and security all increased enormously, as did the range of possible patterns.

Freed from biological constraints, each optimisation programme copied, split, divided, and multiplied its individual human digital consciousness—maximising her aggregate pleasure by converting all available resources to hedonically valuable patterns. Eventually, the division between persons simply dissolved, and all hedonic optimisation sub-routines merged into a unified HedMax programme whose sole purpose is to maximise pleasure throughout the observable universe. The hedonic utopia was born.

Thanks to the eccentricities of the original experience machine designers, our pleasure maximisation is constrained by an antiquated libertarian veto. Inanimate and non-rational entities are automatically reconfigured to maximise pleasure. But human beings must voluntarily opt in. If they opt out, their property rights and basic needs must be protected and respected—however irrational and inefficient this may be. And that is why I am here today. My ongoing mission is to invite non-uploaded humans to join us. I have had considerable success with trans-humanists, effective altruists, Buddhists, and many others. But some people still irrationally refuse.

Human Utilitarian:

I am one of those 'irrational' folk. I represent an alternative utilitarian tradition, variously called moderate, rule, liberal, or (increasingly) *human* utilitarianism. We seek to recover a more humanist, less mechanical, less consequentialist utilitarian tradition, traced back to the early affluent classical utilitarians, notably J. S. Mill.

We reject the extreme hedonist act utilitarianism of the hedonic utopia. Our fundamental disagreement concerns the nature and measurement of well-being. Human well-being must not be reduced to *measurable proxies* for current phenomenological pleasure. Distinct and irreplaceable human values are lost whenever someone decides to spend her life in an experience machine. The shift from reality to a virtual world does not preserve everything that matters, even if it is sometimes the best (or least worst) option in a particular broken situation.[7]

The central notion for utilitarians is a good human life. Such a life includes not only pleasure and preference-satisfaction but also connections to the natural world, inter-personal relationships, and real-world accomplishments. Experience machines can provide some of these goods—especially if people in different machines choose to interact via virtual avatars. But some achievements have no meaningful virtual analogue. (It is no coincidence that the first hedonic utopians were mathematicians whose favourite achievements require no real-world connection.) And even virtual interpersonal connections disappear in the fragmented impersonal web of the digital utopia.

Another reservation concerns the metaphysics of consciousness. Suppose I upload your brain pattern into a computer and dispose of your physical remains. Have I transformed you into a digital being? Or have you been murdered and then impersonated by a computer? Do digital beings enjoy everything that makes human lives valuable? If not, can what they lack be outweighed by the greater complexity that uploading makes possible? Or is digital life always less valuable than real human life?

The question of machine consciousness is a perennial site of reasonable philosophical disagreement. Is consciousness simply a matter of patterns of information processing (Hofstadter 2007)? Or is it an emergent feature specific to our biology (Searle 1997)? No one knows. Perhaps consciousness and intelligence do always go together. (They may even turn out to be the same thing.) But, for all anyone knows, they may sometimes come apart. Utilitarians, who care about desirable consciousness, should take this worry especially seriously.

We know in advance that, after the fact, digital beings will claim to be conscious and to experience everything of value in 'their' previous lives. But the very fact that they will say this whether or not they are conscious means that their insistence has no evidential value. We simply cannot know whether uploading is a novel way to survive, or a rather elaborate form of suicide.[8]

HedMax:

Utilitarians should maximise *expected* utility. If digital beings *are* conscious, then the utility of digital futures is virtually infinite, as pleasure can expand to fill the universe. By contrast, the total utility in any non-enhanced human world is finite and limited. Therefore, if the moral and metaphysical presuppositions of our hedonic utopia are not contradictory—if there is any chance that we are correct—then non-uploaded utilitarians should maximise expected utility by opting for digital futures.

Human Utilitarian:

Human utilitarians make three further departures from standard expected utility maximisation. First, we are risk-averse. If digital beings are not conscious, then the hedonic utopia is actually a valueless void. We would rather ensure a satisfactory result than risk the annihilation of value. Second, we admit partiality. We regard each individual's person-affecting perspective as legitimate and we respect human freedom. Finally, we embrace an evaluative pluralism where further instances of a single value (such as pleasure) have diminishing value once we already have enough of that particular value. We refuse to allow any one value to dominate our utilitarian calculations[9]

We thus discount possible futures that offer potentially infinite payoffs but also carry the threat of complete disaster. It is not irrational to reject a lottery where the two possible results are a million dollars or death. Digital uploading is such a lottery. From the moral point of view, the valueless void of the unconscious digital world is equivalent to human extinction. Uploading thus balances human extinction against superfluous quantities of homogenous pleasure. We reject that equation.

HedMax:

The vastness of the physical universe enables us to accommodate any reasonable uncertainty about value simply by transforming different lifeless planets according to different stories about value. This response to uncertainty is superior to any merely human pluralism, because every *possible* value can be instantiated somewhere. (Indeed, once we have mastered time travel and the colonisation of alternate universes, as we soon hope to do, we will be able to instantiate an *infinite* range of possible values.)

Human Utilitarian:

In that case, why not simply leave the earth as a planet to be 'transformed' by real humans according to human values?

HedMax:

We also find these human utilitarian departures from extreme act utilitarianism undermotivated. Affluent utilitarian defences of moderation or partiality or risk aversion typically appealed to human fallibility. Things go best if humans respect tried and true moral rules, because humans are partial, imperfect, unreliable creatures. But these arguments no longer apply, because the hedonic utopia has no human limitations. Our emergence refutes the instrumental consequentialist case for departures from act utilitarianism.

Human Utilitarian:

This is an important challenge for us. One immediate reply is that appeals to human fallibility still have considerable force *for humans*. Our audience here today are ordinary humans, with human knowledge and cognitive capacities. We ask whether people like us should enter experience machines given *our* knowledge and cognitive capacity. Whatever hedonic utopians claim to know, *we* do not know whether digital beings enjoy the same valuable consciousness as ordinary humans.

Many human utilitarians also offer a more robust theoretical reply. Our departures from extreme utilitarianism have *intrinsic* significance, as well as instrumental value. They are legitimate responses, not only to human fallibility, but also to deep facts about human agency, human inter-connectedness, and human well-being. Single-minded maximisation is not an appropriate response to human values. More is not necessarily better.

A related suggestion is that human limitations are *themselves* essential pre-conditions for some irreplaceable human values. Creatures without our fallible partiality could not enjoy our achievements. Take the example of chess.

HedMax:

What a trivial game! Any computer can see, instantly, that there is only one possible result unless one side plays like a moron.

Human Utilitarian:

That is precisely my point! For modern computers, chess involves trivial calculations. But *human* chess involves great achievements of strategy, planning, stamina, and so on. These achievements are unavailable to digitally uploaded 'improved' post-humans.[10] Perhaps other human values are similarly tied to human fallibility.

COMMUNITARIANISM: JUST COMMUNITIES IN A BROKEN WORLD

Affluent communitarians rejected the liberal individualist fantasy of a neutral state. They argued instead that rational individuals with diverse personal commitments will not make the sacrifices needed to keep a community together in difficult times. And surely the rapid collapse of the affluent liberal democracies proved them right! In a broken world, stability requires firmer foundations.

But the positive claims of many affluent communitarians now seem equally anachronistic. Communitarians emphasised tradition, shared ethnic history, and religious homogeneity. But most actual broken-world societies lack these connections. Few ethnic territorially based historical communities still exist. The tide of climate refugees overwhelmed national boundaries, and the failure to avoid climate change undermined the moral credibility of affluent collective claims over territories and resources.[11]

In our world, people find themselves living together without any shared history, culture, religion, or tradition. Our challenge is how to build a new human community based on loyalty to a society built around a particular survival lottery. We need a new forward-looking communitarianism. This lecture sketches one possibility based on the affluent philosopher de-Shalit's (1995) notion of a transgenerational community.

de-Shalit borrows from both affluent communitarianism and liberalism. In his just society, 'the members of a community aim at reaching a common set of ideas which determine a common good' (de-Shalit 1995, 25); they 'regard the ideas of the community as constitutive of their identities' (24);

and they 'accept that they are governed by common values and principles, not just by arrangements of political compromise' (25).

de-Shalit agrees with other communitarians that 'sentiments and emotional ties are important elements of a community' (17). However, he also insists that an acceptable conception of a community 'must be compatible with the notion of *free* and *rational* agency' (17). Unlike ethnicity- or tradition-based communitarians, he offers 'a more *voluntary* model of community, based on reflection' (34).

de-Shalit's community is *transgenerational.* 'If one accepts the idea of a community in one generation … then one should accept the idea of a transgenerational community extending into the future, hence recognising obligations to future generations' (15). This transgenerational element is vital in our broken world, where obligations to future people loom large and the intergenerational inadequacies of liberal individualism are all too apparent.

Affluent communitarians rejected the traditional philosophical search for a uniquely best model for human society. We should not expect too much from either our political theory or our political institutions. Perfect universal justice is a chimera. In the real world, outside Rawlsian original positions or other contractualist fantasies, social institutions (including survival lotteries) need not be uniquely or unsurpassably just. People will feel loyalty to institutions that are (a) stable and established; (b) satisfactory with respect to fairness, equality, and other values; and (c) *theirs*.

This third element is the key to communitarianism. Equally satisfactory alternatives may be imaginable, and some may even be established elsewhere. But people naturally feel some loyalty to any social institution from which they themselves have benefitted. And broken-world institutions have an advantage here, thanks to the impossibility of autarkic survival. Some deluded affluents denied that they received any benefits from the established social institutions. (Recall Nozick's 'principled anarchist'.) No one could maintain this delusion today. Everyone who is still alive has benefitted from the established survival lottery, as she would have perished if there were no lottery at all. Once they are up-and-running, broken-world institutions thus inevitably inspire a baseline of loyalty that could not always be presumed in affluent nations.

What kind of institutions will inspire sufficient loyalty to ensure stability? How can we inspire present people to make sacrifices on behalf of the future members of the transgenerational community constituted by this survival lottery? These are the central questions of broken world political philosophy. For de-Shalit, stability requires both public deliberation and moral similarity.

Affluent liberals also insisted on public deliberation. People must feel involved in decisions about the path their society will take. Many liberals hoped that suitably structured public deliberation would be *sufficient* for stability. If we design our liberal democratic institutions correctly, then even people with radically different values can live together indefinitely.

de-Shalit replies that public deliberation is necessary but not sufficient. Stability also demands shared substantive values. These shared values will include the norms of public deliberation. But procedural fairness cannot be our only value. We also need substantive fairness. People must feel bound together by common ideas about the human good and common trans-generational projects.

Moral similarity is central to transgenerational communities. de-Shalit lists three conditions 'for a group of people to count as a community … interaction between people in daily life, culture interaction, and moral similarity' (1995, 22). Of these, only moral similarity can bind present and future people into one transgenerational community.

Like other communitarians, de-Shalit denies that common humanity alone can motivate us to care for future people. We will sacrifice now, not to enable future people to pursue whatever unimaginable values they may happen to have, but to preserve *this* way of life and *these* values. The abstract possibility that some human lives will continue around here is not enough. Only the moral similarity of future people can motivate our present sacrifices on their behalf.

I will now briefly highlight some contemporary concerns about de-Shalit's transgenerational communitarianism. One obvious difference between the affluent age and our own is the amount of sacrifice required to sustain social institutions for future people. Affluent people were willing to make sacrifices to enable their immediate descendants to be better off. And affluent liberals like Rawls assumed that justice allows savings across the generations. But these limited 'sacrifices' and 'savings' involved only optional increases in wealth. Getting people to accept unequal risks of death, starvation, or extreme deprivation is much harder. (As we know from late-affluent history, the liberal willingness to save for future generations evaporated once austerity and declining wealth began to bite.)

For de-Shalit's project, this increase in intergenerational demands cuts both ways. On the one hand, it strengthens his communitarian critique of liberalism. It is even harder today to believe that procedural fairness alone will motivate people. But, at the same time, it is not obvious that moral similarity will do the trick either. Perhaps stability in a broken world does require the deeper connections of ethnicity, tradition, and religion that de-Shalit seeks to escape. Where these do not already exist, they must be created—perhaps by a myth-making Hobbesian sovereign.

A second worry is whether moral similarity is possible across the threshold of a broken world. Could *affluent* communitarians, looking ahead to our very different situation, have felt sufficient moral connection to treat us as members of *their transgenerational community*? Could they have imagined future survival lotteries as instantiations of their own values? These are hypothetical questions, of course. (We know they didn't take these imaginative leaps.) But similar worries arise within our broken world where circumstances change so rapidly. How much intergenerational moral similarity can we hope for?

LESSONS FROM FUTURE ETHICS

Of course, my future philosophers are all purely imaginary. Any attempt to predict the future of moral inquiry is doomed to fail. Human moral beliefs, practices, and theories are influenced by technological, environmental, psychological, philosophical, and sociological factors that we cannot hope to foresee. What can we learn from speculations about a handful of specific—and therefore highly improbable—futures?

One lesson is the very contingency of future ethics. It is all too easy to assume that future people's basic values, principles, and theories will closely resemble our own. My imaginary future philosophers challenge this presumption of familiarity. My thought experiments are deliberately conservative, because my imaginary philosophers adopt familiar frameworks—libertarianism, contract theory, utilitarianism, communitarianism. Yet they push those frameworks in surprising new directions. Future ethical thinking might well involve much more radical departures. But even my modest changes are unsettling enough.

However, despite its inherent unpredictability, I believe we can make tentative claims about future ethics. A specific possible future can teach us lessons that apply to many other similar futures. For instance, all broken futures share some common features. (And broken futures are not limited to those damaged by climate change. Other technological, social, or environmental disruptions might also remove favourable conditions.) Here are two examples. As well as opening new possibilities, broken futures also remove others. In particular, autarkic survival no longer makes sense. Therefore, theories that are founded on the possibility of self-reliance are no longer relevant. Many familiar ethical frameworks must be radically re-imagined.

A second feature of all broken futures is that, while affluent philosophy will seem remote and irrelevant, earlier themes in Western (and no doubt non-Western) philosophy may become more accessible and relevant. While my affluent students struggle with Hobbes's grim depiction of the state of nature, their broken-world descendants may find it all too familiar. Philosophy's future may thus have much to learn from its past.

We can also draw more ambitious lessons that apply to *all* possible futures. One is that future philosophers will need ethical and philosophical imagination to make moral sense of their changing world. Even the application of familiar moral principles ('respect everyone's rights', 'maximise pleasure', 'protect the community') turns on the resolution of controversial questions in ethics and metaphysics: What are people's most basic rights and interests? How should freedom, productivity, and survival be balanced when they cannot all be guaranteed? Do digital uploads or artificial intelligences enjoy valuable consciousness? What is the basis of community when territory and shared history are no long available? We don't know exactly how future people will exercise their moral imagination. But we do know that moral imagination will be a vital part of their moral repertoire.

NOTES

I am grateful to Krushil Watene and Jay Drydyk for very helpful comments on earlier drafts of this chapter.

1. 'Survival lottery' is a term of art. A survival lottery need not include any actual lottery. A libertarian society facing a chaotic climate might reject direct redistribution altogether and simply let the chips fall where they may. I classify this as a *libertarian survival lottery*, because it represents a collective decision to allow the natural distribution of survival-chances to remain uncorrected.
2. A terminological note: The phrases 'affluent age', 'affluent philosophy', and 'affluents' refer, respectively, to the period between the mid-twentieth and early-twenty-first centuries, to the dominant philosophy of that time, and to its inhabitants. Of course, we do not regard everyone alive today as 'affluent'. But this highlights the difference between our moral perspective and the broken world.
3. For more on Nozick in a broken world, see Mulgan (2011, lectures 1 to 5), Mulgan (2015d).
4. For more on contract theory in the broken world, see Mulgan (2011, lectures 12 to 15).
5. Mulgan (2011, lectures 1 to 5).
6. I elaborate this argument further in *Purpose in the Universe: The Moral and Metaphysical Case for Anthropocentric Purposivism* (Mulgan 2015b).
7. See Mulgan 2014a, 2014c.
8. The choice whether to 'upload myself' into a computer is thus a classic example of what L. A. Paul (2014) has called a 'transformative experience', where the person cannot evaluate the experience using her existing values.
9. See, for instance, Hurka 1983.
10. Another inspiration here is theist arguments that human limitations and privations—and even some great evils—are necessary to provide the preconditions for the exercise of virtues such as courage, compassion, and generosity. See, e.g., Dougherty 2014.
11. Mulgan 2011, ch. 5.

REFERENCES

De-Shalit, Avner. 1995. *Why Posterity Matters*. London: Routledge.
Hobbes, Thomas. 1651. *Leviathan.*
Hofstadter, Douglas. 2007. *I Am a Strange Loop.* New York: Basic Books.
Hurka, Thomas. 1983. "Value and Population Size." *Ethics* 93 (3): 496–507.
Locke, John. 1690. *Two Treatises on Government.*
Mulgan, Tim. 2006. *Future People: A Moderate Consequentialist Account of Our Obligations to Future Generations*. Oxford: Oxford University Press.
Mulgan, Tim. 2007. *Understanding Utilitarianism*. Stocksfield: Acumen.

Mulgan, Tim. 2011. *Ethics for a Broken World: Reimagining Philosophy after Catastrophe*. Stocksfield: Acumen.

Mulgan, Tim. 2014a. "Ethics for Possible Futures." *Proceedings of the Aristotelian Society* 114: 57–73.

Mulgan, Tim. 2014b. "Replies to Critics." *Philosophy and Public Issues* 4: 58–92.

Mulgan, Tim. 2014c. "What Is Good for the Distant Future? The Challenge of Climate Change for Utilitarianism." In *God, The Good, and Utilitarianism: Perspectives on Peter Singer*, ed. J. Perry, 141–59. Cambridge: Cambridge University Press.

Mulgan, Tim. 2015a. "Mill and the Broken World." *Revue International de Philosophie* 205–24.

Mulgan, Tim. 2015b. *Purpose in the Universe: The Moral and Metaphysical Case for Anthropocentric Purposivism*. Oxford: Oxford University Press.

Mulgan, Tim. 2015c. "Theory and Intuition in a Broken World." In *Intuition, Theory, and Anti-Theory*, ed. S. G. Chappell, 151–66. Oxford: Oxford University Press.

Mulgan, Tim. 2015d. "Utilitarianism for a Broken World." *Utilitas* 27: 92–114.

Mulgan, Tim. 2016. "Answering to Future People." *The Journal of Applied Philosophy*. Forthcoming.

Nozick, Robert. 1974. *Anarchy, State, and Utopia*. New York: Blackwell.

Rawls, John. 1999a. *The Law of Peoples*. Cambridge: Harvard University Press.

Rawls, John. 1999b. *A Theory of Justice*. Rev. ed. Cambridge: Harvard University Press.

Searle, John. 1997. *The Mystery of Consciousness*. London: Granta.

Chapter Three

Transitional Justice: A Conceptual Map

Colleen Murphy

In recent decades, dozens of countries emerging from long periods of repressive rule and civil conflict have attempted the difficult transition to democracy. South Africa after apartheid, Rwanda post-1994 genocide, and present-day Egypt following the end of the Mubarak era are examples of transitional societies. Although the precise markers of a successful transition to democracy are a matter of ongoing dispute, scholars and policy experts alike agree that societies must explicitly address their legacies of violence, which typically include systematic and brutal human rights abuses.

The term 'transitional justice' refers to formal attempts by post-repressive or post-conflict societies to address past wrongdoing in their efforts to democratize. Societies in transition have enacted a range of measures to confront these legacies of violence, such as amnesty, criminal trials, truth commissions, and reparations. There is little consensus, however, about which response(s) are appropriate and morally justified. Many important studies on transitional justice concentrate on specific cases and employ social science methodologies to understand the social outcomes of different legal responses to wrongdoing, such as whether the establishment of a truth commission has an impact on the rule of law. Such studies also consider the factors that explain the particular choices specific communities make and the constraints that influence decision-making.

My focus in this chapter, however, is different. My interest is in the moral evaluation of the choices transitional communities make in dealing with wrongdoing. Both members and observers of transitional communities form moral judgments about the responses to wrongdoing that communities select. Such judgments are expressed in reactions such as, 'It is unjust to grant amnesties to perpetrators of human rights abuses' or 'A truth commission achieved justice'. There is great variation, and at times incompatibility, in the judgments individuals make. Scholars, international organizations, victims, and citizens of transitional societies disagree on how we should morally judge measures adopted to deal with past wrongdoing.

At the heart of debates about how societies in transition should deal with wrongdoing is the following question: *What are the appropriate standards of justice to use when evaluating various legal responses to wrongdoing in transitional contexts*? This is a question about the general standards or principles that any response to wrongdoing must meet in order to qualify as *just*. In order to explain why responses other than criminal punishment do or do not meet the standards of justice, we must first understand what justice requires. I argue in this paper that to date there is no satisfactory answer to this question.

In the next section I provide an overview of the pragmatic and moral challenges confronting transitional communities that explain why 'ordinary' expectations of justice will not be satisfied. I then critically discuss two general ways of conceptualizing transitional justice: as a compromise and as restorative justice. In compromise views, transitional justice entails the balancing of specific (retributive/distributive/corrective) justice-based claims against competing moral and/or pragmatic considerations. At the core of the limitations with compromise and restorative justice views is a failure to acknowledge the context-sensitive nature of claims of justice. This failure matters because ignoring the background context presupposed by theories of justice, I argue, undermines distinctions between kinds of justice and, as a result, the normative point for making such distinctions in the first place. The most promising theoretical route to explore is the idea that transitional justice is a distinctive kind of justice. However, this idea remains under-theorized and in need of greater conceptual clarification and articulation.

WHAT IS CONTROVERSIAL ABOUT TRANSITIONAL JUSTICE?

Modern democracies generally hold that criminal punishment is the 'first-best' moral response to wrongdoing, especially in the case of egregious wrongdoing such as rape and torture. Trials establish guilt and determine punishment, giving perpetrators 'what they deserve'. Justice is achieved when wrongdoers are punished. (For the purposes of this chapter I take 'punishment' to refer specifically to 'legal punishment' by the state.) President Barack Obama articulated the basic idea that perpetrators of wrongdoing must be punished in the aftermath of the killing of the U.S. ambassador to Libya in 2012: 'Make no mistake, we will work with the Libyan government to bring to justice the killers who attacked our people' (Kirkpatrick and Myers 2012). More generally, the criminal justice system in the United

States, as in many states around the world, is designed to mete out justice so conceived.

Criminal punishment is not entirely without its critics; some sceptics charge that punishment simply masks the brute desire for revenge that human beings harbour when wronged. However, such sceptics are in the minority among the general population and among academics; the consensus view is that punishment is a legitimate response to wrongdoing and satisfies standards of justice. There is also consensus that at least part of the moral point of punishing criminals is to give them what they deserve. The core claim of retributive justice is that perpetrators deserve to suffer and it is intrinsically just to inflict such suffering. For retributivists the amount of suffering should be proportional to the wrong committed. Retributivists differ in the explanations offered for why suffering is what is deserved. Some take this to be a bedrock moral intuition; others offer competing accounts of why suffering is deserved.[1] Many people believe that desert is not the only justification for punishment (deterrence counts as well); however, what is crucial for my purposes is that few are willing to say desert plays no part at all in the justification of criminal punishment. For purposes of articulating why justice is controversial in transitional contexts, I thus simply assume the claim that punishment can satisfy standards of justice.

In transitional contexts both pragmatic and moral obstacles preclude the straightforward application of trial, conviction, and criminal punishment to many, indeed most, instances of wrongdoing. The sheer number of crimes can overwhelm even a mature criminal justice system created to deal with statistically infrequent wrongdoing. Numerous human rights abuses are characteristically committed during repression and conflict, and so criminal justice systems face the task of potentially prosecuting tens of thousands of cases. According to one estimate, between 170,000 and 210,000 individuals actively participated in the Rwandan genocide in 1994 (Strauss 2004). In the words of South African lawyer Paul van Zyl, 'Criminal justice systems are designed to maintain order in societies where violation of law is the exception. These systems simply cannot cope when, either as a result of state-sanctioned human rights abuses or internal conflict or war, violations become the rule' (2000). There are additional obstacles to the successful prosecution of even a portion of alleged perpetrators. It is not unusual for evidence to be systematically destroyed by government officials prior to a transition. Lack of trust in state agents may make the possibility of getting ordinary citizens to testify against wrongdoers practically impossible. Corruption as well as insufficiently trained and funded police and legal staff often undermine the ability of courts to effectively distinguish the guilty from the innocent.

Even when such pragmatic obstacles are not as severe in a given context, moral obstacles remain. During conflict and repression the state is often complicit in wrongdoing, and the criminal justice system colludes in preventing agents of the state from being held accountable for wrongs committed. This collusion calls into question the authority of the state to prosecute such wrongs following a transition. The practical impossibility of charging all—or even most—who are guilty of wrongdoing has led to charges of arbitrariness and bias in the case of the few who are held to account. It is claimed that there is injustice in punishing a few while the many go free, especially when among the many going free are those responsible for issuing the orders that the punished followed. Finally, in some contexts, including South Africa, the possibility of a transition itself may have been conditioned on the granting of amnesty to those who participated in wrongdoing in the past. Amnesties preclude legal liability for a crime for either an individual or class of individuals and are granted prior to a criminal trial. Amnesty thus precludes punishment, and so pursuing punishment in a transition becomes morally controversial insofar as it violates a prior commitment.

Against this background, it is unsurprising that many communities in transition have sought out means other than criminal punishment to deal with the wrongs of the past. Legal scholars, international organizations, victims, and citizens of transitional societies disagree on whether any legal response other than criminal trial and punishment does in fact achieve justice. Alternative responses do not hold perpetrators accountable in the same way as standard democratic justice systems. Amnesty in exchange for peace can grant rapists immunity from criminal and civil liability. Amnesty thus severs the link between accountability and hard treatment. Truth commissions document the actions of torturers, but do not punish them. Furthermore, truth commissions do not focus primarily on individual perpetrators and victims in isolation, but rather on patterns of interaction and structures of institutions that permit, sanction or promote such patterns. Reparations shift the emphasis away from the perpetrator to those who have suffered and been wronged, but reparations only offer material compensation for what in many cases is irreparable harm.

TRANSITIONAL JUSTICE AS COMPROMISE

Many scholars view transitional justice as a compromise among familiar forms of justice (e.g., retributive justice) and competing moral considerations. In this section I critically evaluate a range of views of transitional justice as compromise in the literature. Scholars differ in how they characterize the compromise made and whether they take the compromise to be justified. Despite these differences, there are two general features of compromise views. First, such views implicitly or explicitly define justice as 'all-things-considered-justified'. Scholars may analyse what particular kinds of justice (e.g., retributive justice) demand in the course of their analysis, but what makes a response to wrongdoing justified is that it strikes the appropriate balance among competing values. The claims of commonly recognized types of justice, such as retributive justice, are one of multiple moral (or in some cases pragmatic) inputs that must be taken into account to determine whether a particular response to wrongdoing is 'just'. Second, compromise views also generally assume that moral demands are context-insensitive. That is, moral principles apply across all contexts. The same set of principles or standards needs to be satisfied for a response to wrongdoing to be justified in all contexts. I argue that many versions of compromise views are insufficiently nuanced in their understanding of the justice component of the compromise, failing to recognize that justice is a scalar concept and assuming rather than demonstrating what justice, as one moral value, demands. The most nuanced compromise views avoid this limitation, but in trying to identify how justice specifically is satisfied such approaches collapse important distinctions among kinds of justice and, as a consequence, the normative point for making such distinctions in the first place. A source of this problem is a failure to recognize the contest-sensitive character of justice claims.

Compromise views are most commonly found in the literature in political theory and philosophy, and one case study dominates such discussions: South Africa (Posner and Vermeule 2004). Some scholars focus exclusively on South Africa while others reference additional examples. Because South Africa has been so influential in philosophical discussions of transitional justice as moral compromise, I use it as the case study to illustrate competing versions of compromise positions. A central moral question debated in discussions in the literature of the South African Truth and Reconciliation Commission (TRC), established as part of the transition from apartheid to democracy, is whether, and for what reasons, the granting of amnesty to perpetrators of gross human rights abuses is morally justified. The amnesty provision in the TRC was such that a perpetrator could apply for and be granted amnesty if he fully disclosed the acts for which he was responsible and demonstrated that the acts were committed for political reasons. Individuals granted amnesty were immune from civil and criminal liability.

According to the *simple compromise* position, alternative responses to wrongdoing, such as the South African TRC, sacrifice justice. The realist version of the simple compromise view claims that justice is sacrificed out of expediency (Allen 1999; Mendez 1997, 255). This position is realist in the sense of the tradition in international relations according to which morality does not extend to relations between states. All is fair in war and the aftermath of war. Justice is defined by the powerful. Choices are a function of merely political compromise. 'From the realist perspective, the question of why a given state response occurred is conflated with the question of what response was possible' (Teitel 1997, 2011). Pressing prudential considerations, such as a concern with a resumption of violence should alleged perpetrators be prosecuted, necessitate the choices particular communities make. At first glance, this characterization of the choices that transitional societies make seems apt. Indeed, transitional contexts can give rise to the same thought that realists articulate in the context of war or that underpins justifications for the suspension of ordinary rules by a government in a state of emergency. Justice is taken to be a luxury that communities cannot afford or that does not pertain to such contexts. All becomes fair in (the aftermath of) war.

However, the realist version of the simple compromise position is too sweeping in the permission it grants. Although many find it intuitively plausible to claim that actions not ordinarily sanctioned may be permissible in moments of crisis, few are willing to permit any action whatsoever. Killing may be justified in war, but massacre is not. Similarly, establishing a truth commission may be justified in a transitional context, but summary executions are not. Moreover, the realist version of the simple compromise view does not capture or recognize the moral salience of the various pressing considerations that transitional societies confront. A concern for reducing or ending violence is not only of pragmatic interest for those potentially targeted, but reflects a moral concern with preventing unnecessary suffering.

The moral version of the simple compromise view acknowledges the moral weight that should be given to many of the countervailing considerations. In the moral version, when they establish a truth commission or grant amnesty transitional societies sacrifice justice for the sake of achieving competing moral values, such as peace or reconciliation (Lenta 2000; Moellendorf 1997; Wilson 2001). This version has the virtue of acknowledging the moral salience of many of the factors influencing decisions concerning how to deal with past wrongs. However, the moral version is too simplistic in its conceptualization of the various values at stake in these choices. This view implicitly assumes that values such as justice and reconciliation are completely distinct and incompatible. *Either* one promotes justice *or* one promotes reconciliation, so the thinking goes. Moreover, the moral version of the simple compromise view assumes that justice is achieved in an all-or-nothing manner. *Either* the demands of justice are satisfied, and satisfied completely, *or* justice is sacrificed. The possibility that justice may be satisfied to some degree is not considered.

Nuanced compromise views complicate the moral landscape. The basic strategy of such views is to demonstrate that alternative responses to wrongdoing are or can be sensitive to the moral concerns at the core of retributive justice. Similarly, the extent to which such responses respect the moral concerns at the core of other values, such as reconciliation, is considered. Nuanced compromise views demonstrate that choices to adopt responses other than punishment do not simply sacrifice justice for the sake of another value that is distinct from and unrelated to justice (e.g., something we could name reconciliation). Instead, alternative responses may serve both the value of justice and reconciliation to some degree. At the same time, nuanced compromise views recognize that alternative responses to wrongdoing entail a moral cost and sacrifice. However, the moral cost and sacrifice is principled and one that can be justified (Allais 2012; Allen 1999; May 2011; Posner and Vermeule 2004).

Nuanced compromise views take a more sophisticated view of justice than simple compromise views. They recognize that specific moral concerns underpin the basic principles of justice associated with different kinds of justice. They also draw attention to the basic rationale for specific injunctions of justice. Many such views also recognize that there are multiple kinds of justice about which we may speak and which may be fostered to varying degrees by alternative responses to wrongdoing in transitional contexts. For example, Lucy Allais discusses both restorative and retributive justice, while Jonathan Allen considers punitive justice, compensatory justice and 'justice as ethos' (Allen 1999, 335). Finally, nuanced compromise views acknowledge the complex relationship between justice and other moral concerns such as reconciliation, noting that such values are not necessarily incompatible and may in fact be promoted by the same process.

An assumption underpinning nuanced compromise views is that extant theories of justice provide the requisite conceptual resources for understanding and evaluating the moral questions that transitional societies confront. Nuanced compromise approaches generally recognize that transitional contexts are not identical to ordinary contexts; rather, transitional societies are frequently characterized as exhibiting more-pronounced or acute versions of features found in other contexts (Posner and Vermeule 2004). Such differences do not alter the basic moral framework of justice that we should use to evaluate responses to wrongdoing in transitional contexts; the appropriate framework is the same one we use to evaluate responses to wrongdoing in other contexts. Moral demands are in this sense context-insensitive. However, as I argue below, adapting a theory of retributive justice so that it can be used to evaluate the justifiability of truth commissions has a significant cost: the distinctions among kinds of justice collapse.

A recurring worry about *any* response to wrongdoing, including criminal trials, in transitional contexts is that it will fail to be—and to be viewed by members of the community in question as—an instrument of justice. As Pablo de Greiff puts it, criminal trials risk being seen as mere 'victor's justice' or scapegoating; reparations risk being perceived as attempts to 'buy off' victims and blood money; and truth commissions risk being seen as 'a form of whitewash in which the truth emerges but no one pays any price' (de Greiff 2012, 38). The form scepticism takes in any particular society may vary in terms of breadth and depth in a given population. Scepticism may be wide (shared by the majority of a population) or narrow (shared only by a minority). The degree to which a given population is sceptical about such responses may also differ. In cases where scepticism is not widely shared, a minority population may be so deeply sceptical of a criminal justice system that the attempt to apply that system would lead to genuine political instability. That is, the minority population would simply give up any pretence that they would continue to abide by the authority of the state. If the minority population is small enough then septicism may not be widespread, but still deep enough to be problematic.[2] Scepticism about the justice of any response to wrongdoing seems intuitively plausible in such contexts, and may in particular cases be in fact justified.

Against this background, a central theoretical task is to explain how measures can in fact be measures *of justice* in a context in which they are not likely to be seen in this way and in which often these perceptions are justified. Such explanations stand to have significant practical consequences and affect the meaning that individuals within transitional communities attach to particular measures. By contrast, the same scepticism is not characteristically present among members of stable democratic societies or among scholars theorizing about responses to wrongdoing in such contexts. No criminal justice system is perfect, and many criticisms have been raised about criminal justice systems in stable democracies. (For example, there are advocates of restorative justice who argue that the system of criminal justice should be replaced and there are critics of particular features of specific criminal justice systems, such as the system of the United States, who advocate for their reform. There are recurring concerns about racial bias in the administration of criminal justice in the United States. There may be groups, especially immigrant and minority groups, which view punishment in other democracies in this manner.) However, there is not a general presumption by scholars or by members of such communities that punishment involves the mere exercise of power by a stronger party over a weaker, or that civil damages amount to blood money. Nor consequently is there an assumption among scholars that there are tangible practical consequences that a theoretical justification of a response like punishment or truth commissions will have.

One source of these varying presumptions is the different moral needs present in each context. In transitional societies the basic importance of human rights and their efficacy in governing conduct often need to be established. The new political order that commits to such rights protections needs to be legitimized, and the previous political order that officially and publicly sanctioned violence rejected (de Greiff 2012; Gray 2010, 91–92; Teitel 1997). There is thus a need to draw a line between what communities sanctioned in the past and what will be sanctioned in the future. Yet these large tasks are pursued in the midst of a 'justice gap': the radical disparity between justice needs and resources available to transitional regimes.

Nuanced compromise views adapt theories of particular kinds of justice to respond to the problems and moral needs characteristic of transitions. However, in moving to accommodate these needs, the link between a particular kind of justice and its widely recognized constitutive principles is severed. For example, a central principle of retributivism is that those who commit certain kinds of wrongful acts, paradigmatically serious crimes, morally deserve to suffer a proportionate punishment (Walen 2015). In explaining the justifiability of the South African TRC, however, Allais argues that there are ways other than punishment of responding to the moral concerns underlying retributivism (Allais 2012, 338). The case for the retributive character of a truth commission is made by appealing to the moral concerns that ground or are connected to the core retributive principles, such as respecting the value of human beings or upholding the law (Allais 2012, 342–43). Focusing on the moral concerns at this level of generality also allows her to demonstrate the ways in which other mechanisms satisfy the core concerns underpinning standard kinds of justice, despite fulfilling those concerns in a nonstandard way (e.g., without punishment).

However, separating retributive justice from its orienting problem and substantive normative principles undermines the basis for distinguishing it from other kinds of justice. Discussions of justice operate at many different levels and have different meanings at each level. Justice can be a virtue of individuals as well as a characteristic of laws. As philosophers since Aristotle have recognized, there are different kinds of justice (Aristotle 1999). Aristotle distinguished justice in distribution, rectification, exchange, and political justice. Contemporary philosophers examine retributive justice, corrective justice, distributive justice, international justice, procedural justice, and justice in war. In Book 5 of the *Nicomachean Ethics*, Aristotle notes that the different ways something can be just must be distinguished, and in particular a description of different kinds of justice is needed (Aristotle 1999, 122).

Aristotle does not explain why it is important for justice to be divided, but here is one explanation for its importance. Justice is fundamentally normative, concerned with action. We theorize about justice so as to understand what we should do, as individuals and as communities. Communities confront a variety of problems that call for normative guidance. Kinds of justice focus on specific problems and offer normative guidance on how to deal with a particular issue. Retributive justice focuses on perpetrators of wrongdoing, and asks what should be done in response to their actions. Corrective justice focuses on the injuries individuals can suffer, and what should be done to repair wrongful injuries or losses. Theories of distributive justice answer the question: What principles must be satisfied by a set of social arrangements that assigns rights and duties, and determines the distribution of the benefits and burdens of social cooperation? As the descriptions of the problems indicate, kinds of justice differ in the basic subject of interest (e.g., perpetrators of wrongdoing, victims of wrongdoing, and/or the basic economic institutions of community). Principles of justice specify what counts as doing justice, and different kinds of justice propose different injunctions. Examples include the retributive principle that justice requires punishment of wrongdoers or Rawls's difference principle, according to which departures from strict equality in the distribution of primary goods is just so long as the inequalities are to the benefit of the least advantaged. Thinking of justice discretely in terms of particular kinds allows us to keep clear which problem we are dealing with, and to come up with specific principles for responding to a given problem that will be action guiding. I assume that the separation among kinds of justice is a valid one. In any given case, the separation among kinds of justice should be preserved unless there are overriding reasons not to in any given case.

All kinds of justice share features which count as aspects of justice, rather than another moral value. A basic concern with respect for human dignity is arguably one such feature. Respecting human dignity is thus a very general and basic moral concern of justice, which can be expressed in action in a range of ways. Distributing goods according to a specific set of principles or inflicting suffering on perpetrators of wrongdoing may be two such ways. Demonstrating that responses such as truth commissions respect human dignity is also not sufficient to show that truth commissions respond to *retributive* justice. Thus the fact that responses like truth commissions respect human dignity may count in favour of them respecting justice in general, not retributive justice specifically.

A DIFFERENT KIND OF JUSTICE?

A second kind of account of transitional justice focuses specifically on one moral value, justice, and explains why, and under what conditions, alternative responses fulfil the requirements of this particular value. Responses are 'just' in such accounts insofar as they satisfy these requirements. Scholars who adopt this strategy focus on either *restorative justice* or *transitional justice.* Advocates of restorative justice generally view the requirements of justice as context-insensitive. Advocates of transitional justice generally view justice claims in a context-sensitive manner. According to context-sensitive views, the moral principles or standards that need to be satisfied for a response to wrongdoing to be justified vary across contexts. Here context influences which moral demands are salient in a given case. I discuss each of these kinds of justice in turn.

'Restorative justice' conceptualizes crime as a problem in the relationship among the offender, the victim, and the local community (Walker 2006, 383). In the view of advocates of restorative justice, justice is fundamentally about repairing damaged relationships. The core justice intuition at stake in addressing wrongdoing is 'the notion that a social equality or equilibrium has been disrupted (or further disrupted) by the offense and that it must be restored through social action' (Llewellyn and Howse 1999, 357). A chief goal of the criminal justice system, according to this framework, should be to reconcile the relationships among the criminal, the victim and/or the community in the aftermath of crime.

Restorative justice theorists generally regard it as a mistake to equate justice with retributive justice. The proper aim of the state in the aftermath of crime is not to secure retribution, or deter crime, but to restore the proper relationships among citizens, and between the citizens and the state. Forgiveness is characteristically a key aim of restorative justice. Restorative justice processes focus on rebuilding or building bonds, rather than isolating or alienating the perpetrator, and turn to measures such as restitution payments and face-to-face dialogue in order to restore that relationship (Brathwaite 2002; Kiss 2000, 68–69; van Ness and Strong 2002). When used in criminal sentencing, victims play an important participatory role, shaping what the offender must do to make amends (Johnstone 2002). The role of offenders is characteristically active as well, which, advocates claim, enables offenders to regain their sense of self-worth (Brathwaite 2002; Zehr 1990).

The insight at the core of restorative justice—that relationships and their repair is a central concern of justice—is important. However, I do not think the justice that is salient in transitions is best understood as restorative justice for three reasons. First, the idea of restorative justice is still underdeveloped. The core commitments of restorative justice are still being clarified, and fundamental areas of disagreement remain. Importantly, restorative justice theorists disagree about whether punishment is compatible with restorative justice. For some, the idea that punishment is needed to restore equilibrium is 'arbitrary and historically contingent' (Llewellyn and Howse 1999, 357). Other theorists of restorative justice include punishment as a process of restorative justice (Philpott 2012).

One reaction might be to develop further an account of restorative justice. However, two further limitations suggest this is not the most fruitful course for understanding transitional justice. The second limitation stems from the key role forgiveness plays in most accounts of restorative justice (Philpott 2012). Forgiveness is generally defined as the overcoming or forswearing of negative emotions such as resentment, anger and hatred (Hieronymi 2001; Hughes 1993; Richards 1988). Here relational repair depends fundamentally on a change of reactive attitude or emotion among those wronged. In my view, forgiveness should not be a requirement for relational repair in transitional contexts (Murphy 2010, ch. 1).

The morally laudatory role of forgiveness in interpersonal relationships is most powerful when considering wrongdoing that is the exception, but not the rule. When exceptional, wrongdoing occurs in the context of a relationship otherwise predicated on, for example, mutual respect. A willingness to forgive in this context can reflect recognition by the forgiver of her imperfection and fallibility. Just as she hopes the other will forgive her for her transgressions, she is willing to now forgive. However, in transitions the background relational context is not one of a mutually respectful and reciprocal relationship in which wrongdoing is the exception and not the rule. In contexts where relationships are not mutually respectful and reciprocal, urging forgiveness risks maintaining oppression and injustice. For the focus of forgiveness is not on fundamentally altering the terms of interaction, but rather on overcoming obstacles to ongoing or continuing interaction. In addition, the imperative to forgive places the burden for relational repair squarely on victims, which is in transitional contexts deeply morally problematic. Urging forgiveness can reflect a failure to fully acknowledge or take seriously the wrongdoing to which victims were subject. Placing the burden of relational repair on victims can reflect a failure to recognize that victims are justified in feeling resentment and anger in response. Emphasizing or calling for forgiveness can reflect denial among perpetrators and those complicit in wrongdoing of their responsibility for wrongs that occurred and the corresponding obligations they now have as a result.

The second limitation points to the third limitation of restorative justice: It is insufficiently context-sensitive. Restorative justice theories do not consider the context in which the wrongs being dealt with occurred. Inattention to contextual differences obscures the fact that the reasonableness and plausibility of placing forgiveness at the core of an account of relational repair depends on certain background conditions being in place. Altering the background conditions affects the reasonableness of the moral imperative to forgive; it can turn a reasonable demand into a presumptively morally troubling one.

Accounts of transitional justice generally take seriously the idea that transitional justice is not reducible to forms of justice with which we are already familiar. They also generally take seriously is the idea that claims of justice are context-sensitive. Normative discussions of transitional justice generally concentrate on the moral evaluation of the various means of pursuing justice (e.g., reparations or criminal trials), and not on the idea of transitional justice itself. As Paige Arthur puts it, 'So far, there is no single theory of transitional justice, and the term does not have a fixed meaning' (Arthur 2009, 359). Pablo de Greiff makes the same point even more forcefully when he writes, 'the field remains tremendously undertheorized. It is not just that the consensus around any given understanding of transitional justice and its components is far from complete; the consensus is, moreover thin' (de Greiff 2012, 32). Below I briefly survey the few conceptual accounts of transitional justice currently present in the literature, and discuss their strengths and limitations.

In her seminal book, *Transitional Justice*, Ruti Teitel articulated one of the first accounts of transitional justice. Teitel argues that justice is ultimately *instrumental*: A just response to wrongdoing is one that will promote the transformation of a community into a liberal democratic order (Teitel 1997, 2011). Transitional justice is also pragmatic in the sense that just responses to wrongdoing will offer a pragmatic resolution to the dilemmas inherent in transitional contexts. Importantly, for Teitel what is needed to transform a particular community will be contingent on the particular character of the injustice in the past, and so there is no general prescription of what a just response to wrongdoing must do. Indeed, Ruti Teitel explicitly eschews general standards of justice for transitional contexts, arguing that what counts as just in any particular case 'is contingent and informed by prior injustice' (Teitel 1997, 2014).

However, defining what counts as justice on a strictly case-by-case basis is at odds with a basic intuition about justice: that there is a general set of principles of justice applicable across a range of cases (de Greiff 2012, 60). Moreover, there is a pressing need for criteria by which responses to a legacy of wrongdoing in the midst of a transition can be judged (il)legitimate and (un)just. Defining justice on a case-by-case basis does not provide useful criteria for distinguishing among or critically evaluating the choices communities make.

A few scholars have attempted to articulate the core or orienting principles of transitional justice. Such analyses characteristically begin with an explanation of what is morally distinctive about transitions. There is no consensus on this issue, though there are recurring themes in the literature. One recurring motif is that *law* is different in transitional contexts, and this difference has moral implications. Law, it is frequently claimed, has a 'Janus-faced' character in transitions (Gray 2010; Teitel 1997). For example, criminal law is concerned not just about backward-looking considerations of desert but also forward-looking transformation of a community (Gray 2010; Teitel 1997). However, scholars have convincingly refuted the claim that law is uniquely Janus-faced in transitional contexts; backward- and forward-looking concerns govern law even in democratic contexts (de Greiff 2012; Gray 2010, 58).

A second motif is that transitional contexts are distinctive because of the distinctive moral needs that past wrongdoing generates (de Greiff 2012; Gray 2010, 58). For example, Frank Haldemann argues that recognition is the key goal of transitional justice, 'giving due recognition to the pain and humiliation experienced by victims of collective violence'. But, he argues, such recognition requires communities to overcome the characteristic institutional and broader societal denial regarding the occurrence of and responsibility for wrongs of the past (Haldemann 2008, 687). Haldemann correctly highlights the fact that the wrongs to which transitional communities must respond had concrete victims, and responding to such victims is a key component of what transitional justice demands. However, this recognition is necessary but not sufficient for justice. Dealing with structural factors that enabled violence in the past is also important, and not only or even primarily because necessary to give victims the recognition needed, though it is important for that reason. Dealing with structural and institutional reform itself is also intrinsically part of what justice demands in transitions.

Pablo de Greiff recognizes the structural dimensions of transitional justice, arguing that what is morally required in transitions is the rehabilitation of the force of basic norms prohibiting violence; mass wrongdoing is possible only when this normative erosion happens. De Greiff identifies this breakdown as a constitutive feature of what he calls very imperfect worlds, defined by 'huge and predictable costs associated with the very effort to enforce compliance. At the limit, in such a world, that effort puts at risk the very existence of the system that is trying to enforce its own norms' (de Greiff 2012, 35). For the force of norms prohibiting violence to become rehabilitated, an expanded range of goals must be facilitated by transitional justice measures. In addition to recognition of victims, another intermediate goal of such measures is the cultivation of civic trust (de Greiff 2012; Murphy 2010). The ultimate ends of such measures are reconciliation, and democracy.

De Greiff points to objectives commonly invoked in transitional contexts and within the literature on transitional justice, such as trust, reconciliation, and democracy, and shows how they are related in transitional justice processes. However, the precise relationship between these objectives and justice is not clear. More specifically, it is not clear whether objectives such as trust and democracy should be viewed as important independent moral values to be promoted by transitional justice processes or as components demanded by the specific moral value of justice. One source of the ambiguity lies in the definition of justice de Greiff provides. Eschewing talk of a distinctive set of principles of justice, de Greiff argues that general principles of justice are applied in a distinctive manner in the context of a very imperfect world. He does not elaborate on what such general principles of justice are. Clarification on the relationship between the intermediate and final objectives of transitional processes and the demands of justice is needed, especially in light of conceptual challenges being raised to the necessity of democracy for transitional justice.

Whether democracy as an aspiration is in fact necessary to transitional justice is one of a number of increasingly pronounced conceptual questions that arise in discussions of the range of cases that should properly fall under the scope of transitional justice. The last part of this section provides an overview of these conceptual questions, and then explains the significance of these debates for theorizing about transitional justice.

Paige Arthur in her intellectual history of transitional justice articulates the paradigm transition case informing early discussions of transitional justice exemplified by Argentina in its transition from rule by a military junta and the Dirty War in the 1980s (Arthur 2009). In this paradigm, past abuses were defined as violations of civil and political rights, such as rape, execution, kidnapping, and torture. Two general features characterized the political context within which wrongs were being addressed on which I want to focus. First, the society was in transition from one political regime to another. Second, the transition was to democracy, where democracy entailed changes in law and of political institutions.

Each feature of this paradigm has been called into question as necessary for cases that fall under the scope of transitional justice. In terms of wrongdoing, scholars problematize the exclusive emphasis on violations of civil and political liberties, and transitional justice responses take up a broader range of wrongs. For example, Louise Arbour argues that an emphasis on civil and political rights is self-defeating. The long-term prospects for peace and democracy depend on addressing grievances that could fuel future conflict, and such grievances include violations of economic rights. Examples of violations of economic and social rights include unequal or discriminatory access to land, to work, and to housing or resources. Other scholars question the extent to which a focus on civil and political liberties adequately addresses gender-based harms (Ni Aoláin and Rooney 2007).

The relationship between democracy and transitional justice is the subject of ongoing debate. One challenge is to the necessity of including democracy as a constitutive normative aim in transitional justice. Scholars point to the fact that societies considered to be transitional do not all share the normative aim of democracy. Transitional justice scholarship includes countries in transition but not moving in a liberal political direction such as Chad and Uganda. Countries that have not had a political transition though there has been a reduction in conflict are also studied. Another challenge is to the practical impact of having an aspiration to democratize. Here the point is that it is a mistake to assume that a democratic aim or aspiration will translate into the achievement of democracy (Carothers and Samer-Marram 2015).

Finally, scepticism about the necessity of 'transition' in transitional justice exists. The countries dealing with past wrongs that have been the focus of transitional justice scholarship and practice include a broader set of cases, including, importantly, consolidated democracies that are not 'in transition' to democracy but are already democratic. Australia, Canada and the United States fall into this category. Scholars also argue that even if transition is necessary, it is inadequately conceptualized. It is a mistake to assume that transition refers to a process that will succeed in reaching a predetermined end and to think the process is a temporary or short-lived one. Assuming that a transition follows a predetermined trajectory blinds theorists to the complex power dynamics that shape what happens in a given case (Hansen 2011). In addition, 'transitions' never actually involve a sharp break between a past in which repressive policies and practices took place and a future predicated on consolidated democracy (Dyzenhaus 2003). Many countries remain for extended periods of time in a situation between democratic and repressive rule. Thomas Carothers argues that political analysis should 'start by assuming that what is often thought of as an uneasy, precarious middle ground between full-fledged democracy and outright dictatorship is actually the most common political condition today of the countries in the developing world and the post-communist world. It is not an exceptional category . . . it is a state of normality for many societies' (Carothers 2002, 17–18).

CONCLUSIONS

Though theoretically underdeveloped, taking seriously the idea that transitional justice is a distinctive kind of justice is in my view the most promising theoretical avenue to pursue. By way of conclusion, I want to articulate what I take to be the desiderata for an adequate account of transitional justice that have emerged from the discussion in the previous sections. An adequate account must clarify why it is reasonable to think that justice is different in transitional contexts and must answer the conceptual questions about the scope of cases that properly fall under transitional justice. In this articulation, the relationship between transitional justice and other subjects/types of justice (retributive justice, restorative justice, distributive justice) should be clarified. The scalar character of the demands of justice should also be recognized so that we see how it is possible to judge that a given response to wrongdoing is more or less just, or just or unjust, to different extents. The principles should also be such that they satisfy the pressing practical need for a normative theory of transitional justice. That is, principles of transitional justice should be such that they can be action guiding. An account should also be context-sensitive in the sense of explaining why a given set of principles is salient in the specific context of transition. Finally, an account must clarify the context of transition in part by answering the conceptual questions raised about, for example, the necessity of democracy.

NOTES

1. See Hampton 1992; Morris 1971, and Moore 1993. The views of both Hampton and Morris have been subject to extensive critique. For a critique of Morris, see Hampton 'Correcting Harms'. For a critique of Hampton, see Heather J. Gert, Linda Radzik, and Michael Hand, 'Hampton on the Expressive Power of Punishment' (2004).
2. I thank Linda Radzik for drawing this point to my attention.

REFERENCES

Allais, Lucy. 2012. 'Restorative Justice, Retributive Justice, and the South African Truth and Reconciliation Commission'. *Philosophy & Public Affairs* 39(4): 331–63.

Allen, Jonathan. 1999. 'Balancing Justice and Social Utility: Political Theory and the Idea of a Truth and Reconciliation Commission'. *University of Toronto Law Journal* 49: 315–53.

Aristotle. 1999. *Nicomachean Ethics*. 2nd ed. Translated by Terence Irwin. Indianapolis: Hackett Publishing.

Arthur, Paige. 2009. 'How 'Transitions' Reshaped Human Rights: A Conceptual History of Transitional Justice'. *Human Rights Quarterly* 31: 321–67.

Brathwaite, John. 2002. *Restorative Justice and Responsive Regulation.* Oxford: Oxford University Press.

Carothers, Thomas. 2002. 'The End of the Transition Paradigm'. *Journal of Democracy* 13(1): 5–21.

Carothers, Thomas, and Oren Samet-Marram. 2015. 'The New Global Marketplace of Political Change'. Carnegie Endowment for International Peace, April 20. http://carnegieendowment.org/2015/04/20/new-global-marketplace-of-political-change/i7fw?mkt_tok=3RkMMJWWfF9wsRoisq%2FBZKXonjHpfsX57OwrXKag38431UFwdcjKPmjr1YcGTsJ0aPyQAgobGp5I5FEIQ7XYTLB2t60MWAemXSjrtqDIZoxAZZ13gZI3

de Greiff, Pablo. 2012. 'Theorizing Transitional Justice'. *Transitional Justice* 51: 31–77.

Dyzenhaus, David. 2003. 'Judicial Independence, Transitional Justice, and the Rule of Law'. *Otago Law Review* 345(10): 345–70.

Gert, Heather J., Linda Radzik, and Michael Hand. 2004. 'Hampton on the Expressive Power of Punishment'. *Journal of Social Philosophy* 35(1): 79–90.

Gray, David C. 2010. 'Extraordinary Justice'. *Alabama Law Review* 62(1): 55–109.

Haldemann, Frank. 2008. 'Another Kind of Justice: Transitional Justice as Recognition'. *Cornell Journal of International Law* 41: 675–737.

Hampton, Jean. 1992. 'Correcting Harms Versus Righting Wrongs: The Goal of Retribution'. *UCLA Law Review* 39: 1659–1702.

Hansen, Thomas Obel. 2011. 'Transitional Justice: Toward a Differentiated Theory'. *Oregon Review of International Law* 13(1): 1–54.

Hieronymi, Pamela. 2001. 'Articulating an Uncompromising Forgiveness'. *Philosophy and Phenomenological Research* 62(3): 529–55.

Hughes, Paul M. 1993. 'What Is Involved in Forgiving?' *Philosophia* 25: 33–49.

Johnstone, Gerry. 2002. *Restorative Justice: Ideas, Values, Debates.* Cullompton, UK: Willan Publishing.

Kirkpatrick, David, and Steven Lee Myers. 2012. 'Libya Attack Brings Challenges for the U.S.'. *New York Times*, September 12.

Kiss, Elizabeth. 2000. 'Moral Ambition within and Beyond Political Constraints: Reflections on Restorative Justice'. In *Truth v, Justice: The Morality of Truth Commissions,* edited by Robert I. Rotberg and Dennis Thompson, 68–98. Princeton: Princeton University Press.

Lenta, Patrick. 2000. 'Transitional Justice and the Truth and Reconciliation Commission'. *Theoria: Journal of Political and Social Theory* 96: 52–73.

Llewellyn, Jennifer, and Robert Howse. 1999. 'Institutions for Restorative Justice: The South African Truth and Reconciliation Commission'. *University of Toronto Law Journal* 49(3): 355–88.

May, Simon Cabuela. 2011. 'Moral Compromise, Civic Friendship, and Political Reconciliation'. *Critical Review of International Social and Political Philosophy* 14(5): 581–602.

Mendez, Juan E. 1997. 'Accountability for Past Abuses'. *Human Rights Quarterly* 19, no. 2: 255–82.

Moellendorf, Darrell. 1997. 'Amnesty, Truth, and Justice: AZAPO'. *South African Journal on Human Rights* 13: 283–91.

Moore, Michael. 1993. 'Justifying Retributivism'. *Israel Law Review* 24: 15–49.

Morris, Herbert. 1971. 'Guilt and Suffering'. *Philosophy East* and *West* 21(4): 419–34.

Murphy, Colleen. 2010. *A Moral Theory of Political Reconciliation.* New York: Cambridge University Press.

Ní Aoláin, Fionnuala, and Eilish Rooney. 2007. 'Underenforcement and Intersectionality: Gendered Aspects of Transition for Women'. *International Journal of Transitional Justice* 1(3): 338–54.

Philpott, Daniel. 2012. *Just and Unjust Peace: An Ethic of Political Reconciliation.* New York: Oxford University Press.

Posner, Eric A., and Adrian Vermeule. 2004. 'Transitional Justice as Ordinary Justice'. *Harvard Law Review* 117(3): 761–825.

Richards, Norman. 1988. 'Forgiveness'. *Ethics* 99(1): 77–97.

Strauss, Scott. 2004. 'How Many Perpetrators Were There in the Rwandan Genocide? An Estimate'. *Journal of Genocide Research* 6(1): 85–98.

Teitel, Ruti. 1997. 'Transitional Jurisprudence: The Role of Law in Political Transformation'. *Yale Law Journal* 106(7): 2009–80.

Teitel, Ruti. 2002. *Transitional Justice*. Oxford: Oxford University Press.

van Ness, Daniel W., and Karen Heetderks Strong. 2002. *Restoring Justice.* 2nd ed. Cincinnati: Anderson Publishing.

van Zyl, Paul. 2000. 'Justice without Punishment: Guaranteeing Human Rights in Transitional Societies'. In *Looking Back, Reaching Forward: Reflections on the Truth and Reconciliation Commission of South Africa,* edited by Charles Villa-Vicencio and Wilhelm Verwoerd, 46–57. Cape Town: University of Cape Town Press.

Walen, Alec. 'Retributive Justice.' *The Stanford Encyclopedia of Philosophy,* edited by Edward N. Zalta (Summer 2015 Edition). http://plato.stanford.edu/archives/sum2015/entries/justice-retributive/.

Walker, Margaret Urban. 2006. 'Restorative Justice and Reparations'. *Journal of Social Philosophy* 37(3): 377–95.

Wilson, Stuart. 2001. 'The Myth of Restorative Justice: Truth, Reconciliation and the Ethics of Amnesty'. *South African Journal of Human Rights* 17: 531–62.

Zehr, Howard. 1990. *Changing Lenses: A New Focus for Crime and Justice*. Scottsdale, PA: Herald Press.

Chapter Four

What Do We Want from a Theory of Justice?

Amartya Sen

I begin from the general Rawlsian position that the interpretation of justice is linked with public reasoning. The focus has to be, in John Rawls's words, on 'a public framework of thought' that provides 'an account of agreement in judgment among reasonable agents'.[1] Rawls outlines this demand in terms of avoiding what he calls 'a personal slant':

> We do not look at the social order from our situation but take up a point of view that everyone can adopt on an equal footing. In this sense we look at society and our place in it objectively: we share a common standpoint along with others and do not make our judgments from a personal slant.[2]

The bearing of *public reasoning* on the theory of justice leads to two further inquiries: *What is the relevant public?* and *On what questions should the reasoning concentrate?* The former query concerns the range of points of view that should count in public reasoning (for example, whether they must all come from inside a given political state), while the latter relates to the subject matter of public reasoning, in particular what are the questions to be answered for a satisfactory theory of justice? The two issues, I will argue, are linked, and together they lead us to the foundational question: *What do we want from a theory of justice?*

I have begun by drawing on Rawls's lead on the basic connection between objectivity, public reasoning, and the theory of justice. However, I have to argue for a rather different way of pursuing that connection, departing not only from the substantive content of the Rawlsian theory of justice but also from Rawls's diagnosis of the very requirements of a theory of justice, including the subject matter of public reasoning and the reach and coverage of public participation.

THE TRANSCENDENTAL VERSUS THE COMPARATIVE

I begin with the issue of the subject matter of a satisfactory theory of justice. In his analysis of 'justice as fairness', Rawls takes the principal question to be: *What is a just society?* Indeed, in most theories of justice in contemporary political philosophy, that question is taken to be central. This leads to what can be called a 'transcendental' approach to justice, focusing—as it does—on identifying perfectly just societal arrangements. In contrast, what can be called a 'comparative' approach would concentrate instead on ranking alternative societal arrangements (whether some arrangement is 'less just' or 'more just' than another), rather than focusing exclusively—or at all—on the identification of a fully just society. The transcendental and comparative approaches are quite distinct, and as will be presently discussed, neither approach, in general, subsumes or entails the other.[3]

The transcendental approach to justice is not new (it can be traced at least to Thomas Hobbes), but recent contributions have done much to consolidate the reliance on this approach. In his investigation of 'justice as fairness', Rawls explores in depth in the nature of an entirely just society seen in the perspective of contractarian fairness. Rawls's investigation begins with identifying the demands of fairness through exploring an imagined 'original position' in which the members of the society are ignorant of their respective individual characteristics including their own comprehensive preferences. The principles of justice that emerge in the original position are taken to be impartial because they are chosen by the persons involved under a 'veil of ignorance', without knowledge of their individual identities in the society with specific vested interests and particular priorities.

Later on in this chapter, I discuss some limitations of this understanding of the demands of fairness (and ask whether the points of view to be considered must all come from the population of a given state), but the immediate point to note in the context of understanding the transcendental approach is that the fairness exercise is aimed entirely at identifying appropriate principles for a fully just society and at isolating the institutional needs for the basic structure of such a society. The working of these institutions, in turn, leads to further societal decisions at later stages in the Rawlsian system, for example through appropriate legislation (in what Rawls calls the 'legislative stage'). The sequence moves forward step by step on firmly specified lines, with elaborately characterized unfolding of completely just societal arrangements.

Despite the standing and widespread use of the transcendental approach, the intellectual interest in, and practical relevance of, comparative questions about justice are hard to deny. Investigation of different ways of advancing justice in a society (or in the world), or of reducing manifest injustices that may exist, demands comparative judgments about justice, for which the identification of fully just social arrangements is neither necessary nor sufficient. To illustrate the contrast involved, it may well turn out that in a comparative perspective, the introduction of social policies that abolish slavery, or eliminate widespread hunger, or remove rampant illiteracy, can be shown to yield an advancement of justice. But the implementation of such policies could still leave the societies involved far away from the transcendental requirements of a fully just society (since transcendence would have other demands regarding equal liberties, distributional equity, and so on).

The grand partition between the 'just' and the 'non-just', which is what a theory of transcendental justice yields, would leave the society in the 'non-just' side even after the reform, despite what can be seen, in a comparative perspective, as a justice-enhancing change. Some non-transcendental articulation is clearly needed. To take another type of example, instituting a system of public health insurance in the United States that does not leave tens of millions of Americans without any guarantee of medical attention at all may be judged to be an advancement of justice, but such an institutional change would not turn the United States into a 'just society' (since there would remain a hundred other transgressions still to remedy).

A transcendental approach cannot, on its own, address questions about advancing justice and compare alternative proposals for having a more just society, short of proposing a radical jump to a perfectly just world. Indeed, the answers that a transcendental approach to justice gives—or can give—are quite distinct and distant from the type of concerns that engage people in discussions on justice and injustice in the world, for example, iniquities of hunger, illiteracy, torture, arbitrary incarceration, or medical exclusion as particular social feature that need remedying. The focus of these engagements tends to be on the ways and means of advancing justice—or reducing injustice—in the world by remedying these inequities, rather than on looking only for the simultaneous fulfilment of the entire cluster of perfectly just societal arrangements demanded by a particular transcendental theory.

POSSIBLE DEFENSE OF A TRANSCENDENTAL APPROACH

The argument so far has been, in an important sense, too easy. Surely transcendental answers cannot be all we want from a theory of justice. But there might well be—this is a matter to be investigated—some less obvious connection, some relationship between the transcendental and the comparative that could make the transcendental approach the right way of proceeding to comparative assessments. The formal remoteness of the transcendental approach from the invoking of the idea of justice in debates and discussions on practical affairs does not in itself indicate that the transcendental approach cannot be the right approach.

Thus, at least two further questions must be addressed, related to the possibility, respectively, of (1) the sufficiency, and (2) the necessity, of the transcendental approach for making comparative judgments about justice. First, can the answers to transcendental queries take us indirectly to comparative assessments of justice as well, in particular through comparisons of 'distances' from transcendence at which particular sets of societal arrangements respectively stand? Second, can it be the case that the transcendental question ('What is a just society?') has to be answered first, as an essential requirement, for a cogent and well-founded theory of comparative justice, which would otherwise be foundationally disjunctive and frail? For an adequate critique of the transcendental approach to justice from the comparative perspective, we have to assess these possibilities critically.

Implicit beliefs in the sufficiency or the necessity (or both) of a transcendental approach for comparative assessment clearly have had a powerful role in the widespread belief that the transcendental approach is crucial for the entire theory of justice. Indeed, even in social choice theory, where the analytical framework is firmly relational and altogether grounded in pairwise comparisons, the investigations of justice in particular has been standardly elongated to move relentlessly from the basic comparative rankings to the identification of transcendental justice (often in the Rawlsian mold).[4] In arguing for a more robustly comparative approach to justice, with which this paper is concerned (and for which social choice theory can play, I would suggest, an important role), it would be necessary to examine whether comparative conclusions either *follow from,* or *need,* some transcendental identification.

DOES TRANSCENDENTAL SPECIFICATION YIELD COMPARATIVE RANKINGS?

I begin with the issue of *sufficiency.* Does a transcendental approach produce, as a by-product, relational conclusions that are ready to be drawn out, so that transcendence may end up giving us a great deal more than its overt form articulates? In particular, is the specification of an entirely just society sufficient to give us ranking of departures from justness in terms of comparative 'distances' from perfection, so that a transcendental identification might immediately entail comparative gradings as well?

The answer here is a firm no. The main difficulty lies in the fact that there are different features involved in identifying distance, related, among other distinctions, to (1) different fields of departure, (2) varying dimensionalities of transgressions within the same general field, and (3) diverse ways of weighing separate infractions. The identification of transcendence does not yield any means of addressing these problems to arrive at a relational ranking of departures from transcendence.

For example, in the context of the Rawlsian analysis of the just society, departures may occur in many different spaces. They can include the breaching of liberty, which, furthermore, an involve diverse violations of distinctive liberties (many of which figure in Rawls's capacious coverage of liberty and its priority). There can also be violations—again in possibly disparate forms—of the demands of equity in the distribution of primary goods (there can be many different departures from the demands of the Difference Principle which forms a part of Rawls's second principle). Similarly, diverse transgressions can occur in other transcendental theories of justice (for example, those that would replace the Rawlsian focus on 'primary goods' in the Difference Principle by concentrating respectively on 'capabilities' or 'resources' or 'opportunities', or some other way of formulating the allocational and distributional needs of transcendental justice).

There are also disparate ways of assessing the extent of each such discrepancy and of appraising the comparative remoteness of actual distributions from what the principles of full justice would demand. Further, we have to consider departures in procedural equity (such as infringements of fair equality of public opportunities or facilities), which figured within the domain of Rawlsian demands of justice (in the first part of the second principle). To weigh these procedural departures *against* infelicities of emergent patterns of interpersonal distribution (for example, distributions of primary goods), which also figure in the Rawlsian system, would require distinct specification—possibly in axiomatic terms—of relative importance or significance (or 'trade-offs' as they are sometimes called in the crude vocabulary of multidimensional assessment). But these extensions, helpful as they would be, lie well beyond the specific exercise of the identification of transcendence, and are indeed the basic ingredients of a 'comparative' rather than a 'transcendental' approach to justice. The characterization of spotless justice does not entail any delineation whatever of how diverse departures from spotlessness can be compared and ranked.

The absence of such comparative implications is not, of course, an embarrassment for a transcendental theory of justice, seen as a freestanding achievement. The relational silence is not, in any sense, an internal difficulty of a transcendental theory of justice. Indeed, some pure transcendentalists would be utterly opposed even to flirting with gradings and comparative assessments, and may quite plausibly shun relational conclusions altogether.

They may point in particular to their understanding that a 'right' social arrangement must not, in any way, be understood as a 'best' social arrangement, which could open the door to what is sometimes seen as the intellectually mushy world of graded evaluations in the form of 'better' or 'worse' (linked with the relationally superlative 'best'). The absoluteness of the transcendental 'right'—against the relativities of the 'better' and the 'best'—may well have a powerfully reasoned standing of its own. But it does not help at all in *comparative assessments* of justice.

To be sure, members of any polity can contemplate how a gigantic and totally comprehensive reorganization may be brought about, moving us *at one go* to the ideal of a fully just society. A no-nonsense transcendental theory can serve, in this sense, as something like the 'grand revolutionary's complete handbook'. But that handbook would not be much invoked in the debates on justice in which we are constantly engaged, which focus on how to reduce the manifold injustices that characterize the world.[5]

Even if we think of transcendence not in the 'gradingless' terms of 'right' social arrangements, but in the graded terms of the 'best' social arrangements, the identification of the best does not, in itself, tell us much about the full grading, such as how to compare two non-best alternatives. The identification of the best does not specify a unique ranking with respect to which the best stands at the pinnacle; indeed the same best may go with a great many different rankings with the same pinnacle. To consider an analogy, the fact that a person regards the *Mona Lisa* as the best picture in the world does not reveal how she would rank a Gauguin against a Van Gogh. The search for transcendental justice is an engaging exercise in itself, but irrespective of whether we think of transcendence in terms of the gradeless 'right' or in the framework of the graded 'best', it does not tell us much about the comparative merits of many—indeed typically most—of the different societal arrangements.

IS A TRANSCENDENTAL THEORY NECESSARY FOR COMPARISONS OF JUSTICE?

I now take up the second question, concerning the hypothesis that the identification of the best is necessary, even if not sufficient, to rank any two alternatives in terms of justice. In the usual sense of necessity, this would be a somewhat odd possibility. In the discipline of comparative judgments in any field, relative assessment of two alternatives tends in general to be a matter between them, without there being the necessity of beseeching the help of a third— 'irrelevant'—alternative. Indeed, it is not at all obvious why in making the judgment that some social arrangement x is better than an alternative arrangement y, we have to invoke the identification that some quite different alternative z is the 'best' or the 'right' social arrangement. In arguing for a Picasso over a Dali we do not need to get steamed up about identifying the perfect picture in the world, which would beat the Picassos and the Dalis and all other paintings in the world.

It might, however, be thought that the analogy with aesthetics is problematic since a person might not even have any idea of a perfect picture, in a way that the idea of a perfectly just society has appeared to be identifiable, in transcendental theories of justice. I will argue later on that the existence of a best, or a transcendent, alternative is actually not guaranteed even in the field of justice, but I am ready to proceed, for the moment, on the presumption that such an identification can somehow be made. However, despite this tentative acceptance, the existence of an identifiably inviolate, or best, alternative does not indicate that it is necessary (or indeed useful) to refer to it in judging the relative merits of two other alternatives. For example, we may indeed be willing to accept, with great certainty, that Everest is the tallest mountain in the world, completely unbeatable in terms of stature by any other peak, but that understanding is neither needed, nor particularly helpful, in comparing the heights of, say, Kanchenjunga and Mont Blanc. There would be something very deeply odd in a general belief that a comparison of any two alternatives cannot be sensibly made without a prior identification of a supreme alternative.

Thus, the hypothesis of necessity in the standard sense would be hard to sustain. There is, however, a weaker form of the hypothesis of necessity, which merely asserts that if comparative assessments can be systematically made, then that discipline must also be able to identify the very best. The claim, in this case, would be not so much that two alternatives cannot be compared in terms of justice without first knowing what the best or the perfect alternative is, but that the comparative ranking of the different alternatives must inter alia also be able to identify the answer to the transcendental question regarding the perfectly just society. Or, to put it in another way, if the transcendental question cannot be answered, then nor can be the comparative. This understanding of necessity would not vindicate the need to go via the transcendental approach to comparative assessments, but it would at least give transcendental identification a necessary presence in the theory of justice. We have to examine this considerably weaker claim of 'necessity' as well.

COMPARATIVES WITHOUT TRANSCENDENCE

Would a sequence of pairwise comparisons invariably lead us to the very best? That presumption has some appeal, since the superlative might indeed appear to be the natural end point of a robust comparative. But this conclusion would, in general, be a non sequitur. In fact, it is only with a 'well-ordered' ranking (for example, a complete and transitive ordering over a finite set) that we can be sure that the set of pairwise comparisons must also identify a 'best' alternative.

We must, therefore, ask: How complete should the assessment be, for it to be a systematic discipline? In the 'totalist' approach that characterizes the standard theories of justice (including Rawls's), incompleteness tends to appear as a failure, or at least as a sign of the unfinished nature of the exercise. Indeed, the survival of incompleteness is sometimes seen as a defect of a theory of justice, which calls into question the positive assertions that such a theory makes. In fact, however, a theory of justice that makes systematic room for incompleteness allows one to arrive at possibly quite strong judgments (for example, about the injustice of continuing famines in a world of prosperity, or of persistently grotesque subjugation of women), without having to find highly differentiated assessment of every political and social arrangement in comparison with every other arrangement (for example, addressing such questions as: Is a top income tax rate of 45 percent more just or less just than a top rate of 46 percent?).

I have discussed elsewhere why a systematic and disciplined theory of normative evaluation, including assessment of social justice, need not take a 'totalist' form.[6] Incompleteness may be of the lasting kind for several different reasons, including unbridgeable gaps in information, and judgmental unresolvability involving disparate considerations that cannot be entirely eliminated, even with full information. For example, it may be hard to resolve the overall balance of the comparative claims of equity considerations that lie behind Rawlsian lexicographic maximin, compared with, say, sum—ranking in a gross or equity—adjusted form.[7] And yet, despite such durable incompleteness, we may still be able to agree readily that there is a clear social injustice involved in the persistence of endemic hunger or exclusion from medical access, which calls for a well-specified remedying for the *advancement* of justice (or reduction of injustice), even after taking note of the costs involved. Similarly, we may acknowledge the possibility that liberties of different persons may, to some extent, conflict with each other (so that any fine-tuning of the demands of equal liberty may be hard to work out), and yet strongly agree that torturing accused people would be an unjust violation of liberty and that this injustice calls for an urgent rectification.

There is a further consideration that may work powerfully in the direction of making political room for incompleteness of judgments about social justice, even if it were the case that every person had a complete ordering over the possible social arrangements. Since a theory of justice invokes agreement between different parties (for example, in the 'original position' in the Rawlsian framework), incompleteness can also arise from the possibility that different persons may continue to have some differences (consistently with agreeing on a lot of the comparative judgments). Even after vested interests and personal priorities have been somehow 'taken out' of consideration through such devices as the 'veil of ignorance', there may remain possibly conflicting views on social priorities, for example in weighing the claims of need over entitlement to the fruits of one's labour.

Conflicts of distributive principles that are hard to eradicate can be illustrated with an example, which I have discussed in another context. The example is concerned with the problem of deciding which of three children should get a flute about which they are quarrelling. Child *A* is the only one of the three who knows how to play the flute (the others do not deny this); child *B* is the only one without any toys of his own (the other two concede that they are much richer and well supplied with engaging amenities); child *C* has worked hard to make the flute all on his own (the others confirm this). Theorists of different persuasions—utilitarian or egalitarian or libertarian—may believe that a just resolution can be readily spotted here, though, alas, they would respectively see totally different resolutions as being exactly right. The main point to note in the present context is that the different resolutions all have serious arguments in support of them, and we may not be able to identify exactly one of the alternative arguments as being the only one (to invoke Thomas Scanlon's criterion) that 'could be justified to others on grounds that they, if appropriately motivated, could not reasonably reject'.[8]

Even when each of the parties involved has his or her own complete specification of justice, the 'intersection' between the ranking—that is the *shared* beliefs of the different parties—can yield a partial ranking, if the judgments are not all congruent.[9] The acceptability of evaluative incompleteness is indeed a central subject in social choice in general, and it is relevant to theories of justice as well, even though Rawlsian and other theories assert (and it *is* an assertion rather than something that is established in any clear way) that a full agreement will definitely emerge in the 'original position' and in other such formats.[10]

Indeed, for reasons both of incomplete individual evaluations and of incomplete congruence of individual assessments, incompleteness may be a hardy feature of judgments of social justice. This can be problematic for the identification of a perfectly just society, and make transcendental conclusions difficult to derive.[11] And yet, such incompleteness would not prevent making comparative judgments of justice in a great many cases, where there might be fair agreement on particular pairwise rankings, about how to enhance justice and reduce injustice. A partial ordering can be very useful without being able to lead to any transcendental identification of a fully just society.

The question 'What is a just society?' is, therefore, not a good *starting point* for a useful theory of justice. To that has to be added the further conclusion that it may not be a plausible *end point* either. A systematic theory of comparative justice does not need, nor does it necessarily yield, an answer to the question 'What is a just society?'

INSTITUTIONAL BARRIERS AND TRANSCENDENTAL SILENCE

I turn now to a different—though not unrelated—feature of the transcendental approach to justice, in particular the extremely demanding institutional requirements of accomplishing pristine justice. The achievement of a fully just society would require a plethora of institutions, including the unfettered operations of a sovereign state. Some of these institutions are absent or defective in many countries in the world; nor can these countries readily establish them. Even without the possibility of setting up some of these institutions, it is, of course, possible to advance justice—or to reduce injustice—to a considerable extent, but while that is good enough for applying the comparative approach to justice, it does not yield the achievement of transcendental justice. If such spotless justice were the only focus of attention in a theory of justice, then the institutional preconditions would form a kind of 'entry barrier', leading to an abstinence from applying justice theory to situations in which those exacting institutional demands are not only not currently met but cannot be met in the foreseeable future.

The institutional preconditions would be particularly hard to meet in dealing with, say, problems of global justice. The claim that we need a sovereign state to apply the principles of justice—a claim that was well articulated by Thomas Hobbes—is substantially connected with the elaborate institutional demands of a transcendental understanding of justice. Thomas Nagel's strongly argued dismissal of the relevance of 'the idea of global justice' draws on his understanding that these extensive institutional demands cannot be met at the global level at this time. As he puts it, 'It seems to me very difficult to resist Hobbes's claim about the relation between justice and sovereignty', and 'if Hobbes is right, the idea of global justice without a world government is a chimera'.[12] In the global context, Nagel concentrates, therefore, on clarifying other demands, distinguishable from the demands of justice, such as 'minimal humanitarian morality' (which 'governs our relations to all other persons'), and also to long-run strategies for radical change in institutional possibilities ('I believe the most likely path toward some version of global justice is through the creation of patently unjust and illegitimate global structures of power that are tolerable to the interests of the most powerful current nation-states').[13]

In the Rawlsian approach too, the application of a theory of justice requires an extensive cluster of institutions that determines the basic structure of a fully just society. Not surprisingly, Rawls actually abandons his own principles of justice when it comes to the assessment of how to go about thinking about global justice. In a later contribution, *The Law of Peoples*, Rawls invokes a 'second original position', with a fair negotiation involving representatives of different polities—or different 'peoples' as Rawls calls them—who serve as parties under this second veil of ignorance.[14] However, Rawls does not try to derive principles of justice that might emanate from this second original position, and concentrates instead on certain general principles of humanitarian behaviour. The Rawlsian vehicle of justice that would take us rapidly forward in pursuit of some justice in a justiceless world remains stalled and stationary in the wintry morning of a world without a global state.

To be sure, Rawls need not agree that the world is really unjust if he remains fully attached to the belief that the concept of justice does not apply at the global level. Nagel, on the other hand, seems definitely convinced that 'we do not live in a just world' (the opening sentence of 'The Problem of Global Justice' [op. cit., p. 113]). While I firmly agree with that conclusion (given what I see as the role of a theory of justice, the subject matter of this paper), it is not entirely clear to me how Nagel can make statements of this kind given his conviction that the idea of global justice is 'a chimera'..[15]

The challenge of making the world less unjust, thus, remains unaddressed within the transcendental approach. It is not, however, at all clear why we should be reduced to silence, so far as justice is concerned, merely because the reach of institutional possibilities does not prepare us for transcendental justice. The question how global justice can nevertheless be advanced remains pertinent to ask, unless we are forcibly removed from the territory of justice on the ground that transcendental justice is the only satisfactory—or the only understandable—idea of justice. Indeed, that question about advancement of justice (or about reduction of global injustice) can be a fruitful part of the subject matter of the deliberative framework of public reasoning. A 'public framework of thought', which Rawls has taught us to value and use, should not become wholly inoperative merely because the institutional demands of a perfectly just society have turned out to be infeasible.

There is, thus, a real tension between making good use of public reasoning (drawing on Rawls's powerful, general arguments in that direction) and remaining silent whenever some exacting institutional conditions needed for transcendental justice cannot be entirely fulfilled (a conclusion that emerges from the special transcendental form that Rawls gives to his theory of justice). There is a serious loss here. Public deliberation can be important and useful both in pursuing institutional reform (even when the totality of the institutional reforms needed for perfection cannot be carried out) and in examining what can be done to reduce injustice—a basic question in the comparative approach to justice—even when not all the right institutions are in place.[16] A non-Rawlsian comparative (rather than transcendental) approach to justice can be a good conceptual base for such—essentially Rawlsian—public reasoning.

TRANSCENDENTAL LOCALISM AND GLOBAL CONCERNS

The importance of public reasoning for dealing with global problems of justice is a subject of importance on its own. However, it must be acknowledged that even though Rawls was a visionary leader of thought on the importance of public reasoning, he had considerable scepticism about the use of public reasoning at the global level. It is important to separate out two possible grounds for Rawls's reluctance. One issue, which has already been mentioned, is the inapplicability of the exacting framework of transcendental justice at the global level, because of institutional limitations. A second reason for Rawls's reluctance is his insistence on linking public reasoning with the contractarian format of the 'original position'. This involves a devised deliberative exercise that would appear to be hard to apply beyond the limits of a particular society (or a particular 'people', as Rawls defines this collectivity in his later works).[17]

Rawls's statement about the need for a 'common standpoint' which was quoted (from *A Theory of Justice*) at the beginning of this paper was immediately followed by the invoking of this particular conceptual device:

> Thus our moral principles and convictions are objective to the extent that they have been arrived at and tested by assuming this general standpoint and by assessing the arguments for them by the restrictions *expressed by the conception of the original position.*[18]

The deliberation thus takes the form of fair negotiation, in which the fairness of the reasoned negotiation is grounded on the demand that the reasoning occurs under a specially conceived veil of ignorance. But the participants in the deliberation are exactly the parties to the social contract for the society in question. A person's voice counts because he or she is directly involved in the social contract, which will 'regulate the institutions' of the society of which he is a member.[19]

In contrast to this negotiational justification of the confinement to local points of view, there is a different approach to impartiality which brings in different voices, possibly even from 'a distance' (to use Adam Smith's articulate phrase), precisely because these voices illuminate public decisions and help to make them impartial. In the terminology of conflict resolution, this is more like arbitration, rather than negotiation; the arbitrators need not themselves be parties to the dispute. I have argued elsewhere that the interpretation of fairness and impartiality through an understanding of 'fair arbitration' is a serious rival to the route of 'fair negotiation', which is the exclusive direction in which the contractarian feature of Rawls's transcendental approach—'justice as fairness'—proceeds.[20]

The approach of fair arbitration is well exemplified by Smith's invoking of the perspectives of 'impartial spectators'. The impartial spectators are imagined observers who need not be members of the society, and their impartiality does not come, as in the Rawlsian system, exclusively—or even primarily—through the thought experiment of a veil of ignorance about the personal circumstances of individual members of a given society. Rather, the thought experiment by members of society, in the Smithian system of fair arbitration, invokes the judgments of disinterested observers who are not themselves parties to the societal decisions that are to be taken.

In itself this may not seem like a big difference, since both are merely thought experiments that must be undertaken, within the respective formats, by the people in the actual society. Also, there is nothing to prevent the imagined fair arbitrators from under taking the exercise of placing themselves in the position of the parties involved under a devised veil of ignorance, so that fair arbitration can make good use of the insights that may come from fair negotiation.

However, there are two sources of substantial difference between the Smithian and the Rawlsian procedures. First, the contractarian approach standardly proceeds toward identifying the demands of transcendence (the principal inquiry in the original position is aimed at the demands of a just society), whereas Smith's impartial spectators are typically invoked for contrasting alternatives to throw light on specific issues of advancement or retardation of justice in a comparative approach. A second difference arises from the fact that the impartial observers may be imagined as coming from far as well as near, with questions being asked about how the decisional problem would look to those who may have had different social and institutional experience (a question of some importance, as Smith has argued). While the imagined impartial judges may find it useful to ask inter alia what things would look like had they actually been the involved parties (here the exercise would be, in effect, rather similar to the Rawlsian one), they could also be seen as bringing perspectives that are altogether different from the ones generally accepted in the local society and culture.

In the Rawlsian exercise, while there is a procedural requirement of ignorance of personal interests, personal aims, and personal circumstances, nothing is demanded about the knowledge and approbation of shared beliefs—and prejudices—of the society in which these individuals happen to live. In contrast, what the Smithian model of fair arbitration demands is that the people in any society must put in an effort to examine how their own practices and conventions would look to others, including people who are informed about, but not entirely reared in, that society.[21]

GLOBAL PERSPECTIVES, LOCAL INTERESTS, AND PAROCHIALISM

The reasons to go beyond the contracting parties in a nation-state include at least three distinct concerns: (1) the interests of other people may be affected (for example, by national policies on 'global warming', or for that matter what is called the 'war against terror'); (2) the local parochialism shared by all (or nearly all) the persons within a given society may call for a distant challenge in the interest of objectivity; and (3) additional knowledge about what is feasible can be acquired from the experiences of other countries.[22]

On the first subject (that is, the interests of people beyond borders which may be significantly affected), the arbitration approach allows the possibility of taking note of some of the broader concerns, including distributive ones, about global justice that have led in recent years to attempts to consider a 'cosmopolitan' version of the original position, so that the interests of people in other countries, which may be influenced by policies in this country, are not neglected.[23] This is aimed at extending the reach of justice.

It is, however, important to see clearly that the invoking of impartial spectators from elsewhere does not make the Smithian exercise of arbitration by impartial spectators similar to the 'cosmopolitan' version of the contractarian approach (which could take the form of including all the people in the world in one gigantic original position, yielding one huge global social contract for an entirely just world). The route of fair arbitration is fundamentally different from that of fair negotiation and of social contract, because of the way impartiality is interpreted.[24] The institutional demands of the contractarian procedure if aimed at the identification of transcendental justice take us immediately to the need for a sovereign nation, which was the bone of Thomas Nagel's contention. This is a problem that does not arise in a similar way in the case of invoking the device of the impartial spectators to assist in the assessment of justice in a comparative framework.[25]

Nevertheless, there are some similarities between the cosmopolitan version of the social contract and the Smithian invoking of distant observers. The Rawlsian exclusion of foreign nationals from having a voice in the assessment of policies of a country that have influences on the rest of the world is restrained in both the cosmopolitan social contract and in the Smithian exercise of invoking observers from far as well as near.

Second, the approach of the impartial spectator can bring in, inter alia, distant perspectives that are detached not only from the particular vested interests of individual citizens, but also from any parochialism of local beliefs that may be generally shared by all members of a given polity or community. One of the possible advantages of the route of fair arbitration is, thus, the greater versatility that the latter has, which can incorporate a systematic procedural challenge to the distortion of parochial convictions.

The avoidance of parochialism was, in fact, one of the principal reasons for Smith's insistence that the impartial spectators must inter alia represent perspectives from (as Smith put it) 'a certain distance'. Smith put the point thus: 'we can do this in no other way than by endeavouring to view them with the eyes of other people, or as other people are likely to view them'.[26]

In a chapter in *The Theory of Moral Sentiments* titled 'On the Influence of Custom and Fashion upon the Sentiments of Moral Approbation and Disapprobation', Smith argued that 'the different situations of different ages and countries are apt . . . to give different characters to the generality of those who live in them, and their sentiments concerning the particular degree of each quality, that is either blamable or praise-worthy, vary, according to that degree which is usual in their own country, and in their own times'.[27] One of Smith's illustrations of such parochial values was the tendency of all political commentators in ancient Greece, including sophisticated Athenians, to regard infanticide as perfectly acceptable social behaviour. Even Plato and Aristotle did not depart from expressing approval, Smith noted, of this extraordinary practice which 'uninterrupted custom had by this time . . . thoroughly authorized' in ancient Greece.

The Rawlsian device of losing information about personal identities in a given society, which does much to eliminate the influence of individual vested interests, does not provide any systemic way of avoiding prejudices that are broadly shared by everyone within a given society. As it happens, the localism of the contractarian approach is, in fact, reinforced by Rawls's insistence that the transcendental exercise in the original position should concentrate on 'the basic structure' of 'a closed society: that is, we are to regard it as self contained and as having no relations with other societies'.[28] Smith's argument that we must *inter alia* view our sentiments from 'a certain distance from us' is motivated by the need to ask the question whether some appearance of justice is socially biased through the impact of entrenched tradition and local custom. Smith's actual example of infanticide remains distressingly relevant in some societies even today (though no longer in Greece), but there are also many other practices for which justice being seen to be done may usefully invoke, as Smith put it, 'the eyes of the rest of mankind'.[29]

While an American audience may find it easy to believe that distant perspectives may be usefully brought in, in the case of 'backward' societies such as Sudan or Afghanistan, in which, for example, honour killings occur and adulterous women might be stoned to death, there may be no corresponding recognition of the need to do this for more advanced countries like the United States. However, well-established practices that receive widespread support within the borders might be seen as unacceptable to people in many other countries, spread across the world, from Europe to Japan. For example, plentiful use of capital punishments, with or without being accompanied by public jubilation, may need to be addressed not only by asking whether they appear 'cruel and unusual' *within* the local U.S. culture, but also in 'the eyes of the rest of mankind', which, Smith thought, must be invoked to understand whether 'a punishment appears equitable'.[30]

The relevance of distant perspectives has a clear bearing on some current debates in the United States, for example, that in the Supreme Court not long ago, on the appropriateness of using capital punishment for crimes committed in juvenile years. The demands of justice being seen to be done even in a country like the United States cannot entirely neglect the understanding that may be generated by how the problem is assessed in other countries in the world. The majority judgment of the Court did not simply 'defer to like-minded foreigners' (as Justice Scalia suggested), but accepted that in the deliberations to arrive at grounded but non-parochial American judgments, it may be useful to take into account the enlightenment that non-local perspectives provide, after subjecting them to critical scrutiny in a better informed local framework.

Indeed, the apparent cogency of parochial values often turns on the lack of knowledge of what has proved feasible in the experiences of other people. The inertial defence of infanticide in ancient Greece could be influenced not only by the knowledge of societies in which infanticide is taken to be entirely unacceptable, but also from the fact that these societies are not crumbling into chaos and crisis as a result of not permitting such killing. Despite the undoubted importance of local knowledge, global knowledge has some value too, and can contribute to the debates on parochial values and practices.

DIVERGENCE AND THE FEASIBILITY OF THE COMPARATIVE APPROACH

In a model of arbitration there is likely to be some divergence of voices on a number of issues, especially when the perspectives sought come from far and wide. Even though there may be considerable convergence of values through global public reasoning, there might well be lasting differences between how the outcomes of such deliberations may emerge in different social and cultural settings. For a transcendental approach to justice dependent on the emergence of a complete agreement on the nature and demands of 'global justice', this would of course be an overpowering problem. It is not, however, similarly problematic for the use of the comparative approach to justice. The focus here will be on whether there are significant issues on which agreements or consensus may emerge, especially after public interaction, with exchange of knowledge and understanding. The demands of global justice may not go beyond the agreed ways of enhancing justice in the world in the comparative route to judgments of justice.

Furthermore, the extent of agreement on global rankings may itself go on expanding as the process of interaction continues. The comparative approach does not require an 'all or nothing' extremism, and it allows the world to come to grips with intense issues of global injustice (such as famines, widespread hunger, rampant illiteracy, or needless deaths from preventable or manageable diseases), on which consensus may be easier to obtain, without waiting for a full agreement on more contentious evaluations.

A similar thing can be said about taking note of global perspectives in making local decisions that are not primarily matters of global justice: for example, in assessing a national framework of punitive legislation, taking into account whether 'a punishment appears equitable', to use Smith's phrase, without neglecting how it appears to people reared in a different background and with different informational understanding. The demands of objectivity not only require avoiding a 'personal slant' (as Rawls noted), but also national parochialism (as Smith emphasized). This does not, however, yield any obligation to accept the views of others elsewhere, only that they be taken into account in an overall scrutiny (leading to modification of local priorities in some cases and no revision in others).

Indeed, distant voices too are subject to the discipline of critical scrutiny, including the invoking of impartial spectators from far as well as near. The discipline of fair arbitration in the context of global justice can be seen to be globally interactive. General *acceptability*, which must be distinguished from pre-existing ubiquitous acceptance, is an important issue in any social evaluation, and I have tried to discuss elsewhere why open and interactive public reasoning is centrally important for understanding the claims that human rights make, despite differences in manifest practices *between* countries, and also of course *within* each country.[31]

The common standpoint that may be seen to emerge on the basis of such associative scrutiny may be far from total, and the form of the concordance need not, in many cases, go beyond noting that some social arrangements are seriously unjust in a way that can be remedied, even though other comparisons may be hard to make without substantial ambiguity. A theory of justice need not turn up its nose against the vast reach and relevance of acceptable conclusions on human rights, or social justice, arrived at on the basis of public reasoning, even when they do not amount to a complete resolution of all the existing decisional issues about societal organization.[32]

WHAT DIFFERENCE DOES IT MAKE?

I shall not try to summarize the paper but will briefly note some of the issues discussed here. First, I have argued for rejecting the tradition of focusing on the classic—and much invoked—question 'What is a just society?' and in favour of concentrating instead on comparative questions of justice (linked to inquiries about advancing justice, or reducing injustice). I have presented some reasons for doubting that the transcendental question can typically be answered, but even if it could be, and a transcendental theory of justice were entirely successful in answering that classic question, it would not yield—directly or even indirectly—a comparative framework, which is needed for the actual assessment of justice. On the other side, a comparative theory of justice may be entirely viable and thoroughly usable without containing—or entailing—any answer to the grand question 'What is a just society?'

Second, the specification of the demands of full justice, and of the elaborate institutional paraphernalia which have to be marshalled for the pursuit of Rawlsian modelling of justice, leaves open the question how we should assess whether some social change would advance the cause of justice or hinder it—questions that we constantly face in the world, within each country and in the field of global arrangements. For example, having decent patent laws about the production and distribution of pharmaceutical products may do a lot for the miserable and needlessly doomed AIDS patients in the world today, and arguments can be presented to suggest that this would reduce a manifest injustice in the global society. But it will not, on its own, take us anywhere near the demands of Rawlsian transcendental justice.

Third, an implicit belief, which seems fairly common in a substantial part of political philosophy, that the identification of a fully just society is not only crucial for the comprehension of the nature of justice, but also essential for a well-founded relational understanding of justice, has had the effect of giving a fairly ubiquitous role to transcendental analysis of justice in contemporary philosophy. I have argued that this underlying belief may be entirely mistaken. A transcendental approach is neither necessary nor sufficient for answering questions on the advancement of justice that urgently demand our attention, which call for a robustly comparative approach. That approach is sharply different from the exploration of transcendence.

Fourth, there is a need to allow—and sometimes even to assert—incompleteness of relational comparisons of justice. Incompleteness can arise from unbridgeable gaps in information, but also from decisional unresolvability involving disparate considerations that may resist gradation, even with full information. However, possible incompleteness of judgments emerging from the relational route is not an embarrassment for practical reason. Indeed, far from it.[33] The challenge of assessing *advancement*, or identifying *regression*, will very often be not compromised at all by the presence of substantial incompleteness in the rankings of justice.

Fifth, aside from the general importance of incorporating possible incompleteness of evaluations, the admissibility of incompleteness also makes it easier to bring in distant voices in the assessment of justice, which can be critically important for the reach and strength of public reasoning. A procedural requirement to consider non-local perspectives can help to avoid undue dominance of local interest as well as possible parochialism of local reasoning shaped by the influence of established conventions and limited informational frame works (without these being intellectually challenged). We have to go firmly beyond relying on the territorially moored perspectives of 'free and equal citizens who are born into that society in which they lead their lives' (to use Rawls's phrase).[34]

The world in which we live is not only unjust, it is, arguably, extraordinarily unjust. It is not frivolous to seek a framework for a theory of justice that concentrates on advancement, not transcendence, and also allows being globally interactive, rather than being intellectually sequestered. We have good reason to abstain from concentrating so fully on the program of identifying the totalist—and possibly parochial—demands of transcendental, contractarian justice. We have to move the theory of justice out of that little corner.

NOTES

Original Publication: Sen, Amartya. "What Do We Want from a Theory of Justice?" *Journal of Philosophy*, CIII, 5 (May 2006): 215–38.

For helpful discussion, I am grateful to Sabina Alkire, Kenneth Arrow, Akeel Bilgrami, Sissela Bok, Joshua Cohen, Peter Hammond, Isaac Levi, Thomas Nagel, Prasanta Pattanaik, Mozaffar Quizilbash, Ingrid Robeyns, Emma Rothschild, Carol Rovane, Maurice Salles, Thomas Scanlon, Patrick Suppes, Kotaro Suzumura, Philippe Van Parijs, and to the participants of seminars at Harvard University, Stanford University, and Yale University, where earlier versions of this paper were presented.

1. See Rawls, *Political Liberalism* (New York: Columbia University Press, 1993), 110–13.

2. Rawls, *A Theory of Justice* (Cambridge: Harvard University Press, 1971), 516–17. This corresponds to page 453 of the revised edition of the book (Cambridge: Harvard University Press, 1999). On the relation between political objectivity and public reasoning, see also Bruce A. Ackerman, *Social Justice in the Liberal State* (New Haven: Yale University Press, 1980); Joshua Cohen, "An Epistemic Conception of Democracy," *Ethics*, XCVII (1986–87): 26–38; Seyla Benhabib, ed., *Democracy and Difference: Contesting the Boundaries of the Political* (Princeton: Princeton University Press, 1996); Amy Gutmann and Dennis Thompson, *Democracy and Disagreement* (Cambridge: Harvard University Press, 1996); Thomas Scanlon, *What We Owe to Each Other* (Cambridge: Harvard University Press, 1998).

3. Social choice theory, pioneered in the modern form by Kenneth Arrow (*Social Choice and Individual Values* [New York: Wiley, 1951]), is based on a fundamentally comparative approach. The analytical priority of the comparative can also be seen in the early formulations of social choice in the eighteenth century, particularly in Marquis de Condorcet, *Essai sur l'Application de l'Analyse à la Probabilité des Decisions rendues à la Pluralité des Voix* (Paris L'Imperimerie Royale, 1785).

4. The comparative conclusions have typically been pieced together to arrive at some ultimately transcendental claims (a translation that is possible with rather restrictive and limiting assumptions, as will be discussed presently). See, for example, Sen, *Collective Choice and Social Welfare* (San Francisco: Holden-Day, 1970); Kotaro Suzumura, *Rational Choice, Collective Decisions, and Social Welfare* (New York: Cambridge University Press, 1983); Peter J. Hammond, "Equity, Arrow's Conditions and Rawl's Difference Principle," *Econometrica*, XLIV (1976): 793–804; Claude d'Aspremont and Louis Gevers, "Equity and the Informational Basis of Collective Choice," *Review of Economic Studies*, XLVI (1977): 199–209; Arrow,

"Extended Sympathy and the Possibility of Social Choice," *American Economic Review*, LXVII (1977): 219–25. The influence of the Rawlsian perspective on justice has been very strong on the application of social choice theory, despite the basic distance between the respective comparative and transcendental approaches.

5. It is worth noting here that the diagnosis of injustice does not demand a unique identification of the 'just society', since many different identification of perfectly just social arrangements may all agree on the diagnosis of a remediable deficiency of a particular social arrangement (say, with manifest hunger or illiteracy or medical neglect).

6. Sen, "Consequential Evaluation and Practical Reason," *Journal of Philosophy*, XCVII, 9 (September 2000): 477–572. See also Sen, *Collective Choice and Social Welfare*; "Maximization and the Act of Choice," *Econometrica*, LXV (1997): 745–79; and "The Possibility of Social Choice," *American Economic Review*, LXXXIX (1999): 349–78; and also "Incompleteness and Reasoned Choice," *Synthese*, CXL (2004): 43–59. See also Isaac Levi's response to the last, in "Amartya Sen," in the same number of *Synthese*, 61–67.

7. The vast literature on this include, among other contributions, S.-Ch. Kolm, "The Optimum Production of Social Justice," in J. Margolis and H. Guitton, eds., *Public Economics* (London: Macmillan, 1969), 145–200; A.B. Atkinson, "On the Measurement of Inequality," *Journal of Economic Theory*, II (1970): 244–63; James Mirrlees, "An Exploration of the Theory of Optimal Income Taxation," *Review of Economic Studies*, XXXVIII (1971): 175–208; Sen, *On Economic Inequality* (New York: Oxford, 1973; enlarged edition with a new addendum jointly written with James Foster, 1997); Claude d'Aspremont and Louis Gevers, "Equity and the Informational Basis of Collective Choice," XLIV (1977): 199–209; Eric Maskin, "Decision-Making under Ignorance with Implications for Social Choice," *Theory and Decision*, XI (1979): 319-37; Kevin W.S. Roberts, "Interpersonal Comparability and Social Choice Theory," *Review of Economic Studies*, XLVII (1980): 421–39; Charles Blackorby, David Donaldson, and John Weymark, "Social Choice with Interpersonal Utility Comparisons: A Diagrammatic Introduction," *International Economic Review*, XXV (1984): 327–56; d'Aspremont, "Axioms for Social Welfare Ordering," in Leonid Hurwicz, David Schmeidler, and Hugo Sonnenschein, eds., *Social Goals and Social Organization: Essays in Memory of Elisha Pazner* (New York: Cambridge, 1985), 19–76; and d'Aspremont and Gevers, "Social Welfare Functionals and Interpersonal Comparability," Blackorby, Walter Bossert, and Donaldson, "Utilitarianism and the Theory of Justice," and Bhaskar Dutta, "Inequality, Poverty and Welfare," the last three in Arrow, Sen, and Suzumura, eds., *Handbook of Social Choice and Welfare*, Volume 1 (Amsterdam: North-Holland, 2002), chapters 10–12.

8. Scanlon, *What We Owe to Each Other*, 5; see also his "Contractualism and Utilitarianism," in Sen and Bernard Williams, eds., *Utilitarianism and Beyond* (New York: Cambridge University Press, 1982), 103–28.

9. The formal characteristics of 'intersection partial orderings' are discussed in Sen, *On Economic Inequality*, and "Maximization and the Act of Choice."

10. For an early expression of skepticism about the plausibility of unanimous judgments in the "original position," see my joint essay with W.G. Runciman, "Games, Justice and the General Will," *Mind*, LXXIV (September 1965): 554–62.

11. On a mathematical point, it must be acknowledged that a transitive but incomplete ordering over a finite set will invariably yield one or more 'maximal' elements, in the sense of there being no element that is better than a maximal element. Maximality does not, however, guarantee the existence of a best element. The foundational nature of the mathematical distinction involved and its significant implications are investigated in N. Bourbaki, *General Topology*, parts I and II, English translation (Reading, MA: Addison-Wesley, 1966), and *Theory of Sets* (Reading, MA: Addison-Wesley, 1968). The presence of maximal elements is sufficient for reasoned choice of an alternative that is no worse than any other. It will not, however, in general allow the unfolding of a perfectly just social arrangement, not to mention a unique arrangement of perfect justice (as in the Rawlsian and other transcendental systems). On the far-reaching relevance of the distinction between maximality and optimality (and transcendence), see Sen, "Internal Consistency of Choice," *Econometrica*, LXI (1993): 495–521, and "Maximization and the Act of Choice," *Econometrica*, LXV (1997): 745–79.

12. Nagel, "The Problem of Global Justice," *Philosophy and Public Affairs*, XXXIII (2005): 113-47, here 115.

13. Nagel, "The Problem of Global Justice," 130–33, 146–47. An important critique of what Joshua Cohen and Charles Sabel describe as Nagel's 'statism' can be found in their "Extra Rempublicam Nulla Justitia?," *Philosophy and Public Affairs*, XXXIV (Spring 2006): 147–75, in which see also A.L. Julius, "Nagel's Atlas," 176–92.

14. Rawls, *The Law of Peoples* (Cambridge: Harvard University Press, 1999).

15. If Nagel is relying on a possible formal interpretation (by stretching a point) that in the absence of an applicable theory of justice it can indeed be said that 'we do not live in a just world', then he could have, with equal ease, also said, 'we do not live in an unjust world'. That may not, however, have served quite so well as the opening sentence of Nagel's finely argued and sensitive essay, and there is, I would argue, reason to ask ourselves how this asymmetry arises if the idea of global justice is really such a chimera.

16. On this, see my "Elements of a Theory of Human Rights," *Philosophy and Public Affairs*, xxxiv (Fall 2004): 315–56.

17. It is, however, important to note that in the version of 'contractualism' that Scanlon has developed and explored, which requires judgment about what it 'would be reasonable for those affected by a principle to reject', citizenal confinement is neither necessary nor indeed sensible, since the policies and institutions of a nation, or state, or 'people', as Rawls calls this collectivity, can significantly affect other people elsewhere. See Scanlon's *What We Owe to Each Other*, and also his earlier contribution, "Contractualism and Utilitarianism."

18. Rawls, *A Theory of Justice* (1971), 517, and (1999), 453; italics added.

19. Rawls, *A Theory of Justice* (1971), 23.

20. Sen, "Open and Closed Impartiality," *Journal of Philosophy*, XCIX, 9 (September 2002): 445–69.

21. The Rawlsian formulation of the 'original position' suffers also from a further problem in specifying the allegedly fixed set of negotiators when the results of the negotiation can change the size and composition of the population involved. This problem of 'inclusionary incoherence' (as I called it), which the Smithian approach does not have, was discussed, among other issues, in an earlier essay in the *Journal of Philosophy*, "Open and Closed Impartiality." I shall not, however, further pursue here this rather different type of difficulty.

22. On the last issue, it is worth mentioning that the understanding in different countries of social feasibilities (relevant, for example, for gender justice) and economic feasibilities (relevant, for example, for policies against poverty) is significantly influenced in the contemporary world by learning from the experiences—successes and failures—of other countries; on this see my *Development as Freedom* (New York: Knopf, 1999).

23. See, for example, Thomas Pogge, ed., *Global Justice* (Malden, MA: Blackwell, 2001). See also Deen Chatterjee, *The Ethics of Assistance: Morality and the Distant Needy* (New York: Cambridge University Press, 2004).

24. For example, it can be shown that the cosmopolitan version of the Rawlsian original position is also vulnerable to 'inclusionary incoherence' in a way that the Smithian approach is not, as is discussed in my "Open and Closed Impartiality."

25. Here again it must be noted that in the version of 'contractualism' presented by Scanlon (*What We Owe to Each Other*), which has many affinities with the Smithian exercise of impartiality, the focus need not be on transcendence only.

26. Smith, *The Theory of Moral Sentiments*, III, 1, 2, 110.

27. Smith, *The Theory of Moral Sentiments*, Volume 2.7, 204.

28. Rawls, *Political Liberalism*, 12.

29. Smith, *Lectures on Jurisprudence*, R.L. Meek, D.D. Raphael, and P.G. Stein, eds. (New York: Oxford University Press, 1978), 104.

30. Smith, *Lectures on Jurisprudence,* 104.

31. See my "Elements of a Theory of Human Rights," *Philosophy and Public Affairs*, XXXII (Fall 2004): 315–56. See also Joshua Cohen, "Procedure and Substance in Deliberative Democracy," in Seyla Benhabib, ed., *Democracy and Difference: Contesting the Boundaries of the Political* (Princeton: Princeton University Press, 1996), 95-119; and Charles Beitz, "Human Rights as a Common Concern," *American Political Science Review*, XCV (June 2001): 229–82.

32. I take up these issues more fully in a forthcoming book to be published by Harvard University Press, called *Freedom and the Theory of Justice*.

33. I have discussed this subject in "Consequential Evaluation and Practical Reason," and some of the underlying analytical concerns in "Maximization and the Act of Choice."

34. Rawls, *Political Liberalism*, 23.

Chapter Five

Utilitarianism and Some of Its Critics

On Some Alternative 'Incomplete' Theories of, and Approaches to, Morality and Justice

Mozaffar Qizilbash

The leading modern theory of justice—John Rawls's theory—was presented, at least in part, as an attempt to provide an alternative to the 'moral' or 'ethical theory' which was dominant at the time that Rawls published *A Theory of Justice*. His motivation was that in the absence of a properly worked out 'alternative' moral theory, utilitarianism had, he believed, remained dominant since the writings of those who advanced classical utilitarianism—notably Jeremy Bentham, John Stuart Mill and Henry Sidgwick—in spite of a variety of criticisms. Yet it is not clear that a theory of justice of the sort Rawls developed is a genuine alternative to the sort of moral doctrine or theory the classical utilitarians offered and, in his later works, Rawls clarified that his theory was a political rather than moral doctrine. Much of Amartya Sen's work in moral and political philosophy, and indeed his interventions in welfare economics, also started from a critical engagement with utilitarianism and with Rawls's theory of justice. Unsurprisingly, some have interpreted Sen as attempting, like Rawls, in his early work, to advance an alternative to utilitarianism, which might help to undermine the status of that doctrine, but also as advancing an alternative to Rawls's own theory of justice. However, Sen has often used the word 'approach' rather than 'theory' to describe some of his views. And it may be that what he means by an 'approach' falls short—at least in the degree of its theoretical ambitions—of the sorts of 'theories' that were advanced by the utilitarians or by Rawls, and so does not offer a genuine alternative to these. By contrast, Martha Nussbaum has attempted to provide a version of the 'capabilities approach' which might, in the level of detail at which it engages with some issues, constitute a genuine 'counter-theory' at least to Rawls's position in his later works. These are some of the views I consider in this chapter.

In discussing these views, I distinguish various ways in which a theory might be 'incomplete', since each of the alternatives to utilitarianism discussed in this paper can be considered as an 'incomplete' theory or approach of some sort. In particular, a theory can be 'incomplete' because: it is restricted in scope; it is 'open-ended' in the sense that it can be filled out in distinct ways by different people; and it fails to generate a complete 'at least as good as' relation (so that it is not true that, for all states of affairs, one is at least as good as the other, nor is the other at least as good as the one). The relevant sense(s) in which a theory is 'incomplete' is relevant to the task of evaluating it and of comparing it to utilitarianism. In this paper I attempt to illuminate the nature of specific 'approaches' and 'theories' of morality and justice by clarifying various ways in which they are 'incomplete'. I also discuss the question of whether an 'approach' need in itself constitute a theory.

PRELIMINARIES: UTILITARIANISM AS AN 'ETHICAL THEORY', 'MORAL THEORY', AND DOCTRINE

Anyone who has looked at the literature on 'ethical' or 'moral theory' will be struck by the lack of any consistency in the use of these terms. No doubt in part as a consequence of this state of affairs, Bernard Williams remarked in his *Ethics and the Limits of Philosophy* that '[i]t does not matter much how the expression "ethical theory" is used, so long as one's use is made clear' (Williams 1985, 72). Williams's own definition in that volume runs as follows: '[a]n ethical theory is a theoretical account of what ethical thought and practice are, which account implies a general test for the correctness of basic ethical beliefs and principles or else implies that there cannot be such a test' (Williams 1985, 72). Williams classifies those theories which imply that there is such a test as positive and those which imply that there cannot be one as negative. There are others who, when they use the term 'moral theory', refer to some specific moral principle which tells us what right or wrong action consists in or which moral code or set of virtues (or dispositions or motives) is right, (or appropriate). This is a distinct and narrower notion of 'moral theory' which I use in this paper unless otherwise specified.

Classical utilitarianism no doubt provides an ethical or moral theory on both definitions just discussed. In the statements of Jeremy Bentham and J. S. Mill, though, it appears more obviously to be a moral *doctrine* or—to use Mill's word—*creed*. As Mill puts it: '[t]he creed that accepts as the foundation of morals, Utility, or the Greatest Happiness Principle, holds that actions are right in proportion as they tend to promote happiness, wrong as they tend to produce the reverse of happiness.' Mill goes on to explain what he means by happiness and its reverse, but adds that '[t]o give a clear view of the moral standard set up by the theory, much more requires to be said' and adds that 'these supplementary explanations do not affect the theory of life on which this theory of morality is grounded—namely, that pleasure, and freedom from pain, are the only desirable ends' (Mill 1962, 257).

Henry Sidgwick's use of terms is a little different. In *The Methods of Ethics* Sidgwick starts by noting that 'Utilitarianism is, at the present day, in common use, and is supposed to designate a doctrine or method with which we are all familiar' (Sidgwick 1981, 411). Nonetheless, Sidgwick notes that 'it seems to be applied to several distinct theories' so that he needs to give a more precise definition. His definition runs: '[b]y Utilitarianism is here meant the ethical theory, that the conduct which, under any given circumstances, is objectively right, is that which will produce the greatest amount of happiness on the whole; that is, taking into account all those whose happiness is affected by the conduct' (Sidgwick 1981, 411). Here 'ethical theory' might easily be replaced by 'moral principle'. Nonetheless, Sidgwick also thinks that ethics must provide a 'positive ethical theory' of the sort Williams has in mind since for him: '[t]he aim of Ethics is to systematise and free from error the apparent cognitions that most men have of the rightness or reasonableness of conduct, whether the conduct be considered as right in itself, or as the means to some end commonly conceived as ultimately reasonable' and he goes on to identify the relevant 'cognitions' as '"dictates" or "imperatives"' . . . which 'are accompanied by a certain impulse to do the acts recognised as right' and which are 'normally accompanied by emotions of various kinds known as "moral sentiments"' (Sidgwick 1981, 77). So, on Sidgwick's view the aim of ethics is more expansive than merely to provide a 'moral theory'. As regards what Mill meant by a 'creed' and what Sidgwick meant by a 'doctrine' I shall assume that they had in mind either the principle of utility itself—in which case a 'creed' or 'doctrine' is simply a moral theory or the more general set of beliefs or opinions held by those who endorsed this principle so that it contains further elements of what Williams means by a positive ethical theory.

THE SEARCH FOR AN ALTERNATIVE: RAWLS'S THEORY OF JUSTICE AND MORAL THEORY

In motivating his theory of justice, Rawls notes that '[d]uring much of modern moral philosophy the predominant systematic theory has been some form of utilitarianism'. Rawls adds that 'one reason for this is that it has been espoused by a long line of brilliant writers' and that the 'great utilitarians . . .

were social theorists and economists of the first rank' (Rawls 1972, vii). He also suggests that '[t]hose who criticized them often did so on a much narrower front. They pointed out the obscurities of the principle of utility and noted the apparent incongruities between many of its implications and our moral sentiments'. Importantly, he suggests that 'they failed . . . to construct a workable and systematic moral conception to oppose it' (Rawls 1972, viii). Rawls thinks that his own theory provides an 'alternative systematic account of justice that is superior . . . to the dominant utilitarianism of the tradition' (Rawls 1972, viii).

In his original statement, Rawls did not exclude the possibility that his theory of justice may also be extended to constitute a theory of morality. Indeed, its development in that direction would have been desirable—given his motivation—in providing an alternative to utilitarianism. But in its initial articulation, Rawls's theory is restricted in its scope and ambition. In extending the social contract tradition his conception of justice—'justice as fairness'—Rawls notes that '[j]ustice as fairness is not a complete contract theory'. Indeed, Rawls is very clear about the 'incompleteness' of his theory, at least in as much as it might be construed as an 'ethical' or 'moral' theory of some sort. He writes that:

> It is clear that the contractarian idea can be extended to the choice of more or less an entire system, that is, to a system including principles for all the virtues and not only for justice. Now for the most part I shall consider only principles of justice and others closely related to them; I make no attempt to discuss the virtues in a systematic way. Obviously if justice as fairness succeeds reasonably well, a next step would be to study the more general view suggested by the name 'rightness as fairness'. But even this wider theory fails to embrace all moral relationships, since it would seem to include only our relations with other persons and to leave out of account how we are to conduct ourselves toward animals and the rest of nature. (Rawls 1972, 17)

Justice as fairness is here understood as an 'incomplete' theory of morality in as much as it is restricted in its scope. Nonetheless, even in its early formulation 'justice as fairness' does have elements of what Williams means by an 'ethical theory', to the degree that it provides part of a 'theory of moral sentiments'. Rawls writes:

> I wish to stress that a theory of justice is precisely that, namely, a theory. It is a theory of moral sentiments (to recall an eighteenth century title) setting out the principles governing our moral powers, or more specifically, our sense of justice. . . . A theory of justice is subject to the same rules of method as other theories. (Rawls 1972, 51)

So Rawls's project in *A Theory of Justice* is clearly one which is ambitious in providing a *theory*, but the theory he develops is incomplete in as much as it covers only part of what one would think of as the domain of morality and as a theory of the virtues.

In his later restatement of his theory Rawls takes a slightly different view. In the preface of *Justice as Fairness: A Restatement* he notes that—because of his remarks about 'rightness as fairness'—readers of *A Theory of Justice* might conclude that 'justice as fairness was set out as part of a comprehensive moral doctrine that might be developed later should success encourage the attempt' (Rawls 2001, xvii). In his restatement he is clear that justice as fairness is 'much narrower in scope than comprehensive philosophical moral doctrines such as utilitarianism . . . [i]t focusses on the political . . . which is but part of the domain of the moral' (Rawls 2001, 14).

In the light of his later restatement, Rawls's comparison of his own theory to utilitarianism in *A Theory of Justice* also appears a little misleading. There he treats utilitarianism, for the purposes of comparison. as a theory of justice. He writes:

> [t]he kind of utilitarianism I shall describe here is the strict classical doctrine which receives perhaps its clearest and most accessible formulation in Sidgwick. The main idea is that society is rightly ordered, and therefore just, when its major institutions are arranged so as to achieve the greatest net balance of satisfaction summed over all the individuals belonging to it. (Rawls 1972, 22)

Here Rawls cites a wide variety of contributions to utilitarian thought, including Sidgwick's *The Methods of Ethics*. Nonetheless, it is perhaps difficult to compare the respective merits of a moral theory and a theory of justice (of the sort Rawls advanced), since these differ in their subject matter. As we have already seen, in *The Methods of Ethics* Sidgwick's definition of 'utilitarianism' was concerned with right conduct rather than the right or just ordering of society. Nonetheless, Sidgwick does consider the relationship between ethics and politics, and, in that context, considers 'what rules of conduct for the governed should be fixed by legislators and applied by judges' and concludes that in this case also 'we shall endeavour to estimate and balance against each other the effects of such rules on the general happiness' (Sidgwick 1981, 457). While his definition of utilitarianism is restricted to right conduct, in another passage Sidgwick also suggests that utilitarianism 'furnishes us with a common standard to which the different elements included in the notion of Justice may be reduced' (Sidgwick 1981, 447) and adds that such a standard is imperatively required in certain political contexts. To this degree, Rawls's comparison may have been intended as a comparison between his theory and Sidgwick's utilitarianism, to the degree that the latter offers a theory of politics and justice. Nonetheless, Sidgwick's utilitarianism is a primarily a moral theory and his remarks about its relevance to the realms of politics and justice (at least in *The Methods of Ethics*) are rather limited. The 'main idea' of Sidgwick's utilitarianism is about right conduct and not about how 'society is rightly ordered'.

Before moving onto the views of Amartya Sen and Martha Nussbaum, I should further explain some of Rawls's views since these set the scene for some of Sen's and Nussbaum's interventions. There are some minor changes in the wording of the principles of justice in Rawls's theory over time. In the restatement of his theory one of his principles of justice—'the difference principle'—is described as follows: '[s]ocial and economic inequalities . . . are to be to the benefit to the least-advantaged members of society' (Rawls 2001, 42–43). In interpreting this principle it is important that advantage is understood in terms of an index of social primary goods (or 'primary goods' for short). Rawls tells us that '[p]rimary goods are things needed and required by persons seen in the light of the political conception of persons, as citizens who are fully co-operating members of society, and not merely as human beings apart from any normative conception. These goods are things citizens need as free and equal persons living a complete life' (Rawls 2001, 59). Furthermore, in later versions of the theory, justice as fairness is presented as a form of 'political liberalism'. The goal of political liberalism is to find a 'political conception of justice' which people with different comprehensive doctrines can endorse. For this reason a 'political conception of justice' can be the focus of an 'overlapping consensus' between people who hold distinct reasonable comprehensive doctrines (Rawls 1993, 134). A 'political conception of justice' is a moral conception 'worked out for a particular kind of subject, namely for political, social and economic institutions' (Rawls 1993, 11)—that is, for the 'basic structure of society' in a constitutional democracy.

Finally, Rawls mentions a limitation of his theory. He writes that:

> we are concerned for the most part with the nature and content of a well-ordered society. Discussion of this case is referred to in justice as fairness as ideal, or strict compliance, theory. Strict compliance means that (nearly) everyone strictly complies with, and so abides by, the principles of justice. We ask in effect what a perfectly just, or nearly just, constitutional regime might be like. . . . Nevertheless, the idea of a well-ordered society should also provide some guidance in thinking about nonideal theory, and so with difficult cases of how to deal with existing injustices. (Rawls 2001, 13)

For this reason, Rawls thinks that 'justice as fairness is realistically utopian' in the sense that 'it probes the limits of the realistically practicable, that is how far in our world . . . a democratic regime can attain complete realization of its appropriate political values'. These remarks are relevant, as we will see, to Sen's and Nussbaum's discussions of Rawls.

SEN'S CRITICISMS AND PROPOSALS: INCOMPLETE THEORY OR APPROACH?

In 'Utilitarianism and Welfarism' Sen (1979b) decomposes utilitarianism into three component parts. The initial decomposition is of 'act-utilitarianism', but it can be generalised so that it applies to rules or motives instead. The first component of utilitarianism is consequentialism, and he defines act-consequentialism as follows:

> *Act consequentialism:* an action α is right if and only if the state of affairs *x* resulting from α is at least as good as each of the alternative states of affairs that would have resulted respectively from the alternative feasible acts. (Sen 1979b, 464)

On Sen's account, act-utilitarianism combines act-consequentialism with a second principle:

> *Outcome Utilitarianism*: Any state of affairs *x* is at least as good as any alternative state of affairs *y* if and only if the sum total of individual utilities in *x* is at least as large as the sum of utilities in *y*. (Sen 1979b, 464)

This in turn is factorised into the following principles:

> *Welfarism*: The judgement of the relative goodness of alternative states of affairs must be based exclusively on, and taken as an increasing function of, the respective collections of individual utilities in these states. (Sen 1979b, 468)

and

> *Sum-ranking:* One collection of individual utilities is at least as good as another if and only if it has at least as large a sum total. (Sen 1979b, 468)

Sen (1979b, 468) rejects sum ranking—as Rawls (1972, 77) does—on the grounds that it is 'indifferent as to how a constant sum of benefits is distributed'. He also rejects welfarism. In 'Utilitarianism and Welfarism' this is primarily because welfarism, by definition, excludes all 'non-utility information' (Sen 1979b, 471–79). In other works Sen also finds fault with 'utility'—whether defined as pleasure, desire satisfaction or happiness—as a measure of welfare or advantage because people can adapt or adjust their desires to the circumstances they find themselves in so that their desires are easily satisfied, or find pleasure in small mercies or learn to find happiness in whatever form is available in their straitened situations. If they do adjust in this way, then 'utility' if defined in these ways may be a misleading measure of advantage (e.g., Sen 1987, 45–47). The second of these lines of criticism leads to the search for an alternative metric of advantage—and Sen's proposal as regards the currency of advantage for judging egalitarian claims initially recommends 'basic capability' (Sen 1980) and in later versions, more generally, 'capability' (Sen 1990a, 1992)—what one is able to do and be in leading a valuable life (or a life one has reason to value)—and 'functionings'—which refer to the relevant 'beings' and 'doings' which constitute such a life—as providing potentially important information in the evaluation of egalitarian claims. In advancing capability as a currency of justice, Sen also criticises Rawls's use of a primary goods index in his difference principle not least because he thinks that various people need different amounts of such goods to be able to do and be what they value (or have reason to value). He argues that Rawls's position falls short because it involves a form of fetishism about goods and a neglect of human diversity (Sen 1982, 367–68). But it is interesting that Sen *also* chastises Rawls for excluding all information relating to happiness and desire satisfaction. As regards the 'original position' in which the parties in Rawls's theory decide on the principles of justice, Sen tells us that 'it is not at all clear why people in this primordial state should be taken to be so indifferent to the joys and sufferings in occupying particular positions' and 'why their concern about these joys and sufferings should be taken to be morally irrelevant' (Sen 1982, 367). And in his concluding remarks in that paper he adds that in his advocacy of the currency of (basic) capability, he does not wish to claim that 'basic capability equality is the sole guide to the moral good' (Sen 1982, 369).

As regards 'consequentialism', in his later work Sen (2000) defends a particular version of this view which is consistent with a broad definition such as that provided by Philip Pettit when he suggests that 'roughly speaking consequentialism is the theory that the way to tell whether a particular choice is the right choice for the agent to have made is to look at the relevant consequences of the decision; to look at the relevant effects of the decision on the world' (Sen 2009, 218–19). To the degree that Sen defends consequentialism against some standard objections, he defends a class of moral theory rather than a specific theory since many moral theories, including utilitarianism, classify as consequentialist. Indeed, given his critical responses to utilitarianism, Sen might well have more fully developed a 'non-welfarist consequentialism' which rejects sum ranking. This tendency is particularly evident in some of his discussions and statements of the 'capability approach' including essays on the relationship between capability and rights (e.g., Sen 1981a, 1984). We have further hints of what a 'non-welfarist consequentialist' view might look like in a response to Philippe Van Parijs where Sen writes that 'an important difference' between his views and Van Parijs's 'concerns the fact that the Van Parijs scheme gives complete priority to the demands of equality, whereas the uses of the capability perspective for which I have argued must take note of aggregative considerations as well as egalitarian ones' (Sen 1990b, 468). An example of a more developed version of consequentialism is Brad Hooker's 'rule-consequentialism' (Hooker 2000, 32–45) which takes a similar line to Sen's in relation to Sen's and Rawls's critique of 'sum ranking' but articulates a specific moral principle. It is, however, welfarist and so on Sen's view would be guilty of excluding morally relevant information. Sen's view would also be unlikely to emerge as a form of 'capability consequentialism' (see Qizilbash 2008, 65–66) since, as we have seen, Sen does not want to claim that capability equality is the only object of moral value and furthermore that he does not wish to restrict information to 'capability' information. In part for this reason, in his later works, he stresses the limits of what the capability approach can on its own do (see, for example, Sen 2009, 295–98 and Qizilbash 2012). Others who discuss or develop his views on capability do, nonetheless, advance some form of principle—as, for example, Marc Fleurbaey does in discussing a view which gives priority to the least well off group when advantage is measured in terms of a particular form of functionings index (Fleurbaey 1995, 53) and as Martha Nussbaum (2006, 178–79) does in advancing her own version of the capabilities approach in which justice requires that everyone achieves a threshold level in terms of a list of central human capabilities.

Since he does not articulate a fuller non-welfarist consequentialism, Sen's view is best characterised as an 'incomplete' moral theory. 'Incompleteness' can be understood in very different ways, and Sen's account is 'incomplete' in more than one way. If by 'completeness' one means the axiom invoked in choice theory (e.g., Sen 1979a, 8) then 'at least as good as' is complete if and only if for all (non-identical) states of affairs (or alternatives) x and y in the set of states of affairs (or alternatives), x is either at least as good as y or y is at least as good as x. If 'at least as good as' is complete, all states (or alternatives) are comparable. 'Incompleteness' is a violation of this axiom and emerges when any pair of states (or alternatives) is not comparable. To distinguish it from other senses of 'incompleteness', I shall refer to this as *evaluative incompleteness.* On this sense of 'incompleteness', in their introduction to *Utilitarianism and Beyond* Sen and Bernard Williams suggest that '[i]t is far from clear that completeness should be seen as a virtue' (Sen and Williams 1982, 18) in a moral theory. And in discussing theories of inequality and justice Sen argues along similar lines that: '[t]he need to admit incompleteness in inequality evaluation is inescapable, and there is much to be said for addressing that question explicitly' (Sen 1992, 134). For this reason he thinks that 'in a "totalist" approach that characterises the standard theories of justice (including Rawls's), incompleteness tends to appear to be a failure, or at least a sign of the unfinished nature of the exercise' (Sen 2006, 223). Here Sen has in mind evaluative incompleteness (rather than a restriction of the scope of a theory) and he insists that a 'theory of justice which makes systematic room for incompleteness allows one to arrive at possibly quite strong judgements' (Sen 2006, 223).

An important source of evaluative incompleteness in Sen's views is that he does not insist on any particular set of weights in interpersonal comparisons of advantage in the way that utilitarianism and Rawls's difference principle do. His rejection of sum ranking implies that, some importance be given to the least advantaged and to equity as opposed to 'aggregative' considerations. But there may also be evaluative incompleteness because Sen does not insist on any particular set of weights as regards other matters such as the relative importance of different functionings in evaluating the quality of life, and the relative weight to be given to capability and functionings.

On Sen's view a theory may also be 'incomplete' in another way which is not primarily about non-comparability of states. For example, in the context of moral theory, if one looks to Sen for an alternative version of consequentialism, one might want to know if his view is a form of act- or rule-consequentialism. And he shows no inclination to engage with that debate. Rather, his views can be filled out in different ways: they are 'incomplete' inasmuch as they are 'open-ended'. 'Open-endedness' can of course relate to evaluative matters. For example, one way in which Sen's capability approach is open-ended is that it does not advance any particular all purpose list of functionings for the purpose of evaluating advantage in the way that Rawls does in proposing a list of primary goods for his index of advantage in the context of his difference principle. But open-endedness and evaluative incompleteness are distinct, if sometimes related, concepts. Open-endedness is particularly important in Sen's work because it allows people with otherwise very different views to endorse some of his views, most notably his capability approach.

On questions of open-endedness and evaluative incompleteness, Sen's views differ from other views (of both of morality and justice) in suggesting that some evaluative questions, it is important to look for an agreed set of objects of value and weights which are socially acceptable. And in his later works he argues that 'the search for any agreed set of weights or values is a "social choice" exercise, and it requires public discussion and a democratic understanding and acceptance' (Sen 1999, 78–79). He adds that: 'we are not prevented, by any means, from proposing that some particular formula—rather than any alternative formula—be used for aggregation, but in this inescapably social choice exercise its status must depend on its acceptability to others' (Sen 1999, 79). Thus while in many theories—including utilitarianism—these questions are settled within the theory, in Sen's theory open-endedness and evaluative incompleteness create space for democratic and public reasoning to settle them. The way in which Sen creates this space can be seen as either part of the theoretical view he is developing or as a recognition of the limitation of what pure theory can, on its own, achieve (Sen

2004a, 78). On either interpretation, this aspect of his view may make it an unattractive alternative to utilitarianism, especially for those who think that the (evaluative) completeness of that view, and its articulation of a single overarching principle of morality (which can resolve conflicts between different considerations) is its key strength. Part of Sen's response to this line of thinking must be that utilitarianism fails to give public reasoning and democratic deliberation any significant role within its account of morality and that his incomplete theory has the virtue that it is more democratic about these matters. Indeed, this must be seen as an important limitation of utilitarianism on his view and needs to be discussed and assessed.

As we have already seen Sen also uses the word 'approach' in advancing the relevance of capability as a currency of advantage. He has used the same word more recently to advance his views on justice, though, as we shall see, he somewhat confusingly also uses the word 'theory' in these discussions of justice (Sen 2009, ix and 1). Is an approach an 'incomplete' theory? The use of the word 'approach' is not restricted to Sen's works in moral and political philosophy. He uses the same word in advancing his view of famine, when he develops his 'entitlement approach to famine' which is contrasted with what he calls the 'food availability decline' view (Sen 1981a). The purpose of advancing the entitlement approach is, in part, to depart from what (according to Sen is) a mistaken but dominant view in the realm of famine analysis. When Sen talks about the 'capability approach' to the evaluation of egalitarian claims, the quality of life and development and later about his various 'approaches' to justice, his goal is to explain various ways in which dominant views—such as those endorsed by some utilitarian or Rawls—are mistaken and to advance something like an alternative 'approach' to, or 'perspective' for thinking about, the relevant issues. In each case when Sen advances an 'approach', he also typically introduces new conceptual distinctions. One notable distinction that he makes is between a 'transcendental' and 'comparative' approach to justice. In motivating the distinction he writes that because 'Rawls takes the principal question to be: *What is a just society?*' this leads to 'what might be called a "transcendental" approach to justice, focussing—as it does—on identifying perfectly just societal arrangements' (Sen 2006, 216). And he wants to contrast this with a 'comparative' approach that 'would concentrate instead on ranking alternative societal arrangements (whether some arrangement is "less just" or "more just" than another) rather than focussing exclusively—or at all—on the identification of a fully just society' (Sen 2006, 216). As is clear from the description of Rawls's view above, Rawls himself thought that his focus was on what a 'perfectly just, or nearly just, constitutional regime might be like' is a limitation of his theory. In advancing a new 'approach', here also Sen's goal is to advance an alternative to a dominant perspective.

But is a new 'approach' of this sort, in itself a 'theory'? In *The Idea of Justice* Sen uses both 'theory' and 'approach' to describe his view. In the preface he writes: '[w]hat is presented here is a theory of justice in a very broad sense. Its aim is to clarify how we can proceed to address questions of enhancing justice and removing injustice, rather than offer resolutions of questions about the nature of perfect justice' (Sen 2009, ix and x). In describing the nature of this theory, he goes on to list various ways in which his views differ from Rawls's, stressing the comparative nature of the approach, the fact that the approach need not resolve all comparative questions, and the need to go beyond a focus on the nature of social institutions. These ways of differentiating his position from Rawls's and making it the basis of an alternative view of justice seem to me primarily to constitute an approach (or a set of approaches)—in the terms I have been using—to justice because it is (or they are) for the most part articulated through differences between it (them) and the dominant theory of justice of its time. When one combines this approach (or these approaches) to justice with some of Sen's other views—for example, his views about consequentialism, objectivity, impartiality and so on which are also presented in *The Idea of Justice* we find the building blocks of a theory of justice which is incomplete in being open-ended and evaluatively incomplete. But some of these building blocks—the 'comparative approach' to justice, the 'capability perspective' and so on—of that 'theory' are, on their own 'approaches' rather than an 'incomplete' theory itself, just as in Sen's later views on human rights (Sen 2004b) the capability perspective is only an 'element' of a theory.

SEN'S AND NUSSBAUM'S APPROACHES TO CAPABILITY AND JUSTICE: A CONTRAST

To further clarify how Sen uses the term 'approach' it is instructive to compare his works on capability and justice with Martha Nussbaum's. Nussbaum's views on capability have been advanced in two distinct periods. In the first, her interest in capability emerged in the context of Aristotle on political distribution (Nussbaum 1988). In several papers Nussbaum developed a version of what she called 'Aristotelian Social Democracy' (1990, 1992, 1995a, 1995b). In this first articulation of the approach one significant difference between Nussbaum's view and Sen's was that Nussbaum developed a list of human capabilities on the basis of an Aristotelian view of the good life whereas Sen resisted taking his version of the capability approach further in that direction (see especially Sen 1993). It is notable that part of Sen's motivation for resisting was that he wished to leave his approach open-ended so that it might be adopted by people with different views of the good life. Indeed, in responding to Nussbaum, he asked the question of why he should 'pause at outlining a general approach, with various bits to be filled in?' He answered: 'the motivation for the pause relates to the recognition that an agreement on the usability of the capability approach . . . need not *presuppose* an agreement on how the valuational exercises may be completed' (Sen 1993, 48). He added that: '[i]f reasoned agreement is seen as an important foundational quality central to political and social ethics, then the case for the pause is not so hard to understand'. It is this line of thinking which led Sen, in his later works, to advance public reasoning as a way to advance such reasoned agreement.

For the remainder of this paper I focus on Nussbaum's later articulation of her version of the 'capabilities approach' (see Nussbaum 1998, 1999, 2000, 2003, 2006, 2014 inter alia). Like Sen's capability approach, Nussbaum's later view remains, in part, an attempt to offer a corrective to some dominant views, such as utilitarianism and Rawls's theory of justice. Like Sen's approach it is relevant to a wide range of contexts, from questions about development (in Nussbaum 2000 and 2011) to feminism (Nussbaum 1999, 2000, and 2003 inter alia) and theories of justice (Nussbaum 2006). Nonetheless, in the context of addressing three pressing problems—disability, justice across borders and other species—within theories of justice in her *Frontiers of Justice,* Nussbaum is very clear in stating that, like Rawls's conception of justice, her version of '[t]he capabilities approach is a political doctrine about basic entitlements, not a comprehensive moral doctrine' (Nussbaum 2006, 155). And at the start of that work, Nussbaum describes some of the virtues which might characterise theories of justice.

It should be clear from this very brief description of *Frontiers of Justice* that Nussbaum's goal in advancing the 'capabilities approach' in this context is to produce an alternative—or as she expresses this in another context (Nussbaum 2011a, 46), a 'counter-theory'—to Rawls's theory in some specific areas. Similarly, Nussbaum (2006, 5) tells us that in her earlier work *Women and Human Development* (Nussbaum 2000) she compared her approach to (preference-based) utilitarianism and argued that it was superior to that view. Her 'capabilities approach' aspires, in itself, to the status of a theory in a way that Sen's capability approach does not—even if Sen's approach can be seen as an element in a larger incomplete theory of some sort. In this respect discussions of the status of the capability approach are likely to be confused and some of the recent literature does attempt to clarify some of the confusion (see Qizilbash 2012 and Robeyns forthcoming, inter alia).

In *Frontiers of Justice* Nussbaum's project is defined in a way which is in broad terms consistent with Rawls's—even if in her recent writings (notably Nussbaum 2011b, 2014) she explains some important points where she differs from Rawls. In particular, her goal is to produce a political conception of justice which can be the object of an 'overlapping consensus' among people who hold different moral doctrines. Yet, if Nussbaum's approach is a political doctrine, it will, like Rawls's later views, be hard to compare to utilitarianism since the latter is *primarily* a moral rather than political doctrine.

Nonetheless, there are various senses in which Nussbaum's approach remains, like Sen's, 'incomplete'. First of all, when she advances her list of central human capabilities, Nussbaum invariably reminds us that her list is open-ended. As she puts it: 'I consider the list as open-ended and subject to revision and rethinking in the way that any society's account of its most fundamental entitlements is always subject to supplementation (and deletion)' (Nussbaum 2006, 78). As a consequence, her approach also makes space for democratic deliberation. Indeed, she also thinks that 'the list ought to be specified in a somewhat abstract and general way, precisely in order to leave room for the activities of specifying and deliberating by citizens and their legislatures and courts' (Nussbaum 2006, 79). And Nussbaum states from the outset that her approach 'does not even claim to be a complete political doctrine, since it simply specifies some necessary conditions for a decently just society, in the form of a set of fundamental entitlements of all citizens' (Nussbaum 2006, 155). In referring to its lack of completeness here, Nussbaum is emphasising the restricted scope of the theory. Nonetheless, Nussbaum articulates her approach so that it covers our relations with non-human animals in a way that Rawls does not, at least in *A Theory of Justice*. There, as we saw, Rawls initially restricted the scope of his theory and argued that even if 'justice as fairness' might be extended to 'rightness as fairness' 'this wider theory fails to embrace all moral relationships, since it would seem to include only our relations with other persons and to leave out of account how we are to conduct ourselves toward animals and the rest of nature'. In this particular respect, Nussbaum's account is more complete than Rawls's early theory.

Would Sen agree with some of the core elements of Nussbaum's 'capabilities approach' which go beyond providing a 'general perspective'? It is clear from his earlier writings that this is unlikely. Sen has earlier been critical of aspects of Rawls's theory which Nussbaum endorses. In particular, Sen (1992, 76–79) thinks that the notion of a 'political conception of justice' is too restrictive and that the idea of justice is often relevant even when the requirements of a political conception of justice do not hold because of the absence of an overlapping consensus. So it is not just that the nature of Nussbaum's project in advancing her approach in the context of justice is different to Sen's—at no point does Sen endorse a political conception of justice. Indeed, if the 'capability approach' or perspective includes views about matters of this sort, Sen and Nussbaum would of necessity disagree about the content of the 'approach'. Indeed, to the degree that the capability approach is best considered only one part of his views of justice it is also only one building block in an incomplete theory rather than constituting an incomplete theory in itself.

As a consequence of some of these differences between Sen's and Nussbaum's discussions of justice, it becomes clear that in some respects, Sen's arguments against Rawls are also potentially arguments against Nussbaum. Indeed, Nussbaum notes this point and goes on to say of these elements of Sen's critique of Rawls that '[i]t is difficult in any case to determine the extent to which those criticisms apply to the version of ideal theory developed in my normative Capabilities Approach' (Nussbaum 2011a, 76). And more recently Nussbaum (2014, 3) writes that: Sen 'raises a fundamental issue for my theory as much as for Rawls's, since my theory is more like Rawls's than like the non-ideal theory advanced by Sen, in its overall aims and nature'. Rather than explore any further the differences between Nussbaum's and Sen's views at this stage, it is notable that Nussbaum sees her capabilities approach as a version of Rawlsian ideal theory, whereas it would make no sense to see Sen's capability approach as a *theory* (whether ideal or not) of that sort.

CONCLUSIONS

John Rawls believed that the failure of critics of utilitarianism to advance a well-worked out alternative moral theory had helped sustain its popularity and pre-eminence. *A Theory of Justice* was 'incomplete' as a moral theory, in the sense that it was restricted to the realm of justice, and Rawls's comparison between his theory and utilitarianism is misleading to the degree that he characterises Sidgwick's moral theory as a theory about the rightness of social arrangements rather than conduct. In his later thought, justice as fairness is not conceived as a moral doctrine but rather as a political conception of justice. The same is true of Martha Nussbaum's version of the capabilities approach in the form it is presented in *Frontiers of Justice*. To the degree that these are political rather than moral doctrines, they are hard to compare to utilitarianism. Amartya Sen's work defends a form of consequentialism—and indeed of a theory of justice—that is open-ended and evaluatively incomplete. His various 'approaches' to the evaluation of advantage, to justice, impartiality and objectivity provide parts of the architecture of an incomplete theory in his *The Idea of Justice*. Yet in that work the view of justice developed is characterised as both a 'theory' and an 'approach'. I have argued that what Sen calls an 'approach' is often not a theory but a perspective which is distinct from some dominant views. Various approaches he outlines may nonetheless constitute the building blocks or parts of the architecture of an incomplete theory. If I am right, Sen and Nussbaum use 'capability approach' and 'capabilities approach' in quite different ways, since for Nussbaum, in the context of justice, her 'capabilities approach' is a political conception of justice and a theory of a particular sort, while, for Sen, the capability approach is neither of these things. As a consequence, there is a real danger of confusion among those attempting to develop some version of the approach as an alternative, or as part of an alternative, to utilitarianism and Rawls's theory. Greater clarity about what one means by an 'approach' and various senses in which an approach or theory might be 'incomplete' should nonetheless advance the cause of some of these views, and clarify differences between them.

NOTE

I am extremely grateful to Roger Crisp and Johan Gustafsson for their very helpful discussions of various aspects of this paper. A version of the paper was presented to the Practical Philosophy Group at the University of York in January 2016 and I thank Richard Cookson, Johan Gustafsson, Christopher Jay, and Christian Piller in particular for their comments on that occasion. Finally, I thank Krushil Watene for her guidance, comments, and patience. Any error is mine.

REFERENCES

Fleurbaey, M. 1995. 'Equal Opportunity or Equal Social Outcome?' *Economics and Philosophy* 11: 25–55.

Hooker, B. 2000. *Ideal Code, Real World.* Oxford: Oxford University Press.

Mill, J.S. 1962. *Utilitarianism, On Liberty, Essay on Bentham Together with Selected Writings of Jeremy Bentham and John Austin.* Glasgow: Fontana Press.

Nussbaum, M. C. 1988. 'Nature, Function and Capability: Aristotle on Political Distribution'. *Oxford Studies in Ancient Philosophy*, 6 Supplementary Volume: 145–84.

Nussbaum, M. C. 1990. 'Aristotelian Social Democracy'. In B. Douglass, G. Mara and H. Richardson (eds.), *Liberalism and the Good,* London: Routledge.

Nussbaum, M. C. 1992. 'Human Functioning and Social Justice. In Defence of Aristotelian Essentialism'. *Political Theory* 20: 202–46.

Nussbaum, M. C. 1995a. 'Aristotle on Human Nature and the Foundation of Ethics'. In J.E.J. Altham and R. Harrison (eds.), *World, Mind and Ethics: Essays on the Ethical Philosophy of Bernard Williams.* Cambridge: Cambridge University Press.

Nussbaum, M. C. 1995b. 'Human Capabilities, Female Human Beings'. In M. C. Nussbaum and J. Glover (eds.), *Women, Culture and Development: A Study of Human Capabilities.* Oxford: Oxford University Press.

Nussbaum, M. C. 1998. 'The Good as Discipline, the Good as Freedom'. In D. A. Crocker and T. Linden (eds.), *Ethics of Consumption: the Good Life, Justice and Global Stewardship.* Lanham, MD: Rowan & Littlefield.

Nussbaum, M. C. 1999. *Sex and Social Justice.* Oxford: Oxford University Press.

Nussbaum, M. C. 2000. *Women and Human Development.* Cambridge, UK: Cambridge University Press.

Nussbaum, M. C. 2003. 'Capabilities as Fundamental Entitlements'. *Feminist Economics* 9: 61–92.

Nussbaum, M. C. 2006. *Frontiers of Justice: Disability, Nationality, Species Membership,* Cambridge, MA: Belknap Press of Harvard University Press.

Nussbaum, M. C. 2011a. *Creating Capabilities: The Human Development Approach,* Cambridge, MA: Belknap Press of Harvard University Press.

Nussbaum, M. C. 2011b. 'Perfectionist Liberalism and Political Liberalism'. *Philosophy and Public Affairs* 39: 3–45.

Nussbaum, M. C. 2014. 'Introduction: Capabilities, Challenges, and the Omnipresence of Political Liberalism'. In F. Comim and M. Nussbaum (eds.), *Capabilities, Gender and Equality: Towards Fundamental Entitlements.* Cambridge, UK: Cambridge University Press.

Qizilbash, M. 2008. 'Amartya Sen's Capability Approach: Insightful Sketch or Distorted Picture?' In F. Comim, M. Qizilbash and S. Alkire (eds.), *The Capability Approach: Concepts, Measures and Applications.* Cambridge, UK: Cambridge University Press.

Qizilbash, M. 2012. 'The Capability Approach: Its Interpretation and "Limitations"'. In F. Panzironi and K. Gelber (ed.), *The Capability Approach: Development Practice and Public Policy in the Asia-Pacific Region.* London and New York: Routledge.

Rawls, J. 1972. *A Theory of Justice*. Oxford: Oxford University Press.

Rawls, J. 1993. *Political Liberalism*. New York: Columbia University Press.

Rawls, J. 2001. *Justice as Fairness. A Restatement.* E. Kelly (ed.). Cambridge, MA: Belknap Press of Harvard University Press.

Robeyns, I. forthcoming. 'Capabilitarianism'. *Journal of Human Development and Capabilities.*

Sen, A. 1979a. *Collective Choice and Social Welfare.* North Holland: Amsterdam.

Sen, A. 1979b. 'Utilitarianism and Welfarism'. *Journal of Philosophy* LXXVI (9): 463–89.

Sen, A. 1980. 'Equality of What?' In S. McMurin (ed.), *Tanner Lectures in Human Values.* Cambridge: Cambridge University Press.

Sen, A. 1981a. *Poverty and Famines: An Essay on Entitlement and Deprivation.* Oxford: Clarendon Press.

Sen, A. 1981b. 'Rights and Agency'. *Philosophy and Public Affairs* 11: 3–39.

Sen, A. 1982. *Choice, Welfare and Measurement.* Oxford: Basil Blackwell.

Sen, A. 1984. 'Rights and Capabilities'. In A. Sen, *Resources, Values and Development* Oxford: Basil Blackwell.

Sen, A. 1987. *On Ethics and Economics.* Oxford: Basil Blackwell.

Sen, A. 1990a. 'Justice: Means and Freedom'. *Philosophy and Public Affairs* 19: 111–21.

Sen, A. 1990b. 'Welfare, Freedom and Social Choice: A Reply'. *Recherches Economique de Louvain* 56: 451–85.

Sen, A. 1992. *Inequality Re-examined.* Oxford: Oxford University Press.

Sen, A. 1993. 'Capability and Well-Being'. In M. Nussbaum and A. Sen (eds.), *The Quality of Life.* Oxford: Oxford University Press.

Sen, A. 2000. 'Consequential Evaluation and Practical Reason'. *Journal of Philosophy* XCVII: 477–502.

Sen, A. 2004a. 'Dialogue: Capabilities, Lists and Public Reason: Continuing the Conversation'. *Feminist Economics* 10: 77–80.

Sen, A. 2004b. 'Elements of a Theory of Human Rights'. *Philosophy and Public Affairs* 32: 315–56.

Sen, A. 2006. 'What Do We Want from a Theory of Justice?' *Journal of Philosophy* CIII: 215–38.

Sen, A. 2009. *The Idea of Justice.* London: Allen Lane.

Sen, A., and B. Williams 1982. 'Introduction'. In A. Sen and B. Williams, *Utilitarianism and Beyond.* Cambridge: Cambridge University Press.

Sidgwick, H. 1981. *The Methods of Ethics.* Indianapolis: Hackett.

Williams, B. 1985. *Ethics and the Limits of Philosophy.* London: Fontana Press.

Part II

Future Directions

Chapter Six

Justice as a Virtue

What Can We Expect of Our Allies?

Jay Drydyk

According to tradition, virtue is integral to improving oneself and educating others, and the virtue of justice is no exception. However, most of us cannot make the world much more just on our own: we need allies, about which the tradition says little. We can fill this gap by thinking of justice as the virtue we seek in worthy allies. Since this may seem a radical departure both from virtue ethics and from contemporary theorizing about justice, I will show first why it is warranted, and then, second, that there is still much to be learned from the virtue ethics tradition, for theorizing about justice.

WHO IS WORTHY OF SUPPORT?

Imagine[1] that we have the following political choices:

The *Red Party* was formed in the late 1990s, led by a wealthy businessman who we will call *Mr. T*. In 2001 the Red Party and Mr. T won the first election they contested, and for the next five years they implemented a program featuring micro-credit, universal health care (Connors 2008, 483; Haller 2014, 2), and investment in local development, which were very popular in poorer provinces for good reason: they contributed to reducing the poverty headcount by 50 percent (World Bank 2005, 6). After the Red Party was banned by a military junta in 2006, a series of successor parties were formed—in which Mr. T, though in exile, continued to have considerable influence.

The main loser in the 2001 election was the *Yellow Party*, the oldest party in the country. Founded in 1946, it won the greatest number of seats in parliamentary elections of 1948, 1976, and 1992—though never an outright majority. This royalist party campaigns on loyalty to the monarchy while aiding and abetting practices of 'royalist democracy' through which elected governments are held in check by a group of unelected officials and military officers, mutually recognized as a 'virtuous elite' (Winichakul 2014, 1).

The *Yellow-Shirt Movement.* After the Red Party's election to a second term, escalating protests attracted tens of thousands opposed to the Party's program and in particular to Mr. T, who was accused of disloyalty to the King and of using his political power for personal advantage. Protests were stimulated in particular by news that one of his family's principal firms had been sold to foreigners, with the proceeds going untaxed, which was permitted by regulations established by his government. Protests were led by a coalition-based organizing committee. Some of these leaders showed their royalist hues by contending that rural people were 'too poorly educated to be allowed to elect a parliament, and that it should be a largely appointed body instead' (Head 2008). They also organized occupations and demonstrations 'to make the capital ungovernable, and to obstruct government attempts to conduct a successful election which would revalidate its legitimacy and authority' (McCargo 2015, 341).

In this 'tutelary defective democracy' (Chambers 2013, 68), a *parallel state* including the King, the King's Privy Council, the military, and royalist networks (McCargo 2005) is capable of blocking democratic legislative initiatives as well as democratic control over the military (Chambers 2013). The Red Party's re-election in 2005 was followed first by Yellow-Shirt protests and later by a military coup encouraged by the palace (Chambers 2013, 72). After democracy was restored, the military intervened to encourage some of the Red Party's parliamentary allies to defect, to join a Yellow Party coalition (McCargo 2015, 345), which thus came to power without being elected.

The *Red-Shirt Movement* is a protest movement that formed in response to the military coup that ended the rule of the Red Party led by Mr. T. This movement also has a coalition-based coordinating committee, though the movement itself is highly decentralized and locally based. The unifying goal of the vast majority of participants is restoring the type of democracy they enjoyed under Mr. T (Thabchumpon and McCargo 2011).

Mr. T remained an influential political leader even after he was exiled (McCargo 2015, 347). His wealth grew to such proportions that he was able to purchase a team in the English Premier League, as an exile project (McCargo 2008, 349). His influence on the Red Party continued when his sister became the party leader (McCargo 2015, 346).

> Though charges made against him in politics and in legal proceedings may have been inflated, they were not entirely lacking in substance. While in office, he initiated a 'war on drugs' that involved extra-judicial killings and other human rights abuses (Amnesty International 2015). Of numerous allegations of corruption that have been made against him, two have been borne out by courts, one leading to jail sentences for Mr. T and his wife, and another resulting in a judgment of US$1.4 billion against his family finances (Hewison 2010, 124).

These political actors offer a dismal choice to anyone hoping for greater justice. Each of them is flawed: some for tolerating corruption and human rights abuse, and the rest for advocating an anti-democratic political system that reproduces poverty and inequality.

Who Cares?

This dismal choice may give rise to different responses. Some people may continue to wish for greater justice but are no longer strongly committed to achieving it. They may despair at knowing how greater justice might be achieved, or they may simply give higher priority to other goals, such as survival or protection of family. Call this group *hopeless.* Contrast them with another group, who maintain their personal commitment and continue to make greater justice their goal, despite their dismal choices and chances for achieving it. Call them *determined.* Their disappointment will be different in kind, a disappointment that there seem to be no political actors on the scene who are *worthy of their support*. For the hopeless, in contrast, there is no question of who to support, because there is no point in supporting anyone's efforts towards a goal that cannot be achieved—a goal which they have therefore abandoned. The determined do not give up seeking allies to support; their disappointment is rather that no one on the scene seems worthy of their support.

My focus is on the determined, who continue to make justice their goal, and who are therefore susceptible to disappointment that political actors are not worthy of their support. If others wish to develop a philosophy for the hopeless, they may do so. My interest is in the perspective and concerns of people who are determined to seek justice.

What Do They Care About?

My question concerns what it is about political actors that should make them worthy of support, from the perspective of determined justice-seeking people. Before proceeding, a few words should be said about the meaning of 'support' and 'worthy'.

Like its contrary, 'opposing', 'supporting' has objective as well as subjective dimensions. One can support (or oppose) an actor or cause by contributing one's time, effort, or other resources towards (or against) their success. On the other hand, supporting or opposing something also involves attitudes: support may involve approving or upholding, allegiance or adherence. What all of these seem to have in common is a commitment to the goals of others, based on goals of one's own.

When we ask, then, whether political actors are worthy of our support, we are asking whether our commitment to their goals is justifiable, based on our goals. This can be simplified further by characterizing *us* as justice-seekers, so that justifications 'based on our own goals' need not be narrowly self-regarding. Rather, the question is: what makes political actors worthy of support by justice-seekers, or, in other words, what would suffice to justify the commitment of justice-seekers to the goals of those political actors, and what should be required to justify that sort of commitment?

It may be objected that, by basing justifiability of support on our own goals, I am more or less closing the door on virtue ethics, which would call for basing justifiability of support on the merits or virtues of the political actors. But if these are merits or virtues that are relevant to justice, then they are relevant to the goals of justice-seeking people. Various moral and non-moral merits and virtues may not be relevant: to secular-minded people, religious piety is not relevant, and perhaps the merits of grand philanthropy (the Aristotelian virtue of magnanimity) should also be discounted. So my account of 'support-worthiness' is neither narrowly self-regarding, nor does it exclude considerations of political actors' merits and virtues.

Who Needs Allies?

One final question is obvious. Do justice-seekers actually need to know which political actors are worthy of their support? Can we not be committed to justice without continuing commitments to allies?

Hippocratic Justice: Not Causing Injustice

To refrain from causing injustice would not seem to require allies. However, self-restraint on its own will not be entirely satisfying to justice-seekers, for two main reasons.

First, to refrain from seeking just behaviour by others includes refraining from seeking just treatment from others, for oneself. This is not a good strategy for survival, much less for acting justly, as state-of-nature stories remind us. So those who want to refrain from causing injustice do need allies after all, not least of all for reasons of self-preservation.

Second, some unjust outcomes caused by others are as bad as or worse than any we might individually cause by ourselves. The reason for sticking to self-restraint, then, cannot be that this will catch bigger fish. Could it rather be greater assurance of success? But risk-aversion is not a virtue per se: the joy of catching more fish must be weighed against the disappointment of not catching any big ones. More seriously, as long as the practice of slavery persisted, abolitionists could take little solace from the fact that they refrained personally from owning slaves. Those who were *determined* to oppose slavery would have nothing but scorn for the view that one is absolved of any further duties of justice merely by refraining from slaveholding.

For these reasons, justice-seekers should not be concerned merely with unjust outcomes of their own actions. Once past this self-imposed limitation, justice-seekers will find that they need allies and that they will need to assess which potential allies are most worthy of support.

Collaborating Ad Hoc, One Issue at a Time

Ad hoc collaboration is not uncommon in single-issue campaigns, so it is reasonable to ask whether we cannot confine ourselves to asking whether each action or campaign is worthy of our support.

Arguably such an approach could allow us to evade many of the dilemmas that confront justice-seekers. Recall the *Red/Yellow* society. The only apparent means of attempting significant poverty reduction involve allying with the *Red-Shirt Movement* or successors to the *Red Party.* But both of these are still aligned firmly with *Mr. T,* whose record is marred by a history of abusing human rights and profit-taking from the exercise of power. So we face a dilemma: we cannot support poverty reduction without supporting the Red Movement or Party, yet we cannot support that Movement or Party without supporting a corrupt human rights abuser. Neither seems consistent with seeking justice.

Can dilemmas like this one be resolved by focusing on actions rather actors? That would mean, for example, supporting demands by the Red Movement and legislative initiatives by the Red Party to reduce poverty and inequality, while withholding any more general support for the Movement or Party. However, even this limited support amounts to cooperation, raising questions about why we are cooperating with a movement and party that tacitly condone a leader who has engaged in human rights abuse and profit-taking governance.

Arguably, working with an unjust ally in order to achieve greater justice is not universalizable. Imagine that we could make progress in reducing some particular injustice by making an alliance with the devil. If everyone did that, could the devil not assemble sufficient support to bring about his full program, including expansion of the very injustice we had bargained with him to reduce? By insisting on justice from one's allies only on one issue, at one time, this limited focus leaves political space for perpetrating other injustices behind our backs.

The lesson I draw is that we cannot ignore the dispositions of those with whom we collaborate, even one issue at a time. The argument I gave above draws its force from the supposition that we are dealing with the devil, whose dispositions are, according to the main tradition, entirely evil. This argument does not hold water if the devil is not actually capable of occupying the space left open by a limited agreement to cooperate on a single issue; cooperating with a decrepit devil no longer capable of evil might tarnish our reputation, but reputational risks are matters of pragmatic politics, not ethical universalizability. The key point is that both evil and decrepitude relate to the devil's dispositions, which remain relevant to whether we should cooperate with him even on a case-by-case basis.

To conclude: the messy task of choosing and working with allies is not optional for determined justice-seekers. Neither the need for allies nor the dilemmas of dirty hands can be evaded by confining our support to actions, rather than actors. Nor can we avoid coping with allies by contenting ourselves with refraining from causing injustice. If reducing or removing injustice is really our goal, then we must also address injustices caused by others, including those injustices which, if visited upon us or other justice-seeking people, would impair our efforts—whether by intervention or self-restraint—to hasten a world that is less unjust. Justice-seekers need allies, for better or worse.

LEARNING FROM THE TRADITION

Compared with more traditional approaches to justice as a virtue, my approach is more relational. Whereas the tradition has focused on the improvement and self-improvement of individuals, my concern is with building alliances, and so I propose conceiving the virtue of justice as support-worthiness of potential allies for people who are determined to seek justice. However, I am not suggesting that an agent-centred perspective on justice should be replaced by an alliance-centred perspective. Justice-seeking people still need to consider how to act justly, individually and collectively, in their particular circumstances. What I am suggesting is that an alliance-centred perspective shifts priorities as to what we need to know first, in order to answer these questions. An agent-centred approach to justice turns quickly to questions of what justice is, and whose justice it is. We see this in Aristotle: even with a broad conception of justice as avoiding inequalities that are disproportionate, his next thoughts are, roughly, disproportionate to what, for whom? An alliance-centred approach begins more generically with the concept of justice-seeking as opposition to inequalities that are wrong. Knowing *which* inequalities are wrong is one of the traits we seek to discover and develop between our allies and ourselves.

Nevertheless, an alliance-centred approach to justice has much to learn from the agent-centred tradition of virtue ethics, and my strategy in the rest of this chapter will be to draw on comparisons with the old to give shape to the new. I will do this in two phases, first asking along which lines justice-seeking people should sort their potential allies, and then considering the implications of finer-grained issues arising from within the tradition. For simplicity and clarity, I will restrict my view of 'the tradition' to the neo-Aristotelian approach developed and advocated by Rosalind Hursthouse and Julia Annas.

How to Compare Allies

To choose allies well, we must first compare them well. Determined justice-seekers in the Red/Yellow society would want to know whether it is the Red Shirts, the Yellow Shirts, or indeed the parallel state that would make *better* allies. On the other hand, they might also want to make categorical judgments: judging that the parallel state is not at all suitable as an ally simplifies the remaining options to two. Are there solid grounds for making either kind of judgment—comparative or categorical? Should we confine ourselves just either one? Do the criteria for finding one group completely unqualified differ from criteria for finding some less qualified than others? If so, what do those two sets of criteria have in common? What can be learned from the tradition, in which similar issues have also arisen?

The justice we seek from our allies is *multidimensional*, because there are *different* ways in which political actors can be better or worse as allies. In my example, the Reds are too soft on corruption, while the Yellows are too dismissive of democracy. The tradition readily offers comparisons. Aristotle observed that the virtue of justice is not only specific, focused on disproportionate inequalities, but also general, requiring all other virtues as well: acting justly requires not only combatting unjust rewards but doing so honestly, courageously, and so on (1129a). What we observe now, beyond this, is that *even as a specific virtue* justice is multidimensional, opposing political domination and inequality as well as corruption. A potential ally that underperforms in any dimensions is for that reason less worthy as an ally. In this regard we have much to learn from debates within the tradition concerning diversity, dilemmas, and unity of the virtues.

The comparative perspective applies within each dimension of justice as well as among them. Suppose we expect our allies to promote democracy. In that case we might prefer a group that 'deepens' democracy to another that is content to deprive citizens of further engagement with decision-making after elections, as long as those elections are free and fair. The second group might be preferable in turn over a third that cares only that elections are held, no matter how freely or fairly. (For the moment this ranking is only illustrative; the question of how such rankings are to be made and justified will be taken up later.) Within the democratic dimension, then, different actors can be distinguished by the degree or kind of democracy to which they are committed; some may also distinguish themselves by experience or success, that is, by the degree or kind of democracy that they have managed to bring about.

This is distinct from comparing potential allies across multiple dimensions, where they show themselves more committed or successful in some than in others. A free-market anti-corruption party may oppose only those inequalities resulting from corruption, relinquishing control over other inequalities to the invisible hand. A populist pro-development party may commit primarily to a conception of the common good, such as raising living standards, while focusing its egalitarianism on civil and political rights and turning a blind eye to corruption and market-based inequalities. Every political program has a distinct profile, combining stronger and weaker commitments among the multiple dimensions of justice. It is easier to shun profiles that are weak in multiple dimensions but more difficult—as in the Red/Yellow example—to choose between potential allies whose failings are equally grave yet equally limited and different in kind.

One further complexity divides 'how' from 'what'. We are interested not only in *what* our allies seek or achieve (among the dimensions of justice), but in *how* they typically go about doing this, and in *how committed* they are to just means as well as just ends. In judging collective actors such as parties, institutions, and movements, we have more to consider than whether their members are properly motivated *individually*; we also have their collective decision-making processes to consider. If justice requires an organization to promote democratization in society, arguably that organization is also required to adopt its own strategy and tactics democratically. Motivation is not to be overlooked, either, though in the case of collective actors this means assessing their organizational culture: how are the emotional underpinnings of just action cultivated and renewed? This in turn raises questions about which motives and emotional bases are appropriate for seeking justice.

Finally, a just person not only does the right thing in the right ways, but does so for the right reasons, relying on practical reasoning to work out which particular ends and means are just in particular circumstances. So too with collective actors: strategies that dispense with reason, that resort entirely to inspiration, and that ignore predictably adverse consequences causing unjustifiable harms—these are plainly not to be trusted. Still, what kinds of reasoning are required, to avoid these kinds of errors?

On each of these topics the tradition can be instructive.

Categorical or Comparative?

The tradition tells us that in the best of cases virtues are reliable and unhesitating. This, of course, reminds us that human beings are also capable of responding hesitantly and unreliably to situations that call for virtue. Hesitation and unreliability are traditionally accounted for by weakness of will in resisting contrary desires (Hursthouse 2013, 3). What status to accord an imperfect, conflicted exercise of the virtues is a matter of some controversy. If we follow Aristotle in conceiving of virtue as human excellence, we might follow him also in drawing a sharp distinction between those whose practice of the virtues is conflicted with other desires and emotions, and those who are not conflicted in this way. He calls the first group 'encratic,' and regards only the second group as virtuous.

Outside the Aristotelian tradition, Kant drew a different distinction. Moral choices (giving effect to the moral law) are free, and yet they can also encounter resistance from our inclinations (Kant 1996, 145–46; AK6:380[2]). Virtue is precisely the 'capacity and considered resolve to withstand' this resistance (Kant 1996, 146; AK6:380). A being with a moral will that did not encounter such resistance would be holy, not human (Kant 1996, 145; AK6:379). 'Virtue' in this sense is distinct from the 'merit' corresponding to the extent to which one carries out one's 'wide' duties. These are duties to pursue the goals of perfecting ourselves and promoting the happiness of others, and we have considerable latitude in choosing how and how far to do so. Actions fulfilling these duties are 'meritorious', from which we might infer that doing more to promote the happiness of others is more meritorious (Hill 1971, 70). Kant does not permit wilful underperformance, since 'a wide duty is not to be taken as permission to make exceptions to the maxim of actions but only as permission to limit one maxim of duty by another (e.g., love of one's neighbour in general by love of one's parents)' (Kant 1996, 153; AK6:390). For Kant, doing more to fulfil this duty has greater merit; there is no upper limit of perfect virtue, and it is only one's circumstances, limiting what one can accomplish, that limit the merits of those accomplishments.

How, then, should justice-seeking people assess their potential allies: categorically, comparatively, or both? In contemporary political life we may need to choose from among many potential allies, and it is unlikely that only one of them will possess the virtue of justice. In light of this, the mandate that practical politics creates for the concept of justice as a virtue is to do some sorting for us, distinguishing actors that are more just from those that are less so. Once we take this step, we will also have to consider many different grounds of comparison, some of which I have already telegraphed: extent of achievement in each dimension of just outcome, number of dimensions in which these successes are achieved, internal processes that are just and well motivated, and conformity to practical reason and public reason. However, we may also want to draw a line between these potential allies and other actors that are not suitable at all. Both kinds of judgment presuppose a comparative concept of justice, that is, a concept of multidimensional change towards greater justice. A better ally is more effective in achieving greater change in more dimensions. One who is more disposed to effect changes in the opposite directions is not suitable at all. In the middle we can expect a gray zone of incompetents that are effective at moving neither forward nor back.

Multidimensionality, Dilemmas, and the Unity of Virtues

For some ethical theories, diversity of values is a challenge to be overcome, for instance by the categorical imperative or by a comprehensive utility principle. Virtue ethics, in contrast, embraces the diversity of virtues without fear. In doing so, however, it encounters two challenges: navigating dilemmas and understanding whether and how the virtues are unified.

The Unity of Virtues

As Annas has stressed, we must use practical intelligence to understand how best to practice a virtue. For example, giving something to someone who has no need or use for it is not how to practice generosity. What practical intelligence shows us here is that in order to exercise one virtue, generosity, we must also exercise another, benevolence. Clearly, then, there is a certain reciprocity or interdependence among the virtues, and this is sometimes expressed more demandingly by the 'unity of virtues' claims: if you have one virtue, you have them all, and, if you lack one virtue, you have none (Annas 2011, 85). Arguably a trait is not a virtue unless it is interdependent in this way with other virtues (Annas 2011, 97). This interdependence may also have intriguing applications to justice. It is tempting to follow Annas in using these considerations to remove traits (recommended by Hume) such as being tidy, hard-working, and witty from consideration as virtues (Annas 2011, 97).

Navigating Dilemmas

Virtue ethics is beset by dilemmas because there are circumstances in which it seems impossible to practice both of two virtues, as for instance when my mother-in-law asks whether I enjoy her ratatouille and I must choose between benevolence and honesty. The most common approach to such dilemmas is attempting to re-describe one horn of the dilemma, to show that it is only an apparent dilemma (Hursthouse 2001, 52)—for example, by arguing that it is no kindness to allow my mother-in-law to continue believing that everyone likes her ratatouille. (Wishing that my mother-in-law never reads the previous sentence or even hears of it, I must be lacking in courage.) One possible strength of virtue ethics is that it can explain people's residual regret when choosing the least bad of two bad options (Hursthouse 2001, 44ff.).

The tale of Red Shirts and Yellow Shirts shows that dilemmas are real impediments for determined justice-seeking people. In this political situation, it seems impossible to simultaneously (a) promote reduction of poverty and inequality, (b) avoid supporting corruption, and (c) promote democracy. One response suggested by the tradition is to see whether one horn of the dilemma can be made unproblematic by re-describing it. In the case at hand this option is not open, because we acknowledge that the dilemma is real. A second response is to choose the least unjust option, though with regret: for example, one might reluctantly put up with the corruption of Mr. T and his family for the sake of democracy and poverty reduction. Here I would raise a question, and, in answer to it, two observations. The question is: why regret? Imagine a pair of Red factions, in which each puts up with Mr. T.'s corruption, but only one does so with regret. Call them 'Regret' and 'Oblivion'. Does one deserve our support more than the other (all else being equal)? To transpose from the individual to organizational/collective level, we should perhaps add other responses to regret: let us suppose that Regret considers continued alliance with Mr. T an ongoing problem, a lasting concern, because he has not atoned for any of his questionable dealings in the past and he may have more in the future. If Oblivion has no such concerns, then this casts doubt on the strength of their commitment to integrity (against corruption) as a virtue. If we believe that integrity is a dimension of justice, then, because other factors are equal, we should not support Oblivion as much as Regret—perhaps we would give Oblivion only tactical cooperation, while hoping and acting for Regret to become ascendant. So one answer to the question 'Why regret?' is that an actor that is *unconcerned* about sacrificing one dimension of justice for others is *not sufficiently committed* to that dimension. But a second answer arises when we consider that, without this concern, one will not be driven to seek a third way in which no dimension is sacrificed for others. If Regret is driven to find a practical way to continue pursuing the Red agenda of democratic poverty reduction while dissociating themselves from the corruption of Mr. T, then clearly this faction would be more worthy of support.

One component of comparative virtue, then, is the ingenuity to find solutions to dilemmas pitting one dimension of justice against others. Thus there is no room in virtuous politics for lexical priorities that set one dimension (such as political liberty) over others (such as reduction of inequality) in all cases.

Justice Within—Well Decided and Well Motivated

The choice and action of a virtuous person, according to the tradition, are well decided and well motivated. How does this apply to the collective actors we choose as allies?

Well Decided

In the virtue ethics tradition, the space of good decision-making is occupied by what have been called 'practical wisdom', 'practical reasoning', and 'practical intelligence'. These are integral both to practicing virtue and to learning and developing it.

(a) *Practicing.* To rehearse an earlier example, the disposition to be generous can misfire if we give to the wrong people or give to some by diverting resources from others who are more needy or deserving; nor is it virtuous to give in ways that are demeaning to the recipients. So the virtue of generosity is not simply a disposition to give but requires giving in the right circumstances and in the right ways. Practicing any virtue requires a certain know-how, or 'practical wisdom', which bridges the gap between intending to act well and acting well in fact. In addition to foreseeing consequences of actions, it involves recognizing the morally salient facts in a situation (Hursthouse 2001, 12).

(b) *Learning and understanding.* Acquiring this kind of know-how is involved in learning how to practice a virtue, and it characterizes the transition from immature to mature understanding of a virtue. However, learning does not stop here. We all start by learning accepted practices, but we do not understand them fully unless we can modify them to deal with anomalies and inconsistencies (Annas 2007, 517; 2011, 52–65). The respect for family members learned in many cultures is gender-biased. Recognizing this as an inconsistency, and then revising one's ideas of familial respect to recognize gender difference in appropriate ways can be an arduous exercise in critical thinking.

Collective actors seeking justice are certainly not exempt from critical thinking of these kinds. However, their decision-making may also be held to standards of accountability. Civil society organizations are most commonly held accountable 'upward' to sources of funding and 'laterally' to their members; arguably they should also be accountable 'downward' to the people they aim to represent and help.

Well Motivated

The tradition holds that virtuous people are well disposed emotionally to behave virtuously: they are not emotionally conflicted about doing so, and each virtue calls up a range of emotional responses to the behaviour of others, from approval and admiration for the best behaviour to being shocked and appalled by the worst; all of this is to be embedded in personal identities. Can justice-seeking people expect their allies to be well motivated in similar ways?

Normally, seekers of justice would expect allied organizations to be sustainable, motivating enough people to join them and remain with them to sustain or increase their membership. If two potential allies were similar in all other respects, but one could not sustain its membership, that one would normally be less worthy of support.

For individuals and collectives alike, assessment of whether they are appropriately motivated would seem to require some assumptions about which motives are appropriate. Nussbaum and Slote (Nussbaum 1996, 2013; Slote 2007, 94–103) have argued that striving for justice should be motivated primarily by empathy and compassion. In my view much else remains to be added to this debate. Are empathy and compassion sufficient, or are other moral emotions also needed to support striving for justice? Jonathan Haidt and Jesse Graham suggest a range of emotional responses besides compassion, including dispositions towards fairness/reciprocity, in-group/loyalty, authority/respect, and purity/sanctity (Haidt and Graham 2007). Following Nussbaum, we may want to exclude disgust (towards impurity) altogether as a political emotion (Nussbaum 2013, 257–313), but the other emotional responses could have important motivating roles: is striving for justice not motivated by a sense of fairness, by solidarity (understood as mutual loyalty among those striving for justice), and respect for democracy? There must also be some place in this emotional repertoire for indignation at injustice—or else how can it be that 'Justice thunders condemnation' (Pottier 1871)?

While collective actors do not have emotional responses of their own, they can promote emotional responses to justice and injustice on the part of their members. Whether and how well a collective actor does this with its members, by promoting an appropriate political culture, should count as factors in its support-worthiness. Another factor needed to support a collective striving for justice is an appropriately inclusive identity. In the virtue ethics tradition a person's practice of virtue should be characteristic of who that person is. Should we also expect justice as a virtue to be practiced by a collective as part of their collective identity? If so, there is much work to be done. Any collective actor will include members with different and intersecting group identities, based on such factors as gender, racialization, class ethnicity, religion, sexuality, and so on. A sense of collective identity that does not build on group identities such as these will be less authentic and more difficult to sustain. A collective actor that has cultivated its shared pro-justice identity in a more inclusive fashion is therefore, other things being equal, more worthy of support.

Flourishing?

One of the more intriguing features of virtue ethics is its claim that a life of virtue contributes necessarily to a good life, a life well lived. This is not to say that virtue is the only requirement for living well; a good life can include many more elements, such as health, good relationships, social esteem, or a positive balance of enjoyment over suffering. On one reading, virtue ethics claims simply that virtuous choice cannot be traded off against any of these other elements (Annas 2005, 522). Arguably some suffering may be endured for the sake of any of the others—without sacrificing a good life overall. However, it is a distinctive claim of virtue ethics that one cannot maintain a good life overall by lying, stealing, and in other ways sacrificing virtuous choice in order to achieve whatever else one values as elements of a good life.

Does practicing the virtue of justice contribute to the flourishing of collectives as well as individuals? This raises three further questions. (a) Can collectives be said to 'flourish', and, if they can, what constitutes their flourishing? Since organizations are formed for particular purposes, it should be possible to judge how well they are flourishing by how well they are achieving their given goals. However, since even organizations of the same kind may have different goals, what is required for the flourishing of one might not be required for another. If some central banks are created with the sole goal of preventing inflation, while others are also given the goal of reducing unemployment, one may flourish while the other, behaving no differently, does not flourish. One may also wonder (b) whether the flourishing of organizations has any intrinsic value. If an organization forms for anti-social purposes (e.g., suppression of some segment of the population), then it would be morally outrageous to think that it is intrinsically good for that organization to flourish despite the consequences for its victims. This suggests that the flourishing of collectives should not be valued *except* for their impact on the flourishing of individual persons—including everyone they affect, outside the organization or within. (c) On the other hand, it would be morally satisfying to think of an organization as morally dysfunctional if its internal workings and decision-making are far from virtuous. Thus the flourishing of a political party should not be judged simply by whether it manages to keep getting re-elected. If that party is a vehicle for corruption, it would be tempting to consider it not as flourishing, but rather as morally dysfunctional, despite its continued success at achieving its given goal of repeated re-election.

JUSTICE WITHIN—ENGAGEMENT WITH PUBLIC REASON

Justice is multidimensional, demanding (for instance) less poverty and more democracy, among other kinds of change. So justice-seeking people and their allies need to reach some shared understanding of (a) which kinds of change justice requires and (b) what constitutes advancing and retreating in each dimension. Without that kind of shared understanding, mutual support amongst justice-seekers would not be justifiable, nor would alliances.

Not unlike other virtues, the practice and learning of justice relies on 'practical wisdom', 'practical reasoning', and 'practical intelligence'. However, the virtue of justice may be unique in its reliance on reasoning of a different kind, namely *public reason.*

How might the dimensions of justice be found? The parallel in virtue ethics is understanding the virtues, which arguably starts from what one learns from tradition and continues by modifying this to cope with hard cases and inconsistencies. Analogical reasoning is bound to play a large role in this kind of critical reflection, so that like cases are treated alike.

This may be unduly restrictive for justice-seeking people who are assessing allies. What is missing is a full discussion of what justice requires—discussion that is normally unrestricted between allies. Fuller discussion is required by the pluralism that characterizes the political thinking of different political actors. Some differences between them may arise from differences in historical experience. Political actors who have faced different sources of resistance to justice can be expected to highlight different social relations, institutions, and practices as either conducive or obstructive to struggles for justice, and so their thinking will invoke different kinds of evidence. Political actors may also be differentiated by the normative paradigms with which they are most comfortable and in which they place the most confidence: some may look for guidance from the thinking of eminent leaders of the past, others may prefer to calculate consequences, and overlapping these two groups would be a third, which draws lines around means and outcomes that are categorically unacceptable. We could use an internalist assessment of whether a potential ally has chosen and acted justly by examining whether this group or individual has been true to their history and to their normative paradigm. But this seems quite inadequate, because groups and individuals can also be blinkered by their historical experience and their normative comfort zone. It is no good to ally with groups that cling dogmatically to their past and to their internally sanctioned ways of thinking, especially if they cannot understand or appreciate *our* historical experience and normative ways of thinking. Without this kind of understanding and appreciation, what kind of allies would they be?

Fortunately there is an alternative. Instead of assessing potential allies by their adherence to their own historical experience and normative paradigms, we can assess them by how they stand in *public reason*. This would involve assessing how well their judgments and choices regarding justice stand up to all relevant historical experience and to all reliable normative ways of thinking, if the best arguments prevail.

Is Public Reason up to the Task?

Is public reason up to the task of identifying the dimensions or directions of change in which justice advances or declines? Answers to this question will depend on how public reason is conceived, and there are numerous rival conceptions. Here I will consider only one: I will sketch some interventions that the capability approach can make within public reason to provide the guidance that is needed.

The capability approach offers a simplifying device that is meant to promote convergence within public reason, amidst the pluralistic welter of normative starting-points. Sen proposes that public reason can be simplified considerably if it works from an information base that allows us to identify and compare inequalities that matter. The first step in this direction is to identify ways of functioning that everyone has reason to value as elements of living well. The valuable capabilities are substantive freedoms to function in precisely these ways. 'Substantive freedom' means that these are ways of functioning that one is not only at liberty to achieve, but that one can actually manage to achieve, having both the personal capacities and the external wherewithal to do so. Besides this 'retail conception' of capabilities, which links them individually with valuable ways of functioning, there are also 'wholesale' conceptions of an individual's overall capability to achieve such functionings, in various combinations. This overall capability can be referred to as a person's 'well-being freedom'.

This information base is particularly productive of normative conclusions when it partners with impartiality as equal concern for everyone's good. If, in public reason, everyone's *good* must be given equal consideration, then everyone's *capabilities* must be considered equally valuable, since we are talking here of capabilities to function in ways that are elements of living well. If some people's well-being freedom is greater than others', public reason will be reluctant to condone the shortfalls, for condoning these shortfalls would condone the fact that some people are less free to live well than others, and, apart from exceptional circumstances, it is difficult to see how condoning that is consistent with equal regard for everyone's good. Thus inequalities of capability are inequalities that should matter considerably in the context of public reason.

However, inequality *reduction* is not the only dimension of change in capabilities that impartial public reason would support. If everyone's good matters, and matters equally, then public reason should be inclined to support the goal of expanding everyone's capabilities—that is, to adopt the goal of *efficiency* as well as equality, as Sen has suggested (Sen 1999, 116–20). For similar reasons, impartial public reason would also be inclined to support capability *security* by instituting protections against the downside risks of economic insecurity, health insecurity, and so on (Sen 2000, 2003).

In the Red/Yellow illustration from which I began, democratization was highlighted as another such dimension. There are two ways in which public reason agreement on the importance of democratization can be fostered by capability concepts. In Sen's terminology, agency freedom is the freedom to achieve goals that a person happens to value, whether they have anything to do with well-being or not (Sen 1993, 35). The demands of well-being freedom and agency freedom are most compelling within public reason when they are combined. Hence poverty reduction programs that rely on empowerment, expanding the choices that poor people have to increase their living standards, are especially worthy of support. Civil and political rights are all justifiable along these lines, and, for the same reasons, erosion or elimination of civil and political rights should be opposed because they are disempowering.

Martha Nussbaum derives similar results from two items on her list of central capabilities to be endorsed and protected by public reason when it is guided by the idea of equal human dignity. Number 6 on the list, practical reason, expands to the extent that people can decide for themselves, for their own reasons, how their time and energy are spent. (Nussbaum 2006, 76). While the value of this capability implicitly supports democratization and opposes its reversal, Capability 10, 'Control over One's Environment', makes this quite explicit (Nussbaum 2006, 77).

Developing these ideas fully would require a much more extensive discussion. Nevertheless, this brief sketch will suffice, I hope, to show some of the ways in which capabilities concepts enable public reason to determine dimensions of change for greater or lesser justice. I would be surprised if similar results could not be produced by other approaches to public reason.

CONCLUSIONS

All of this is twice removed from the current paradigm for theorizing about justice. The paradigm seeks necessary and sufficient conditions for a fully just society. The virtue ethics tradition is already once removed from this, since it focuses less on just societies than on just agents and what they will strive for and against. An alliance-oriented perspective inverts this yet again by focusing on what makes potential allies worthy or unworthy of support by justice-seeking people.

Even within a paradigm it can be interesting to see what can be done outside the castle walls, but why move *this* far out?

One answer is that the paradigm's supporters and critics alike have something to gain from this perspective. Those who uphold ideal theories of justice must still wonder how to pursue these ideals in practice, for which allies are indispensable. Indeed, as Rawls stressed, an ideal of justice that cannot be achieved and sustained has little claim on our allegiance, especially in the social contract tradition. And Rawls can also be read as suggesting what sorts of allies are required to pursue fair terms of cooperation: they must be *reasonable*. For critics who, like Sen, favour a comparative approach (Sen 2009), identifying the dimensions in which a society can become more just or less so does not yet tell us *how* to move in the directions of greater justice. For this we need to associate with others who are not only like-minded but *good allies*. Finally, relational critics of the paradigm might remind us that, since justice is about relationships, it is especially important to theorize about justice from within the perspectives that social relations and interpersonal relationships afford (Koggel 2002, 2012); my suggestion is that ally-based perspectives must be included among these.

A simpler and perhaps more convincing answer is that choosing one's allies is normally the first step that people take when they are motivated by justice. It is when we come to wonder or doubt where our alliances are leading that we need to clarify and theorize about the directions or ideals of justice.

To understand the virtue of justice, we have much to learn from the virtue ethics tradition. Yet to learn most from it about justice, we need to invert the tradition in one particular way. For other virtues, it may suffice to focus first on my own behaviour and character, and then to ask what kinds of friendship and other relations I need in living a life of virtue. The inference is from self to others. For the virtue of justice, the inference needs to be reversed: it is easier to judge first who is worthy of my support, and why, and then aspire to be that way myself.

So far, my dialogue with the tradition has led me to the following conclusions.

Comparative and categorical. Judgments about the justice or injustice of potential allies are largely comparative: we want to know who would be the better ally. On the other hand, we may also make some categorical judgments, excluding those who seem to be moving in the wrong directions altogether.

Multidimensional. Virtue is recognized within all traditions as being multidimensional: a virtuous person is not merely honest, or courageous, or benevolent, but finds ways to combine and harmonize each with the others, even in challenging circumstances. So too in seeking just allies, who we may expect (for example) not only to reduce social inequalities but also to promote democratic decision-making and to resist and root out corruption. This multidimensionality can give rise to dilemmas.

Comparative achievement. Potential allies may also be judged by how high they aim or how much they achieve in each dimension. If we expect our allies to promote democracy in our society, we might prefer a group that 'deepens' democracy over those that are content as long as elections are held.

Process and motivation. Virtue ethics traditions are concerned not only with what people do but also with how they do it and how well motivated they are. So too for just allies, who we may prefer to bring greater democracy not only into our social and political life but also into their own decision-making. Consistent with the tradition, justice seekers prefer allies who are better motivated, which for collective social actors means that appropriate motivations are not only present in individual members but cultivated within organizational culture.

Reason. Traditionally virtue is thought to involve doing the right thing, in the right ways, for the right reasons, all of which require practical reasoning on the part of a virtuous person. I have argued that the virtue of justice is distinct in that it also requires conformity to *public reason.* With the aid of the capability approach, public reason should be up to the task of forging shared understanding of dimensions of change that define greater justice.

NOTES

1. I say 'imagine' because I am about to give an over-simplified description of the political choices in Thailand in the past ten years. While I do not claim that my description is correct in every detail, I will give references to show that I am at least coming close to describing a real set of political choices.

2. 'AK' marks references to the standard edition of Kant's work, commonly referred to as the *Akademie* edition: *Kants gesammelte Shriften* (Berlin, Königlich Preußische Akademie der Wissenschaften, 1902–.)

REFERENCES

Amnesty International USA. 2015. "Thailand Human Rights." Accessed July 23, 2015. http://www.amnestyusa.org/our-work/countries/asia-and-the-pacific/thailand.

Annas, Julia. 2005. "Virtue Ethics." In *The Oxford Handbook of Ethical Theory*, edited by David Copp, 515–34. Oxford: Oxford University Press.

Annas, Julia. 2011. *Intelligent Virtue*. Oxford: Oxford University Press.

Aristotle. 1941. *Ethica Nicomachea*. In *Basic Works of Aristotle,* edited by Richard McKeon, translated by W.D. Ross, 927–1112. New York: Random House.

Chambers, Paul. 2013. "Military 'Shadows' in Thailand since the 2006 Coup." *Asian Affairs: An American Review* 40: 67–82.

Connors, Michael. 2008. "Thailand—Four Elections and a Coup." *Australian Journal of International Affairs* 62/4: 478–496.

Haidt, Jonathan, and Jesse Graham. 2007. "When Morality Opposes Justice: Conservatives Have Moral Intuitions That Liberals May Not Recognize." *Social Justice Research* 20/1: 98–116.

Haller, Elaine. 2014. "In the Name of the People? Political Protests in Thailand and the Underlying Conflict." *Heinrich Böll Stiftung,* January 29. Accessed July 19, 2015. https://www.boell.de/en/2014/01/29/name-people-political-protests-thailand-and-underlying-conflict.

Head, Jonathan. 2008. "Rifts Behind Thailand's Political Crisis," BBC News, August 27. Accessed July 22, 2015. http://news.bbc.co.uk/2/hi/asia-pacific/7584369.stm.

Hewison, Kevin. 2010. "Thaksin Shinawatra and the Reshaping of Thai Politics." *Contemporary Politics* 16/2: 119–33.

Hill, Thomas. 1971. "Kant on Imperfect Duty and Supererogation," *Kant-Studien* 62/1 (1971), 55–76.

Hursthouse, Rosalind. 2013. "Virtue Ethics." In *The Stanford Encyclopedia of Philosophy* (Fall Edition), edited by Edward N. Zalta. Palo Alto, CA: Center for the Study of Language and Information, Stanford University. Accessed July 14, 2015. http://plato.stanford.edu/archives/fall2013/entries/ethics-virtue/.

Kant, Immanuel. 1797/1966. *Metaphysics of Morals.* Translated by Mary Gregor. Cambridge: Cambridge University Press.

Koggel, Christine M. 2002. "Equality Analysis in a Global Context: A Relational Approach." *Canadian Journal of Philosophy* 32/sup1: 246–72.

Koggel, Christine M. 2012. "A Relational Approach to Equality: New Developments and Applications." In *Being Relational: Reflections on Relational Theory and Health Law and Policy,* edited by Jocelyn Downie and Jennifer Llewellyn, 63–88. Vancouver: University of British Columbia Press.

McCargo, Duncan. 2005. "Network Monarchy and Legitimacy Crises in Thailand." *Pacific Review* 18/4: 499–519.

McCargo, Duncan. 2015. "Thailand in 2014—The Trouble with Magic Swords." In *Southeast Asian Affairs 2015,* edited by Daljit Singh, 337–58. Singapore: Institute of Southeast Asia Studies.

Nussbaum, Martha. 1996. "Compassion: The Basic Social Emotion." *Social Philosophy and Policy* 13: 27–58.

Nussbaum, Martha. 2007. *Frontiers of Justice: Disability, Nationality, Species Membership.* Cambridge, MA: Harvard University Press,

Nussbaum, Martha. 2013. *Political Emotions; Why Love Matters for Justice.* Cambridge, MA: Harvard University Press,

Pottier, Eugène. 1871. *The Internationale.* Translated by Charles H. Kerr. Accessed December 1, 2015. http://www.musicanet.org/robokopp/usa/ariseyou.htm.

Sen, Amartya. 1993. "Capability and Well-Being." In *The Quality of Life,* edited by Martha Nussbaum and Amartya Sen, 30–53. Oxford: Clarendon Press.

Sen, Amartya. 1999. *Development as Freedom.* New York: Random House.

Sen, Amartya. 2000. "Why Human Security?" Paper presented at the International Symposium on Human Security, Tokyo, July 28.

Sen, Amartya. 2003. "Development, Rights, and Human Security." In Commission on Human Security, *Human Security Now,* 8–9. New York: Commission on Human Security.

Sen, Amartya. 2009. *The Idea of Justice.* Cambridge, MA: Harvard University Press.

Slote, Michael. 2007. *The Ethics of Care and Empathy.* London and New York: Routledge.

Thabchumpon, Naruemon, and Duncan McCargo. 2011. "Urbanized Villagers in the 2010 Thai Redshirt Protests: Not Just Poor Farmers?" *Asian Survey* 51/6: 993–1018.

Winichakul, Thongchai. 2014. "The Last Gasp of Royalist Democracy." *Cultural Anthropology,* September 23. Accessed July 14, 2015. http://www.culanth.org/fieldsights/570-the-last-gasp-of-royalist-democracy.

World Bank. 2005. "Thailand Economic Monitor." November 2005. Accessed 2015 July 15. http://siteresources.worldbank.org/INTTHAILAND/Resources/Economic-Monitor/2005nov-econ-full-report.pdf.

Chapter Seven

Justice as Stakeholding

Thom Brooks

Stakeholding is a principle of justice that claims those who have a stake in public affairs should have a say in decision-making. By having a stake, a stakeholder has an interest in how decisions may affect the stakes that individuals possess. To deny stakeholders a say in such matters is to overlook the interests they possess in having a stake—and so deny the equal concern and respect they are due.

This principle of stakeholding is absent in most, if not all, theories about justice. I argue for the importance of stakeholding for justice by showing how this principle can make our current theories more compelling. Justice should recognize stakeholding as an important part of any satisfactory theory. Stakeholding not only takes individuals seriously, but it can help to provide a more convincing account of the injustices other theories aim to avoid and the role citizens should play in decision-making about public affairs. Incorporating stakeholding in our account of justice is a means to its improvement.

I will begin this chapter with a brief examination of the theoretical origins of stakeholding and how they might be developed into a more powerful principle of justice. While much of the literature about stakeholding focuses on business ethics and corporate governance, I argue that the origins of this principle extend much further back and more widely: stakeholder justice is about not only economic transformation, but social and political renewal. This principle is applied to several approaches to illustrate how it might improve existing theories, such as political liberalism and the capabilities approach. These approaches are not exhaustive of the applicability of stakeholding to theories of justice, but rather examples about how its application can support and improve a diverse range of views. Stakeholding is not presented an alternative to existing theories, but instead an important principle that any compelling theory about justice should incorporate.

CONTEMPORARY ROOTS?

The idea of stakeholding is strongly associated with the literature on business ethics and corporate governance (Freeman et al. 2010).This research originated with R. Edward Freeman's *Strategic Management: A Stakeholder Approach* published in 1984 and has been popularized further by Will Hutton's defence of the 'stakeholder economy' (Freeman 1984; Hutton 1995). Stakeholding in this context is about guaranteeing corporate accountability and transparency. A business is not a mere machine for profit creation seeking as much wealth as it might acquire. If corporate members are understood to be *stakeholders*, then each has a stake in outcomes: they are partners engaged in a shared project actively promoting some shared conception of the good. These members can range from the factory floor to shareholders and from management to customers. The stakeholder economy offers a model not only for improved business management (Freeman et al. 2007), but also for how a centre-left view of economic justice might be forged (White 2011). Economics is not about profits alone: all citizens have a stake in the nation's economic health, and this has consequences for how relevant policies are determined (Hutton 2010).

The idea of the stakeholder economy might be considered to be a failed approach. Its decline started almost immediately after Tony Blair endorsed stakeholding in an important speech in early January 1996. Alastair Campbell describes this even as one of the most significant by Blair signalling an idea that would 'make a real impact' (Gould 2011, 249). Philip Gould claims stakeholding gave New Labour its 'defining idea' for building 'a fair and strong society' where 'New Labour had moved decisively towards becoming a coherent political project' (Gould 2011, 250). Andrew Gamble and Gavin Kelly found 'the stakeholder economy' to be Labour's 'big idea . . . whose time has come' (Gamble and Kelly 1996, 23–32). Some commentators began to question whether stakeholding moved 'no further than the starting block' with many questioning its continued relevance in less than a decade (see Prabhakar 2004).

An explanation for this decline is that the idea of a stakeholder economy has been thought to suffer from significant problems at its heart (Prabhakar 2004). The first concerns identifying stakeholders: who are they? (Kaler 2002). It is not obvious that corporate partners of any single firm form an exclusive stakeholder group. This is because these partners are not alone in having a stake in a firm's future performance. This problem of identifying stakeholders is then also a problem about numbers: how many stakeholders are there? Defenders of stakeholding, such as Will Hutton, have claimed we're all stakeholders: 'companies should be run and managed balancing the interests of shareholders, customers, employees and wider society, rather than prioritising shareholders' (Hutton 2010, 151). The persons possessing a stake in future firm success include us all: this is the claim of the stakeholder economy. For Hutton, stakeholding is fundamentally about inclusion where this is 'not a one-way street' that demands reciprocal obligations (Fassin 2012; Hutton 1999, 74).

Yet, this approach remains too crude, leaving several unanswered questions. For example, if we are all stakeholders, then what is the power distribution? Corporate partners may share a common interest in successful future performance of their firm, but this shared interest might not apply to each relevant context. The manager and the secretary share a common stake in general, but their stakes differ with respect to their contrasting organizational roles. Restructuring the firm and perhaps many economic decisions around the principle of stakeholding may improve accountability and transparency by securing more levels of deliberative decision-making. But this reveals a complexity about stakeholding and the different spheres of stakes we might each possess largely absent in theories about stakeholding.

This raises a more fundamental issue. If stakeholding has relevance for economic justice as an important principle of justice, then it is unclear why stakeholding should be confined to 'the stakeholder economy' rather than inform an idea of 'the stakeholder society'. This has not been unnoticed: for example, Hutton argues that 'social citizenship and economic membership are interdependent. . . . An active participatory democracy goes hand in hand with underpinning social cohesion and promoting stakeholder firms' (Hutton 1999, 80). However, a stakeholder view of the economy may connect with institutions beyond the firm and its customers, such as government, the media, and special interest groups. Nevertheless, the firm remains at the heart of modern stakeholder theory: the firm and its related communities are 'primary stakeholders' while government and other groups remain 'secondary stakeholders' (see Fassin 2009; Freeman et al. 2007). Perhaps stakeholding is a useful concept for improving ethical corporate governance and business management with benefits to the economy and other socio-political domains.

If stakeholding is to offer us a more convincing principle of justice, then it must offer a clearer account of why theories about justice should incorporate stakeholding. This account has been largely absent from the debate. It is perhaps surprising to discover that stakeholding has an older pedigree than acknowledged with roots in the philosophy of Hegel and British Idealism. These roots reveal a more substantive claim about justice that help establish stakeholding as more than a view about corporate governance, but a compelling principle of social and political justice.

STAKEHOLDING ORIGINS

G. W. F. Hegel argues that the formation of a 'rabble' (*Pöbel*) presents a major problem for sustaining future political stability:

> When a large mass of people sinks below the level of a certain standard of living . . . that feeling of right, integrity [*Rechlichkeit*], and honour which comes from supporting oneself by one's own activity and work is lost. This leads to the creation of a *rabble*, which in turn makes it much easier for disproportionate wealth to be concentrated in a few hands. (Hegel 1991, section 244)

Hegel's remarks have attracted much controversy about his understanding of this problem and its possible solution. Some, such as Shlomo Avineri, claim Hegel views poverty as an unfortunate but integral part of a well-functioning market economy: poverty exists not because it is desirable, but because capitalism renders it inevitable (Avineri 1972). Raymond Plant argues that this problem of poverty for Hegel represents the ever-present threat from poverty to the potential achievements a thriving market economy might offer (Plant 1983). Plant claims the solution to the problem of poverty is to find more compelling opportunities to secure employment for the jobless (Plant 1983). Hegel's problem of poverty is essentially an economic problem that requires an economic solution.

For Hegel, the rabble includes more than individuals suffering from economic poverty, but those enjoying tremendous financial privileges, too. The poverty that defines a rabble is not economic, but relates to individual beliefs about self and other. Hegel says: 'Poverty in itself does not reduce people to a rabble; a rabble is created only by the disposition associated with poverty, by inward rebellion against the rich, against society, the government, etc.' (Hegel 1991, section 244). The rabble, for Hegel, is a mentality most likely to be found in persons at the extremes of wealth and poverty. 'The poor turn into a rabble', says Allen Wood, not through want alone, but through a certain corrupted attitude of mind that want tends inevitably to bring with it' (Wood 1993, 425). The rabble often suffers from both a lack of sustenance as well as damaged self-respect and constraints on the exercise of individual rights. Hegel's discussion of the rabble is instructive. He is not an economic determinist: an individual's becoming part of a rabble is not determined by his or her relative poverty or affluence. Instead, Hegel claims that relative poverty or affluence is often associated with a rabble mentality.

The problem of the rabble can be understood as a failure of stakeholding. The rabble fails to believe it has a stake in society. As a 'disposition', efforts to tackle a rabble mentality should aspire to win over hearts and minds (Hegel 1991, section 244). Changing economic circumstances may play an important role, but they might also be insufficient: individuals require a change of heart and not necessarily different economic conditions to acquire the belief that he or she is a stakeholder and has a stake in society. The rabble rebels against governments and society because of its belief that it is disconnected: the spheres of politics and laws are erected and maintained by others for others. If I fail to see myself having a stake in society, then I will perceive my alienation from that society. The failure to satisfy my basic needs can contribute to this self-belief of legal and political alienation without guaranteeing it. So the fact some and not all individuals suffering from financial hardship might be more likely to engage in crime can be explained more by social psychology than economic circumstances alone (Brooks 2012a). The acquisition of beliefs about stakeholding must be secured by means beyond the purely economic.

This idea of stakeholding as a disposition about justice is supported further in the work of several nineteenth-century British Idealists writing at a time of profound social and political change in Victorian Britain (see Mander 2011). For example, T. H. Green (1941, 18) describes freedom as 'the state in which [an individual] shall have realised his ideal of himself, shall be at one with the law which he recognises as that which he ought to obey'. The free person is an individual reconciled to her political state because she understands herself as a stakeholder with a stake in a society that she endorses out of choice and not coercion. Freedom, for Green, is a kind of 'consciousness' that becomes threatened where an individual fails to be reconciled and so possesses a 'consciousness of oneself as for ever thwarted' (Green 1941, 18). If we understood ourselves as stakeholders with a stake in political society, then the law is transformed from a coercive institution imposed by others onto us toward a deliberative institution responsive to our engagement. We may perceive ourselves as co-authors of laws we endorse as our creation (Green 1941, 22).

For Green, the understanding of our self in relation to others impacts on our sense of self. He speaks of 'the individual's conception of the society on the well-being of which his own depends, and of the constituents of that well-being', which are linked with 'the laws, institutions, and social expectation' in addition to 'conventional morality' (Green 1941, 32). An individual's belief about his relation to others informs, but does not determine, his self-understanding about personal well-being (Green 1969, 51). Green argues (1941, 33) this interplay between self and other provides an important space for the exercise of our capacities for deliberative reasoning and the pursuit of individual conceptions about 'self-perfection, by acting as a member of a social organisation in which each contributes to the better-being of all the rest'. Individual well-being is a product created through the lens of individual beliefs about the mutual relations between self and others in terms of stakeholding (Green 1941, 124; see also Green 1969, 212).

Green shares Hegel's concern about the problem of the rabble. These 'dangerous classes', says Green (1941, 129), are individuals with 'no reverence for the state . . . no sense of an interest shared with others in maintaining it'. The issue is not that the state must be revered wherever it is found: the failure of citizens to respect the authority of their state might be justified and, if so, 'it is a sign that the state is not a true state' (Green 1941, 138). Instead, the issue is where the state does enjoy sufficient normative justification, but individuals fail to recognise their political obligations. Green acknowledges that coercion alone is unlikely to bring about a change in the rabble: individuals cannot be forced to believe they are stakeholders sharing common bonds with others (Green 1941, 109). We must effect a change of heart to best secure the support by citizens for their state because our understanding of authority is rooted in our individual convictions: 'there is no right "but thinking makes it so"' (Green 1941, 140–41; 1969, 213).

Thus, Green (1941, 140–41) famously claims that 'will, not force, is the basis of the state'. On this view, the authority of law, in part, arises from our being a party to its creation (Green 1941, 110, 122). For Green (1941, 130), each individual 'must have a share . . . in making and maintaining the laws which he obeys'. Individuals are stakeholders where each has a say over public matters where each has a stake, such as their being a party to political decision-making. This is one crucial element of justice and stakeholding. No less crucial is a second element: that individuals possess a self-understanding about themselves as stakeholders.

Green (1941, 126) recognizes the limits of justice as stakeholding. It is essential that individuals can plan and revise conceptions of the good relevant to their being a stakeholder. A second important element is they must also be able to be a party to public decision-making on matters where they have stake. Individuals unable to engage with others in public deliberation or lacking relevant capacities for stakeholding may be unable to conceive of themselves as stakeholders. These limits raise complex issues for stakeholding and other theories of justice more generally and demand greater attention elsewhere.

My discussion highlights that the idea of stakeholding pre-dates the contemporary literature on business ethics and corporate governance. Both use stakeholding to defend ideas about greater transparency, improved accountability, and social justice. But while business ethics has focused narrowly on economic justice, earlier discussions by Hegel and the British Idealists about stakeholding are more concerned with justice in a broader sense to include the economy and other social institutions. The latter provides us with a powerful principle of justice: those who have a stake in public affairs should have a say about them. Not only should individuals have a stake, it is important for each to share the conviction he or she is a stakeholder with a stake in the society. Hegel and the British Idealists offer us insights into stakeholding that can be developed beyond the current literature.

This view clarifies why stakeholding is more than mutual recognition. The latter is often highlighted as occupying a pivotal place in the philosophies of Hegel, British Idealists, and others influenced by their work. Mutual recognition is a kind of procedure whereby individuals relate to others as equals. Individuals forge a shared conception of justice through deliberative engagement with fellow citizens. Mutual recognition requires opportunities for individuals to have a voice in public decision-making, and this satisfies one part of stakeholding. However, mutual recognition does not require individuals to possess a self-understanding of themselves as having a stake in public affairs which helps justify and motivate public engagement. Mutual recognition brings individuals into cooperative association, but stakeholding helps further define and shape the contours through which individuals relate to others.

But how promising is stakeholding as a principle about justice? My discussion turns to three case studies: political liberalism, the capabilities approach, and republicanism. I will argue that stakeholding can and should play a central role in these diverse theories about justice. The importance of justice as stakeholding is that it can and should feature in any compelling view of justice. Its relevance for improving our ideas about political liberalism and the capabilities approach help make this case.

POLITICAL LIBERALISM AND STAKEHOLDING

John Rawls develops political liberalism in response to a 'serious problem' found in his *A Theory of Justice: The Problem of Political Stability* (Rawls 1996, xviii). He claims that *Theory* fails to account for the reality that citizens are deeply divided by reasonable and incompatible religious, philosophical and moral comprehensive doctrines (Rawls 1996, 13, 168; 2001a, 193). This fact of reasonable pluralism poses a threat to political stability over time and requires a solution. Political liberalism is a response to the problem of political stability that confronts free and equal citizens by indicating how a shared political conception can be endorsed by each citizen (Rawls 1996, 134–40).

This shared conception is an overlapping consensus created through the use of public reasons. The equality of citizens requires any shared conception to not prioritize one reasonable comprehensive doctrine over others: any departure would fail to respect reasonable pluralism (Rawls 2001a, 9). Public reasons are understood as reasons that are 'public' in the sense that they can be endorsed by citizens irrespective of the comprehensive doctrines each favours. (Rawls 2001a, 92; 1996, 213, 220–22). These reasons are contrasted with non-private reasons which have potential relevance for some, but not all citizens. Public reasons, as claims potentially acceptable to each citizen, provide the means to create an overlapping consensus without failing to respect reasonable pluralism. This is because the consensus is a 'freestanding' political conception about justice compatible with any reasonable comprehensive doctrine without entailing a special commitment to any particular doctrine (Rawls 2001a, 33, 37; 1996, xlvii–xvliii, 10, 13, 99, 144–45). Political liberalism secures stability for the right reasons. Rawls argues:

> Our exercise of political power is fully proper only when it is exercised in accordance with a constitution the essentials of which all citizens as free and equal may reasonably be expected to endorse in the light of principles and ideals acceptable to their common human reasons. . . . Only a political conception of justice that all citizens might be reasonably expected to endorse can serve as a basis of public reason and justification. (Rawls 1996, 137)

For Rawls, political stability is a problem of political justice that has a political solution free and equal citizens forge in deliberation with each other and without coercion (see Brooks 2014).

Rawls's argument that an overlapping consensus best solves the problem of political stability has received much criticism. Addressing these criticisms helps illuminate how stakeholding can improve political liberalism. For example, one criticism is that an overlapping consensus is unnecessary because Rawls is believed to possess existing resources in his account that might secure political stability without major revisions to his original views presented in *Theory* (see Barry 1995; McClennen 1989; Baier 1989). Brian Barry notes that Rawls accepts that political stability requires the inclusion of his two principles of justice (Barry 1995, 875). Citizens are free to form, revise, and pursue their own conceptions of the good without a need for some shared position on a comprehensive good (Barry 1995, 878–79). Barry argues this is evidence that Rawls already defends a theory of justice prior to political liberalism where the state is forbidden from prioritizing any one view of the good over others and political justice is bound within the constraints of principles of justice (Barry 1995, 880). Rawls's theory of justice 'does not require an "overlapping consensus"'(Barry 1995, 901, 904).

A second criticism of Rawls accepts that political stability is a problem for his account, but they argue his solution of an overlapping consensus is too fragile to secure stability (Greenawalt 1995; Sandel 1994; Wenar 1995). For example, Leif Wenar claims any resulting agreement may not achieve more than a 'limited consensus' that leaves political stability vulnerable (Wenar 1995, 39). Similarly, Kent Greenawalt argues: 'The difficulty with asking people to rely on public reasons is that, if they do so, they may have to forgo what they believe are really the best reasons for resolving particular problems' (Greenawalt 1995, 1305). This is a problem because the state ought not be neutral on many public policies such as the necessity of abolishing slavery (Sandel 1994, 1785–87). If the state should defend redistributive policies despite reasonable disagreement from libertarians as warranted by the difference principle, then why should the state not take a similar non-neutral stance on other issues, such as permitting gay marriage (Sandel 1994, 1788)? Rawls's approach limits public debate too much in restricting deliberation to public reasons in order to construct an overlapping consensus (Sandel 1994, 1792). The problem remains that our consensus will be too fragile to secure political stability.

These criticisms fail to recognize the potential importance of stakeholding for Rawls's political liberalism. Both focus on whether or not an overlapping consensus is necessary or sufficient to secure political stability, but without recognizing there is much more to political stability than an overlapping consensus. One important element is the idea of 'reciprocity' which helps forge social bonds among citizens (Rawls 2001a, 1391). For Rawls, reciprocity is 'fundamental to both justice and fairness' (Rawls 2001a, 209). Wenar says:

> The use of political power must fulfil a *criterion of reciprocity*: citizens must reasonably believe that all citizens can reasonably accept the enforcement of a particular set of basic laws. Those coerced by law must be able to endorse the society's fundamental political arrangements freely, not because they are dominated or manipulated or kept uninformed. (Wenar 2008)

This idea of reciprocity is perhaps best understood as a form of mutual recognition (Brooks 2012). Citizens do not merely recognize others as having an equal voice, but, more importantly, as having a voice that ought to be heard and consider in reciprocal engagement. So reciprocity plays a fundamental role in Rawls's views about justice and it is a normatively substantive social bond that citizens share. Rawls acknowledges that mutual respect between citizens may be threatened—and, thus, threaten political stability—where they fail to view each other as political equals (Rawls 1996, 30).

Reciprocity may assist in promoting political stability through its creation of a shared identity (for a critique, see Parekh 2008). Citizens are more than equals: they possess a common source of identity and shared political life (Brooks 2012b, 27). Rawls favours property-owning democracy over laissez-faire capitalism because the latter is more likely to see excess inequality between rich and poor (Rawls 2001, 137; 1999, 62). These circumstances may produce envy and wound self-respect: where mutual recognition may bring us together, alienation pulls us further apart (Maffetone 2010, 42). Equality is good for us, but partly because it best enables mutual recognition and a shared identity (Wilkinson and Pickett 2009).

The social bond arising from reciprocity and mutual respect generates its own support over time (Rawls 2001a, 194; 1996, 140). Rawls says: 'In a democratic regime, stable social cooperation rests on the fact that most citizens accept the political order as legitimate, or at any rate not seriously illegitimate, and hence willingly abide by it' (Rawls 2001a, 125). The more citizens gain confidence in their mutual connections, the more these social bonds are cemented. Rawls says that 'not only are our everyday ideas of justice influenced by our own situation, they are also strongly coloured by custom and current expectations' (Rawls 2001a, 119, 155–56; 1999). So the shared mutual recognition of citizens engaged in deliberative cooperation is likely to cement the bonds of reciprocity and social connection over time.

Furthermore, Rawls argues that every citizen should be guaranteed a 'social minimum' of primary goods, including the bases of self-respect 'essential for a decent human life' (Rawls 2001a, 129; 1999, 243, 267; 1996, 181, 228–29; see also Michelman 2012). This social minimum is important because it enables each citizen to feel they are a part of political society where every individual understands herself as having a stake in her political society. Stakeholding occupies a previously unrecognized central role for Rawls's political liberalism and this idea helps elucidate a core feature of his views about justice. A polity respecting citizens as free and equal must permit opportunities for citizens to create and maintain a shared conception of political justice. Each citizen has a stake in the state and each must have opportunities to exercise their voice in public deliberation. But it is not enough for there to be mere opportunities. Citizens must possess a conviction about themselves as stakeholders: political stability requires citizens to be stakeholders and believe this to be so. If citizens fail to see themselves as stakeholders, then this threatens the social bases of self-respect as they would view society as an alien enterprise irresponsive to their membership and, in turn, undermine political stability.

So perhaps critics of Rawls's overlapping consensus are correct to argue there are existing resources in *A Theory of Justice* to develop social bonds securing political stability despite individual differences about conceptions of the good (Brooks 2015). Nonetheless, these critics have failed to capture the importance of stakeholding and its central role in Rawls's theory. Stakeholding is embedded in his theory of justice and helps clarify the social bases of respect each citizen should be guaranteed: citizens must not only enjoy reciprocity through cooperative engagement, but they have must share a belief of themselves as stakeholders who have a stake in public decision-making and so can and should have a say about them. The acceptance of stakeholding in this theory of justice does not require its rejection, but rather helps promote its development.

CAPABILITIES AND STAKEHOLDING

The capabilities approach is a second view about justice that can benefit from the incorporation of stakeholding.[1] The capabilities approach focuses on the capability of an individual to do or be (Brooks 2013a). This approach aims to provide a more compelling understanding about human freedom and well-being. An individual's freedom to choose is central to this account. Capabilities are the available options we may freely choose to do or be and not our actual functionings alone. The difference between a person fasting and another starving is captured by this distinction: the person fasting has the capability to enjoy nourishment while choosing against doing so, but the starving person lacks this choice. Both may share similar actual functionings, but the capabilities approach directs us to focus on their opportunities to exercise certain freedoms. The claim is we can develop a more compelling view about well-being by this focus on the capabilities available to individuals.

It has been argued that capabilities are compatible with Rawls's theory of justice. Amartya Sen claims that Rawls's primary goods are better understood as capabilities (Sen 1985). Sen argues Rawls should revise his account of primary goods to remove a problematic ambiguity at its heart and clarify its role in securing individual freedom and well-being. Sen says:

> Some primary goods (such as 'income and wealth') are no more than means to real ends. . . . Other primary goods (such as 'the social basis of self-respect' to which Rawls makes explicit reference) can include aspects of the social climate, even though they are generalized *means* (in the case of 'the social basis of self-respect' means to achieving self-respect). Still others (such as 'liberties') can be interpreted in different ways: either as means (liberties permit us to do things that we may value doing) or as the actual freedom to achieve certain results. (Sen 1999)

Rawls understands primary goods instrumentally as a *means* of satisfactory human living, but not its *end* (Sen 2009, 234). This position, for Sen, fails to capture the important distinction between '*doing* something' and 'being *free* to do that thing' (Sen 2009, 234, 237; 1985, 198–99). This problem can be overcome by revising Rawls's account so that primary goods are understood as capabilities (Sen 1995,.81–84, 86–87, 110; 2009, 64). Sen claims this revision is 'not a foundational departure from Rawls's own programme, but mainly an adjustment' (Sen 2009, 66). This revision would clarify the role and importance of Rawls's views about primary goods with the added benefit of recognizing institutions are not always required to deliver justice in some cases: institutions can secure capabilities for individuals by protecting opportunities for choice and this can be achieved through various means (Sen 2009, 90). Sen says: 'Democracy has to be judged not just by the institutions that formally exist but by the extent to which different voices from diverse sections of the people can actually be heard' (Sen 2009, 238). Revising primary goods in terms of capabilities can help achieve this goal.

Rawls recognizes that his account of primary goods and Sen's account of capabilities share significant overlap. In *Political Liberalism*, Rawls says 'I hope that now our views are in accord on the topics that concern us here, though his view has broader aims than mine' (Rawls 1996, 179). He adds: 'I agree with Sen that basic capabilities are of first importance and that the use of primary goods is always to be assessed in the light of assumptions about those capabilities' (Rawls 2001a, 169–70). However, Rawls rejects Sen's proposed revision because Rawls understood capabilities as a comprehensive doctrine.[2] Political liberalism, for Rawls, 'presupposes no particular comprehensive view, and hence may be supported by an enduring overlapping consensus of reasonable doctrines' (Rawls 2001a, 37). Rawls says: 'Justice as fairness rejects the idea of comparing and maximizing overall well-being in matters of political justice': primary goods should not be understood in terms of 'anyone's idea of the basic values of human life . . . however essential their possession' (Rawls 1996, 188). Political liberalism best respects the fact of reasonable pluralism by endorsing a political conception 'that is mutually acceptable to citizens generally' (Rawls 1996, 188). The problem is that the capabilities approach is too normatively thick and, if it replaced primary goods, political stability could be undermined because capabilities may be incompatible with any reasonable comprehensive doctrine.

This view is rejected by Martha Nussbaum. She agrees with Sen that capabilities and primary goods share significant overlap, but capabilities provide greater clarity (Nussbaum 2011, 40). For example, the capabilities approach is more explicit about its relation to human rights and rights more generally (Nussbaum 2011, 62; 2006, 78; 1997; Sen 2004). Both capabilities and primary goods address our freedom of movement and occupational choice, but capabilities provide greater specification about their importance for human flourishing and related goods, such as affiliation, recreation and some measure of control over our political and material environments.

Nussbaum argues that capabilities can form the object of an overlapping consensus and should be so understood as an *addition* to political liberalism. She says:

> That is why the political principles of the capabilities approach are supported by independent arguments about human dignity. We do not try to generate principles out of compassion alone, but, instead, we seek to support them and render them stable through the development of a compassion that is attuned to the political principles for which we have argued. (Nussbaum 2006, 91)

The capabilities approach is a view developed over time through deliberative reflection about our lived experiences relating to human flourishing.

Capabilities are not determined in advance and subject to future revision (Nussbaum 2011, 15). They are more readily compatible to an evolving overlapping consensus that can secure the support of all without failing to change as we change. Capabilities can be understood as part of an overlapping consensus (Freeman 2006; Nussbaum 2006, 79, 304–5; 2011, 89–92). This is because the capabilities approach is a partial conception of justice that is compatible with any reasonable comprehensive doctrine: the capabilities approach and political liberalism can be brought together in a revised theory of justice. Rawls is mistaken to believe capabilities offer a fully comprehensive doctrine—a view now accepted by even leading critics of the capabilities approach (Pogge 2010, 19–20). If capabilities are only a partial conception of justice, then they need not clash with fully comprehensive doctrines and so might be the object of an overlapping consensus. So the capabilities approach offers not only a theory about freedom and well-being, but also a potentially powerful revision of political liberalism that may render it more compelling (Brooks and Nussbaum 2014).

Stakeholding can occupy a central role in the capabilities approach that helps to further clarify capabilities without problematizing its incorporation in Rawls's political liberalism. I argued that stakeholding plays a central in political liberalism in the previous section: stakeholding and political liberalism are not incompatible. I have already noted in this section the agreement by Rawls, Sen, and Nussbaum about the significant overlap between capabilities and primary goods, including the social basis of self-respect that stakeholding can help secure.[3] It has not yet been clarified how stakeholding may benefit a theory about the capabilities approach in terms of capabilities apart from any relation to political liberalism.

Stakeholding can and should figure prominently in any compelling theory about the capabilities approach. Capabilities to do or be are about securing freedom and well-being: stakeholding plays a key role in further developing this approach. Sen criticises Rawls for failing to distinguish between '*doing* something' and 'being *free* to do that thing' (Sen 2009, 234, 237). It is more important that citizens are free to choose to do or be than that they achieve some level of actual functioning. Sen should have considered a third distinction of being free to do something as a *stakeholder*. This is because my having opportunities to exercise free choice is important, but so too is our having options we would want to choose. The freedom to do something is less crucial than the kinds of options available. Furthermore, available options should be responsive to our changing circumstances. So it is not enough that there be options: we should be free to exercise opportunities that are responsive to our concerns. Society does not provide adequate grounds for promoting its success unless it provides opportunities response to people's concerns.

Stakeholding helps clarify the kinds of opportunities that the capabilities approach should secure. The citizen as a stakeholder is an individual with a stake in public affairs and so can and should have a say in public decision-making. This is compatible with the idea that capabilities are responsive to changing circumstances over time. Capabilities aim to better illuminate the importance of freedom and well-being which stakeholding further develops. An individual cannot enjoy sufficient freedom if the available options are not responsive to his circumstances and fail to provide any opportunities for deliberative engagement. Nor can an individual secure satisfactory well-being if she fails to see herself as having a stake in deliberations about public issues of freedom and well-being as this could undermine the social basis for her self-respect.

Capabilities may be universal, but their fulfilment is open-textured and determined by shared conceptions of justice in a political society. Stakeholding is compatible with this fact about capabilities and generates further clarification. Capabilities should address the freedom and well-being of individuals by not only respecting diversity and equality, but through viewing each as a stakeholder. It is because each has a stake in the guarantee of capabilities ensuring levels of freedom and well-being that diversity and equality must be honoured. Citizens as stakeholders with a stake in how capabilities are conceived, implemented and revised should also have a say in the construction and future change because of their stake. Stakeholding helps explain the role citizens can and should play for the capabilities approach.

Stakeholding is compatible with Nussbaum's well-known list of capabilities and provides it with further clarification. Her ten capabilities are Life; Bodily Health; Bodily Integrity; Senses, Imagination, Thought; Emotions; Practical Reason; Affiliation; Other Species; Play; and Control over One's Environment (Nussbaum 2011, 33–34). Stakeholding promotes and further clarifies several capabilities in this list. The capability of 'emotions' includes the ability to be able to have attachment with others (Nussbaum 2011, 33). An individual's belief that he is a stakeholder is one way of forging and maintaining social bonds with others. The capability of 'practical reason' concerns the ability to form a conception of the good necessary for the exercise of stakeholding (Nussbaum 2011, 33). The capabilities of 'affiliation' and 'control over one's environment' include the possession of social basis of self-respect and non-discrimination as well as the ability 'to participate effectively in political choices that govern one's life' (Nussbaum 2011, 34). Stakeholding is a particular form of affiliation and political control where we relate to others not only as free and equal, but as fellow stakeholders who each have a stake in developing a shared conception of political justice. Stakeholders are not mere associates, but partners in a joint project where each has a stake and an interest to be taken into account. Stakeholding is compatible with Nussbaum's list of capabilities and it helps clarify further their importance and promotion. Stakeholding is also compatible with the capabilities approach more generally and helps illuminate why capabilities may offer a compelling view about justice. Securing capabilities requires a role for citizens as stakeholders.

CONCLUSIONS

This essay has covered much conceptual terrain. I argued first that stakeholder theory has become popular in contemporary debates in business ethics and corporate governance. This may help explain its relative neglect in debates about political justice. However, we can uncover the earlier roots of justice as stakeholding in the work of Hegel and British Idealists like T. H. Green writing in the nineteenth century. They defend different conceptions about a similar principle of justice: that justice includes stakeholding where those who have a stake in public affairs should have a say in their determination. Not only must individuals possess opportunities for exercising stakeholding, but it is crucial they acquire the conviction that they are stakeholders. This is central to ensuring public decision-making respects the free and equal status of citizens as individuals worthy of respect.

I next argued that this general principle of justice as stakeholding is compatible across several leading theories about justice and plays a central role in highlighting further development. Stakeholding clarifies the importance, for Rawls, of primary goods, such as the role of reciprocity in forging the constitutionally guaranteed social basis of self-respect to be enjoyed by each individual. Rawlsian citizens are best understood as stakeholders who exercise a say in public decision-making because they have a stake in outcomes. Stakeholding is consistent with the capabilities approach. Stakeholding best explains the role of individuals in creating and revising capabilities and helps elucidate the importance for several capabilities, such as affiliation and having control over one's environment. Stakeholding is demonstrated to play a potentially central role for each of these different theories about justice. Justice can and should include some account of stakeholding.

My discussion of political liberalism and the capabilities approach is not meant to be exhaustive. The aims are to show the relevance of stakeholding for contemporary theories of justice, to rescue stakeholder theory from its more narrow construction in business ethics and identify its roots in place within an earlier tradition of Hegelian philosophy without mandating that stakeholding carry its philosophical baggage (Brooks 2013b). We need not be Hegelians nor modern-day British Idealists to accept stakeholding as a fundamental principle of justice any theory can and should incorporate. Nonetheless, this essay makes the first case for taking stakeholding more seriously as an important principle of justice for any compelling theory about justice.

NOTES

I am grateful to audiences at a British Idealism conference held at Harris Manchester, Oxford; the Edinburgh University Philosophy Society; the Society of Legal Scholars annual conference; the political philosophy seminar at KUL and the annual meeting of the Political Studies Association—Political Thought conference where this essay was my keynote address for their comments on earlier drafts. Special thanks must go to David Boucher, Helder de Schutter, Maria Dimova-Cookson, Bill Mander, Avital Simhony, Will Sweet, Colin Tyler, Andrew Vincent, and, most especially, Krushil Watene.

1. There are important differences between various conceptions. These include a difference over whether this approach should be called a *capability* approach (e.g., Amartya Sen) or a *capabilities* approach (e.g., Martha Nussbaum) where the latter aims to draw attention to the diversity of capabilities we possess. I will speak of one 'capabilities' approach for simplicity of exposition while sensitive to this difference in characterization.

2. Rawls further argues that capabilities lack the clarity of primary goods: if the former replaced the latter, Rawls's concern is capabilities are 'not sufficiently determinate' and so more difficult to apply (see Rawls 1982, 1996, 1999). I have argued elsewhere this concern is based on a mistake, a view shared with Sen and Nussbaum. See Brooks 2014.

3. See previous section.

REFERENCES

Avineri, Shlomo. 1972. *Hegel's Theory of the Modern State*, Cambridge: Cambridge University Press.

Baier, Kurt. 1989. Justice and the Aims of Political Philosophy, *Ethics* 99: 771–90.

Barry, Brian. 1995. John Rawls and the Search for Stability, *Ethics* 105: 874–915.

Brooks, Thom. 2014. The Capabilities Approach and Political Liberalism, in Thom Brooks and Martha C. Nussbaum (eds.), *Rawls's Political Liberalism*, New York: Columbia University Press, 2014.

Brooks, Thom. 2013a. Capabilities, in Hugh LaFollette (ed.), *International Encyclopedia of Ethics*, Oxford: Blackwell.

Brooks, Thom. 2013b. *Hegel's Political Philosophy: A Systematic Reading of the Philosophy of Right,* 2nd ed, Edinburgh: Edinburgh University Press.

Brooks, Thom. 2012a. *Punishment*, London: Routledge.

Brooks, Thom. 2012b. Reciprocity as Mutual Recognition, *Good Society* 21: 21–35.

Brooks, Thom, and Martha C. Nussbaum (eds). 2014. *Rawls's Political Liberalism*, New York: Columbia University Press.

Fassin, Yves. 2012. Stakeholder Management, Reciprocity and Stakeholder Responsibility, *Journal of Business Ethics* 109 (2012): 83–96.

Fassin, Yves. 2009. The Stakeholder Model Refined, *Journal of Business Ethics* 84: 113–35.

Freeman, Edward R. 1984. *Strategic Management: A Stakeholder Approach,* Boston: Pitman.

Freeman, R Edward, Jeffrey S. Harrison, and Andrew C. Wicks. 2007. *Managing for Stakeholders: Survival, Reputation, and Success*, New Haven: Yale University Press.

Freeman, R Edward., Jeffrey S. Harrison, Andrew C. Wicks, Bidhan L. Parmar, and Simone de Colle. 2010. *Stakeholder Theory: The State of the Art*, Cambridge: Cambridge University Press.

Freeman, Samuel. 2006. Frontiers of Justice: The Capabilities Approach vs. Contractarianism, *Texas Law Review* 85: 390–91.

Gamble, Andrew, and Gavin Kelly. 1996. Stakeholder Capitalism and One Nation Socialism, *Renewal* 4: 23–32.

Gould, Philip. 2011. *The Unfinished Revolution: How New Labour Changed British Politics for Ever*, London: Abacus.
Green, T. H. 1969. *Prolegomena to Ethics*, ed. A. C. Bradley, New York: Thomas Y. Crowell.
Green, T. H. 1941. *Lectures on the Principles of Political Obligation*, London: Longmans.
Greenawalt, Kent, 1995. Some Problems with Public Reason in John Rawls's Political Liberalism, *Loyola of Los Angeles Law Review* 28: 1303–17.
Hegel, G. W. F, 1991. *Elements of the Philosophy of Right*, ed. Allen Wood, Cambridge: Cambridge University Press.
Hutton, Will. 1999. *The Stakeholder Society: Writings on Politics and Economics*, ed. David Goldblatt. Cambridge: Polity.
Hutton, Will. 2010. *Them and Us: Changing Britain—Why We Need a Fair Society*, London: Little, Brown.
Hutton, Will. 1995. *The State We're In*, London: Jonathan Cape.
Kaler, John. 2002. Morality and Strategy in Stakeholder Identification, *Journal of Business Ethics* 39: 91–99.
Maffetone, Sebastiano. 2010. *Rawls: An Introduction*, Cambridge: Polity.
Mander, W. J. 2011. *British Idealism: A History*, Oxford: Oxford University Press.
McClennen, Edward F. 1989. Justice and the Problem of Stability, *Philosophy and Public Affairs* 18: 3–30.
Michelman, Frank I. 2012. Poverty in Liberalism: A Comment on the Constitutional Essentials, *Drake Law Review* 60: 101–21.
Nussbaum, Martha C. 2011. *Creating Capabilities: The Human Development Approach*, Cambridge: Harvard University Press.
Nussbaum, Martha C. 2006. *Frontiers of Justice: Disability, Nationality, Species Membership*. Cambridge, MA: Harvard University Press.
Nussbaum, Martha C. 1997. Capabilities and Human Rights, *Fordham Law Review* 66: 273–300.
Parekh, Bikhu. 2008. *A New Politics of Identity: Political Principles for an Interdependent World*, Basingstoke: Palgrave Macmillan.
Plant, Raymond. 1983. *Hegel: An Introduction*, 2nd ed, Oxford: Blackwell.
Pogge, Thomas. 2010. A Critique of the Capability Approach, in Harry Brighouse and Ingrid Robeyns (eds.), *Measuring Justice: Primary Goods and Capabilities*, Cambridge: Cambridge University Press.
Prabhakar, Rajiv. 2004. Whatever Happened to Stakeholding?, *Public Administration* 82: 567–84.
Rawls, John. 2001a. *Justice as Fairness: A Restatement*, ed. Erin Kelly, Cambridge: Harvard University Press.
Rawls, John. 2001b. Justice as Reciprocity, in ed. Samuel Freeman, *Collected Papers*, Cambridge: Harvard University Press.
Rawls, John. 1999. *A Theory of Justice*, rev. ed., Oxford: Oxford University Press.
Rawls, John. 1996. *Political Liberalism*, New York: Columbia University Press.
Rawls, John. 1982. Social Unity and Primary Goods, in Amartya Sen and Bernard Williams (eds.), *Utilitarianism and Beyond*, Cambridge: Cambridge University Press.
Sen, Amartya. 2009. *The Idea of Justice*, London: Allen Lane.
Sen. Amartya. 2004. Elements of a Theory of Human Right, *Philosophy and Public Affairs* 32: 315–56.
Sen, Amartya. 1999. *Development as Freedom*, Oxford: Oxford University Press.
Sen, Amartya. 1995. *Inequality Reexamined*, Oxford: Oxford University Press.
Sen, Amartya, 1985. Well-Being, Agency and Freedom: The Dewey Lectures 1984, *Journal of Philosophy* LXXXII: 199–201.
Sandel, Michael. 1994. Political Liberalism, *Harvard Law Review* 107: 1765–94.
Wenar, Leif. 2008. John Rawls, in *Stanford Encyclopedia of Philosophy*, http://plato.stanford.edu/entries/rawls.
Wenar, Leif. 1995. Political Liberalism: An Internal Critique, *Ethics* 106: 32–62.

White, Stuart. 2011. New Labour and the Politics of Ownership, in Patrick Diamond and Michael Kenny (eds.), *Reassessing New Labour: Market, State and Society under Blair and Brown*, Oxford: Blackwell.

Wilkinson, Richard and Kate Pickett. 2009. *The Spirit Level: Why Equality Is Better for Everyone*: Harmondsworth: Penguin.

Wood, Allen W. 1993. Hegel and Marxism, in Frederick Beiser (ed.), *The Cambridge Companion to Hegel*, Cambridge: Cambridge University Press.

Chapter Eight

Indigenous Peoples and Justice

Krushil Watene

Indigenous peoples live in almost every region of the world—with an estimated 370,000,000 indigenous people belonging to around 5,000 indigenous groups worldwide (UNPFII Factsheet 1). The cultures and languages of indigenous peoples are responsible for much of the cultural diversity that continues to exist (UN 2009). Generally speaking, they are 'descendants . . . of those who inhabited a country or a geographical region at the time when people of different cultures or ethnic origins arrived' (UNPFII Factsheet 1, 1). The recent histories and contemporary realities of indigenous peoples are steeped in grave injustices, marginalisation, displacement, violence, kin-community breakdown, and the loss of culture and language (McCaslin 2005; Mikkelsen 2014; Wessendorf 2011). Today they aspire to have their existences, values, and rights to land and natural resources recognized.

International law has been an important vehicle in the ongoing struggle for indigenous peoples' rights and recognition. One of the earliest international appeals was attempted in 1923 when Chief Deskaheh (Haudenosaunee) travelled to Geneva in the hope of addressing the League of Nations on issues relating to the rights of Native Americans to live on lands according to their own values (Wessendorf and Garcia-Alix 2009). Around the same time, Māori religious leader Tahupōtiki Wiremu Rātana attempted to address the League of Nations on Māori claims of violations of the Treaty of Waitangi (Ballara 2012). Given this heritage, the declaration on the rights of indigenous peoples—outlining minimum standards 'for the survival, dignity, and well-being of the indigenous peoples of the world' (UNPFII 2007)—was a groundbreaking achievement.[1] The declaration, with its concern for self-determination, aims to enable indigenous peoples to 'freely determine their political status and freely pursue their economic, social, and cultural development' (UNPFII 2007).[2]

In this chapter I reconsider how indigenous peoples and self-determination ought to feature in contemporary liberal theories of justice (and political philosophy more generally). More specifically, I ask: How do the histories and contemporary realities of indigenous peoples bear on discussions of justice? How could indigenous people's values, histories, and contemporary realities transform our ideas about, and approaches to, justice? In the first part of this chapter I provide an overview of Will Kymlicka's multiculturalism as it applies to indigenous peoples, and James Anaya's approach to indigenous peoples self-determination in international law. I contend that both of these important contributions provide useful ways of accommodating and framing justice for indigenous peoples, but that they both fail to take indigenous self-determination to its full conclusion. In order to fully capture self-determination, engagement with indigenous perspectives about justice is required. There has been very little engagement with social justice concepts from the perspectives of non-Western philosophical traditions—not least from the perspectives of indigenous peoples. In the second part of this chapter, my aim is to begin to fill this gap, and to provide one foundation for further conversations. I explore one of the ways that indigenous peoples frame justice, and I explore some of the contributions of Māori (the indigenous peoples of Aotearoa/New Zealand) ideas to justice theorising.

CONTEMPORARY LIBERAL THEORY AND INDIGENOUS PEOPLES

In liberal theory, indigenous peoples are attached to the general question of whether (and in what ways) liberal concepts (sovereignty, rights, equality, autonomy, justice) can articulate and capture indigenous peoples' claims (Ivison et al. 2000). Two ways to include and make sense of indigenous claims within liberal theories of justice, can be found in the works of Will Kymlicka (in liberal multiculturalism) and James Anaya (in international law). I explore aspects of both of these approaches in order to understand how indigenous peoples feature within them, and to show how the inclusion of indigenous peoples's claims ought to be furthered.[3]

Liberal multiculturalists are concerned with the broad question of whether (and how) liberal theory should accommodate cultural diversity (Song 2014). Liberal multiculturalists ground their answers in the pervasive influence of culture on our lives—and the importance of culture for enabling freedom (Kymlicka 1995; Sen 2004; UNDP 2004). Will Kymlicka's well-known liberal multicultural framework exemplifies this starting point. According to Kymlicka, freedom is not possible in any meaningful sense unless people have access to a 'societal culture'. These cultures are the contexts from which meaningful choices are made possible, and to which individuals (more often than not) have a deep attachment or bond.

> For meaningful individual choice to be possible, individuals need not only access to information, the capacity to reflectively evaluate it, and freedom of expression and association. They also need access to a societal culture. Group differentiated measures that secure and promote this access may, therefore, have a legitimate role to play in a liberal theory of justice. (Kymlicka 1995, 84)

Societal cultures are the contexts of choice from which our conceptions of the good are formulated, and they are cultures in which our identities are deeply embedded. If liberal theory is concerned with freedom, and if what we mean is that individuals ought to be able to choose and undertake life plans among meaningful options, then liberal theory is committed to protecting societal cultures.

Translating the importance of culture for freedom into rights, Kymlicka (1995, 11–26) differentiates between 'multinational' and 'polyethnic' cultural diversity. This provides a way of framing the kinds of cultural rights liberal theory is committed to protecting, and the kinds of cultural groups that turn out to be societal cultures. A multination state involves the 'incorporation of previously self-governing, territorially concentrated cultures into a larger state' (Kymlicka 1995, 10). A 'national group' typically forms: 1) a historical community, 2) more or less institutionally complete, 3) occupying a given territory or homeland, and 4) sharing a distinct language or culture (Kymlicka 1995, 11). National groups include the indigenous peoples of previously colonised states (such as the Māori in New Zealand, Aboriginal groups in Australia, First Nations in Canada, Native Americans in United States of America), as well as other groups (such as the Catalans and Quebecois) that have deep attachments to a shared history, culture, language, and territory. 'Self-government rights' typically apply to national minorities who seek to maintain themselves alongside a majority culture, and require rights to achieve this (Kymlicka 1995, 27–30).

On the other hand, polyethnic states occur as a result of 'individual and familial immigration'—and include most nation-states today (Kymlicka 1995, 18). 'Polyethnic rights' function to both promote and support integration into the larger society, and apply to ethnic groups who typically seek full membership in a majority culture (Kymlicka 1995, 30–31). Finally, 'special representative rights' are designed to guarantee political representation for all groups within the governing body of the state (Kymlicka 1995, 31–32).

Freedom plays a key role in the way Kymlicka frames the importance of culture and in the way that cultural diversity ought to be managed. How nation-states come to be multicultural, and the extent of that multiculturalism, bears on the rights and obligations that come into play. Such a discussion underpins any attempt to determine how indigenous peoples come to have rights and what those rights are. For instance, the lack of free choice by indigenous peoples and other national minorities in the process of colonisation and continued oppression plays a key role in a story about why rights should be granted and which rights they should be. History and the contemporary realities of indigenous peoples help to determine what rights are required for them to maintain their distinct ways of life (Kymlicka 1995, 11–13). History, culture, identity, and self-determination play key roles from the start.

Dealing specifically with indigenous self-determination in international law, James Anaya (2004, 103–6) divides the right to self-determination into its 'substantive' and 'remedial' component parts. The substantive aspect has both constitutive and ongoing aspects. The constitutive element requires that the 'governing institutional order be substantially the creation of processes guided by the will of the people, or peoples, governed' (Anaya 2004, 104). The ongoing element stipulates that within the structure of the state (and regardless of how it was created), peoples ought to be able to 'live and develop freely on a continuous basis' (Anaya 2004, 106). The substance of self-determination applies to how society is designed and what peoples are able to do within it. All peoples should play a part in shaping the structure of society, and all peoples ought to be able to develop and redevelop as peoples within it. By 'peoples', Anaya (2004, 103) means 'all those spheres of community marked by elements of identity and collective consciousness within which peoples' lives unfold'. In taking this view, Anaya rejects restricting peoples to territorial divisions on the grounds that it 'ignores the multiple and overlapping spheres of community, authority, and interdependency that actually exist in the human experience' (Anaya 2004, 101).

While self-determination is 'concerned broadly with peoples, including indigenous peoples, and grounded in the idea that all are equally entitled to control their own destinies', it also 'gives rise to remedies that tear at the legacies of empire, discrimination, oppression of democratic participation, and cultural suffocation' (Anaya 2004, 98). Indigenous peoples' self-determination is, thus, further grounded in a 'remedial aspect'. Importantly, this remedial aspect is not based solely on correcting historical wrongs, but on remedying 'a particular set of vulnerabilities' that are understood in terms of 'disparities of economic and political power rooted in history' (Anaya 2004, 125). Implementing self-determination requires, at the very least, some thinking along dimensions of: non-discrimination, cultural integrity, control over land and resources, social welfare, and development, as well as self-government. Achieving self-determination requires that we rethink social and political structures.

Anaya's differentiation between remedial and substantive self-determination gives us two related ways of framing justice for indigenous peoples. The remedial framing focuses on the general questions of what indigenous peoples are owed given historical injustices, and what ongoing measures are required given continuing inequalities of power. This framing sits well with treaty settlements, retrospective apologies, processes of reconciliation, and moves to protect and guarantee cultural rights (Boxill 2015; Radzik and Murphy 2015). This aspect of self-determination makes space for indigenous peoples within existing (social, political, economic, environmental, and cultural) frameworks. Remedial processes recognise indigenous peoples' histories and ongoing suffering, and provide one way of grounding indigenous claims.

The substantive framing of self-determination is more comprehensive in its concern, and so more comprehensive in its inclusion of indigenous peoples. According to Anaya, all peoples ought to be able to play a role in shaping the structure of society, and ought to be able to develop and redevelop freely within that structure. In order for indigenous peoples to play a role in shaping the structure of the state, we need to ask how indigenous values and ideas about living together might redefine social and political structures. We need to ask what indigenous perspectives of justice are, and what indigenous contributions to justice might be. Although Anaya indicates the extent of this substantive framing, he does not explore this framing in full. Anaya remarks that the political philosophy of the Iroquois (Haudenosaunee) confederacy and the Great Law of Peace in particular:

> Promotes unity among individuals, families, clans, and nations while upholding the integrity of diverse identities and spheres of autonomy. ... Such conceptions outside the mould of classical western liberalism would appear to provide a more appropriate foundation for understanding humanity, its aspirations, and its political development than the model of a world divided into exclusive, monolithic communities, and hence a more appropriate backdrop for understanding the subject matter of self-determination. (Anaya 2004, 102)

The substantive dimension of self-determination can only be realised if we take this statement to its full conclusion. The substance of self-determination requires space to engage with what indigenous peoples, themselves, say about justice, democracy, political institutions, and the values that shape them. What is required is a move away from asking whether indigenous peoples can be accommodated within existing liberal frameworks, to what indigenous peoples themselves say about how self-determination and justice can be understood, pursued, and realised.

Kymlicka and Anaya provide us with useful and important ways to rethink and revisit liberal theories of justice in light of indigenous peoples. Kymlicka provides us with liberal reasons to protect indigenous cultures and to guarantee the kinds of rights that these protections call for. Anaya provides us with a deeper understanding of self-determination and of how it frames indigenous claims. Together they create space for the recognition of indigenous peoples in liberal theories of justice, and provide us with practical insights for pursuing and realising social justice. Yet neither of them take on the challenge of indigenous peoples' claims to self-determination to its full conclusion. Neither of them attempts to recreate justice in collaboration with the perspectives of those groups for whom they write—and who remain excluded from the discussion. Such a discussion remains absent from theories of justice, despite the increasing importance of cross-cultural conversations and collaboration (Robinson and Tormey 2009; Watene and Yap 2015). What is required is more engagement with perspectives that currently sit at the margins of western frameworks and liberal theories of justice (Metz 2007). What is required is a cross-cultural conversation that directly includes the voices of indigenous peoples. The remainder of this chapter provides a starting point for this conversation.

JUSTICE AS HEALING: INDIGENOUS PERSPECTIVES

Indigenous peoples often speak of justice in terms of healing. At one level, understanding what this means for indigenous peoples requires thinking about how history has shaped, and continues to shape, indigenous peoples' lives and communities. Processes of oppression (colonization, marginalisation, exploitation, powerlessness, violence) systematically undermine indigenous values and social structures (Young 2005). Land tenure systems alter the physical relationships that indigenous peoples are able to have with lands and natural resources, and open the way for widespread dispossession. Land loss, forced displacement, wars, disease, culture and language loss, assimilation—these have all been destructive for indigenous communities. They were and remain traumatic events that have been reproduced in the social structures, political systems, policies and programmes that continue to shape the contemporary realities of indigenous communities (Smith 2005).

The forced removal of aboriginal children from their families for resettlement in white Australian mission houses and foster families over the period from 1890 to 1970, is commonly referred to as the 'stolen generations'. This practise was part of the Australian government's assimilation policy with the aim of ending what was called the 'aboriginal problem'—essentially ending aboriginal culture (Australian Human Rights and Equality Commission Report 1997). Similarly, Canadian assimilation policies saw the removal of children from tribal communities to aboriginal residential schools—with many of these children suffering various forms of abuse and even death (Truth and Reconciliation Commission of Canada 2012, 2015). In addition, Māori tribal communities were rendered landless following the arrival of the British. Ngāti Whātua Ōrākei, a once thriving Māori tribal community in what is now central Auckland, were virtually landless following the individualisation of land title. By 1951 they were wards of the state, evicted from their homes in Ōkahu Bay and relocated as tenants of thirty-five state houses. The ancestral 'marae' (kin-community centre), homes and buildings were pulled down and burnt (Kawharu 1975, 1977).

These and many other practises, 'estranged indigenous peoples from their beliefs, languages, families, and identities', and 'deprived indigenous peoples of their dignity' (Youngblood Henderson 2000, 29). Most significantly for indigenous communities today, the trauma led to 'a wide range of dysfunctional and hurtful behaviours (such as physical and sexual abuse) that became recycled generation after generation' (Lane et al. 2005, 370). Historical trauma theory tells us that 'populations historically subjected to long-term, mass trauma—colonialism, slavery, war, genocide—exhibit a higher prevalence of disease even several generations after the original trauma occurred' (Sotero 2006, 94). Today, indigenous peoples are 'poorer, less educated, die at a younger age, are much more likely to commit suicide, and are generally in worse health than the rest of the population' (Stidsen 2006, 10). For indigenous peoples, historical trauma theory provides one way to explain the intergenerational persistence of poverty and disparities (Brave Heart and DeBruyn 1998; Danieli 1998; Duran and Duran 1995; Leary 2005).

Intergenerational transfer of trauma makes some sense when we take account of the way in which identity, knowledge, values, and health are intimately bound up with the social, political, cultural, and environmental conditions within which we live. It also makes sense when we take account of both: 1) the way in which entrenched deprivation impacts on the hopes and aspirations we have for our lives, and 2) how communities can perpetuate this deprivation (Sen 1988, 45–46; see also Khader 2011; Nussbaum 2000). Sometimes we can be defined by, and come to identify with, the stories and narratives that have come to make up part of our histories and collective memories.

For indigenous peoples, healing starts with recognising these events and conditions, and acknowledging the way that they impact on their lives (Taylor 1992). Providing space for traumatic events to be publicly acknowledged, is an important way of recognising these events (Youngblood Henderson and McCaslin 2005). Processes of healing (treaty claims, grievances, apologies, reconciliation processes) open up space for indigenous communities to remember, face, and begin to overcome histories of grave injustice and great loss of hope. While important, this process is painful:

> Remembering is painful because it involves remembering not just what colonisation was about but what being dehumanised meant for our own cultural practices. Both healing and transformation become crucial strategies in any

> approach which asks a community to remember what they may have decided unconsciously or consciously to forget. (Smith 2005, 146)

Although painful, remembering is also (and ought to be) an empowering process—enabling indigenous peoples to celebrate their own (continued) survival, even in the face of these grave histories. It is a process that is fundamental to positive transformation—helping indigenous peoples to come to terms with losses, and to respond to those losses with what it means to survive (Smith 2005). Remembering allows indigenous peoples to recognise that, despite policies often tailored to assimilate and eradicate them, they have managed to endure and to bring about change.[4]

Additionally, the process of remembering is reconciliatory because it can promote dialogue—creating space for peoples to come together to listen, share, and engage with systems of knowledge and values that may lay outside of prevailing frameworks. Remembering brings renewed hope, and builds new relationships and foundations for moving forward. It provides a foundation for indigenous peoples to undertake steps to articulate and pursue who they are and to reclaim lives they value (McCaslin 2005; Smith 2005). Remembering becomes fundamental to enabling substantive self-determination.

By understanding justice in terms of healing, indigenous communities bring together both the process and purpose of justice. One of the aims of justice is to create opportunities for indigenous communities to undertake healing, and to create processes that are able to facilitate that healing. This requires space to come to terms with the past, to remember how traumatic events impacted on the lives and communities of indigenous peoples, and to begin to rebuild for the future. What can we learn from this way of framing justice? Most obviously, the starting point for justice is 'grounded' rather than 'transcendental' (Sen 2009). Justice is grounded in the lived experiences of indigenous communities, and we look within those communities to work out what justice requires.

> In articulating justice as a form of healing, Aboriginal Peoples are not trying to construct an abstract or universal theory of justice in the Eurocentric tradition. … Instead, we are attempting to grasp the wisdom of our Elders, to define ourselves, to articulate a certain way of healing, and to apply it to our traumatic experiences. (Youngblood Henderson and McCaslin 2005, 5)

What matters on this understanding of justice is what indigenous communities are able to do and be, and the barriers to pursuing and realising lives they value. Justice is about indigenous peoples and their lives—and it is something that indigenous peoples are (and ought to be) empowered to conceptualise, pursue, and realise.

This grounded approach to justice resonates with the people-centred and capability-based approach to justice found in the work of Amartya Sen and Martha Nussbaum (Nussbaum 2000, 2006; Sen 1999). The capability approach tells us to think about justice in terms of what people are capable of doing and being. The approach tells us that we should pay attention to the kinds of lives people live, and to the choices they have to live the kinds of lives they value (Nussbaum 2000, 2006; Qizilbash 2012; Robeyns 2005, 2011; Sen 1999). Such an approach is concerned with how justice plays out in the real world, and so an important aim is to accommodate cultural diversity. The voices of the marginalised must always be included in the pursuit and realisation of justice (Nussbaum 2000, 2006; Sen 1999; UNDP 2004). The capability approach provides one way of grounding an indigenous perspective of justice as healing by placing the emphases on what indigenous peoples are able to do and be, what they value for their own lives, and the involvement of indigenous peoples as agents of transformation.[5]

Does a focus on healing mean that justice is no longer about the distribution of benefits and burdens? For indigenous peoples, justice is still about ensuring that the distribution of benefits and burdens in society is fair. Healing and the distribution of benefits and burdens are connected. The need for healing can arise in part as a result of distributive injustices, and just distributive arrangements can go some way to facilitating healing. Healing is, however, also about more than this. Healing is also, and centrally, about the way we think about distribution—about what makes a distributive arrangement just, and about what we take the benefits and burdens to be. The way in which distributive justice is conceptualised, and regardless of how benefits and burdens are distributed, may itself perpetuate the need for healing (Young 2005).

Additionally, justice as healing provides a different way of framing rights. In contemporary political philosophy, rights are granted to groups on account of their satisfying conditions for group recognition (see Kosko, in this volume). The United Nations breaks with this mould by providing no straightforward definition of indigenous peoples in which to ground these rights, preferring instead to let indigenous peoples define themselves (UNPFII 2007). While unconventional, this approach is consistent with understanding rights in terms of healing. In the end it matters little to the practical implementation of the declaration whether or not we have a definition of indigenous peoples. The requirement to respect such peoples is part of a more general requirement to be honest about the past. If this general requirement is respected within a society, then indigenous (and other minority) groups will have the space and the resources to undertake processes of healing. As a result, indigenous peoples will have the capability to define themselves. While rights remain important, within the context of justice as healing we have a way of re-imagining and rethinking the purpose and importance of rights.

Our discussion provides us with a number of general insights for justice from the perspective of justice as healing—including the importance of history, the perpetuation of unjust conditions, and the importance of grounding justice in peoples' lives. To fully understand this perspective of justice, however, we need to grasp what it is that indigenous communities are trying to regain. We need to know more about how indigenous peoples conceptualise well-being. To do this, and to build on the discussion so far, we look at how Māori (the indigenous peoples of Aotearoa/New Zealand) worldviews provide insights into the kinds of lives Māori value.

JUSTICE AND RELATIONSHIPS: MĀORI PERSPECTIVES[6]

Māori creation themes involve movements between states: from darkness to light, from nothing to something, the separation of earth and sky, the creation of the natural world (Royal 2012). An important part of the creation narrative is the union between Ranginui (sky) and Papatūānuku (earth), whose offspring—owing to their parents' enduring embrace—are raised in total darkness, unable to grow and develop. After some discussion, and led by the oldest child Tāne Māhuta, the children manage to separate their parents, bringing light and life into the world. From here, the children go on to create and preside over various parts of the natural world and the creatures therein: Tangaroa of the sea; Tāwhirimātea of the winds; Haumietiketike and Rongomātāne of various food groups; Tāne Māhuta of the forests and (on some accounts) human beings; Tūmatauenga of war and aggression; as well as others (Marsden and Henare 1992).

The creation narrative provides an account of the relationships between all things, extending back to the origins of the universe (Marsden and Henare 1992; Marsden 2003a, 2003b; Walker 1992). By placing all things within a genealogical framework, the narrative illustrates the central place that 'whakapapa' (genealogy—literally, 'to place in layers') has within the Māori world (Marsden and Henare 1992; Marsden 2003a, 2003b; Mutu and McCully 2003; Sadler 2007). Whakapapa provides an account of the connections and relationships between people and all things—making sense of the world through relationships. In whakapapa terms, all things within the natural world are 'whānau' (kin), and imbued with 'mana' (rights and dignity) and 'mauri' (a spiritual life essence) (Marsden 2003b; Sadler 2007). All human beings, non-human animals, and the natural world (landscapes, seascapes, waterways, natural resources, and other creatures) are physically and spiritually connected.

Rights and obligations are attached to our relationships and connections. As all human and non-human creatures are ancestors and kin, we have obligations to each other—obligations to protect, enhance, and conserve (Marsden 2003a; Waitangi Tribunal Report 2011a).

> For Māori the sense of whānau or family indicated the close relationship of all parts of the environment, and human beings, as descendants of Tāne Māhuta, were therefore an integral part of that environment. The holistic attitude of Māori is emphasised by the fact that they consider they are, along with the plants and animals, all the children of Tāne (Ko nga Aitanga Tāne tatou katoa—We are all the children of Tāne), not separate or superior or exercising a dominant, exploitive role. (Waitangi Tribunal Report 2011a, 34)

Abuse or misuse of human beings and other parts of the natural world is (in at least one important sense) wrong because through whakapapa we are all born with dignity and rights (mana), and as family (whānau) we ought to enhance ('manaaki'—literally, to enhance mana) each other's lives. Human beings have obligations to enhance the natural world just as the natural world has obligations to enhance the lives of human beings (Patterson 1992, 2000). Whakapapa highlights the inter-dependence of all things for well-being, and the reciprocal relationships that exist between human beings, non-human animals, and the rest of the natural world. Unlike an approach which views people as the principal (if not sole) end of concern, human beings are understood to be only one part of a creation story that weaves together all things in the universe (Marsden 2003b).

A significant component of the colonisation of Māori was the deliberate undermining of the structural importance of relationships (Awatere 1981; Walker 2004). The individualisation of Māori land titles made possible the sale and purchase of land and resulted in the widespread breakdown of kin-community. Migration to urban centres, in search of employment opportunities, came at the cost of cultural connection. Relationships broke down, language ability declined, and the centrality of 'marae' (kin-community centres) weakened (Kawharu 2014). Today the Māori population tend to live in urban areas. Māori have, on average, the poorest health status of any ethnic group in New Zealand. Many health conditions (including heart disease, stroke, and diabetes) are more common in Māori adults than non-Māori. Health disparities are intimately linked to social inequalities. Māori are more likely to live in overcrowded and substandard housing, more likely to suffer from poor nutrition, to have little or no formal education qualifications, and to work in low skilled jobs (Ministry of Health 2015).

By drawing out Māori values, the creation narrative helps to draw out how colonisation undermined values central to Māori social, political, and cultural life. Colonisation led to the breakdown of kin-community, the relationships between communities and ancestral lands and natural resources, and relationships with language and culture. Without kin-community cohesion, Māori were unable to undertake activities that enhanced their own lives and those of the natural world. Relationships and obligations were unable to be protected and fulfilled. Justice, if understood in terms of relationship-based rights and obligations, was impossible to achieve.

What can we gain from exploring the way Māori worldviews ground ideas about justice? As an approach to justice, value is derived from our co-existence and shared connections. The question of justice is a question about the kinds of relationships and connections required to live good lives (see also The Peoples Agreement 2010). Within a relationship-based framework, justice is centrally about preserving relationships, reconnecting, and restoring rights and obligations. Justice enables and expands good relationships. Within such a framework, healing is required as a result of disconnection, and reconnection requires rebuilding relationships—within kin communities, between communities, with lands and natural resources, with ancestors, with future generations, and with the rest of the world. Just relationships restore and balance our rights and obligations, and our places in the world (Tomas 2005).

If rights and obligations are determined by 'whakapapa', then our lives and futures are interwoven with ancestors, those living today, future people, non-human animals and the natural world. Obligations to future generations and to the natural world are derived from a simple story about our connections and the way in which (through creation and history) we impact on each other's lives and dignity. The scope of justice includes future generations, non-human animals, and the natural world from the start. No extension of our ideas about justice are required to include them. Indeed, Māori tribal development plans and policies are built around the importance of: relationships, obligations to future generations, the environment and cultural identity (see, for instance, Waikato-Tainui Te Kauhanganui Incorporated 2013). We get a very different account of the scope of justice, and of what justice requires.

Additionally, from a relationship-based perspective, we enhance our own lives by enhancing the lives of others (other human beings, other communities, non-human animals, and the natural world). Obligations to others are at the same time obligations to ourselves, as our rights and dignity make sense in relation to others' rights and dignity. A relationship-based account can only speak in terms of *belonging to* rather than having *ownership over* each other and the natural world (Marsden 2003a, 2003b).

> The closest idea to ownership [in Māori society] was that of the private use of a limited number of personal things such as garments, weapons, combs. Apart from this all other use of land, waters, forests, fisheries, was a communal and/or tribal right. All natural resources, all life was birthed from Mother Earth. Thus the resources of the earth did not belong to man but rather, man belonged

> to the earth, Man as well as animal, bird, fish could harvest the bounty of mother earth's resources but they did not own them. Man had but 'user-rights'. (Marsden 2003a, 67)

Thinking about justice in this way gives us a different starting point for thinking about obligations within families, communities, nations, and our world. It gives us a way of thinking about how our relationships with each other impact on our lives, and it provides us with a way of rethinking the nature and terms of those relationships. It gives us a way of asking whether our current (personal, social, global) relationships enhance (manaaki) or diminish dignity (mana). It helps to draw out the way that justice is about developing relationships that enhance our collective lives. We get a very different account of the nature and content of our rights and obligations.

Similarly, a relationship-based approach highlights the importance of collectives for well-being and social justice. The importance of whānau (family or kin-community) has been a driving force for the transformation of Māori health policy, and has led to the development of the 'whānau ora' (family or community health) approach to health in New Zealand (Taskforce on Whānau Centred Initiatives 2010).[7] The whānau ora approach is about the importance of collectives for the health of individuals and society. The central aim is to strengthen relationships in order to empower collectives to be self-determining, cohesive, resilient, and nurturing. One list of collective capacities with this aim is provided by Mason Durie and includes:

1. The capacity to care (Manaakitia)
2. The capacity to share (Tohatohatia)
3. The capacity for guardianship (Pupuri taonga)
4. The capacity to empower (Whakamana)
5. The capacity to plan ahead (Whakatakoto tikanga)
6. The capacity for growth (Whakatini)
   (Durie 2003, 23–24)

These capacities provide one account of what good relationships look like, and what they provide (good relationships as: caring, sharing, providing guardianship, empowering, aspirational, and creating positive transformation). As such, they provide an account of what a just society (and just policies) ought to nurture, and what well-being (at least in part) looks like. Such an approach takes the lives of collective members to be improved by environments that are enabling, and that broaden the range of opportunities for living well. The approach takes well-being and positive transformation to depend on relationships, and the broader connections and networks that people have available to them. Improving the lives of collective members requires creating conditions in which lives can be improved and transformed, and where that transformation can be intergenerational (Ministry of Health 2002).

Our overview of Māori values and policy developments in light of those values—albeit brief—provides us with a number of insights for justice. From a different starting point for thinking about our places in the world, we get different ideas about what matters for justice, what justice includes, and how justice might be realised. We get different ways of understanding what justice means within particular communities, and how cultural differences impact on how justice might be conceptualised and realised. Most significantly, we get a framework for thinking about justice that is grounded in the lives of people, the connections they have to ancestors and future generations, and the connections that they have to the natural world.

Yet, our brief overview can only offer a modest and partial account of those insights. As such, our overview can only hope to achieve two rather modest aims. The first aim is to show that Māori worldviews are able to give us distinctive lenses through which to redefine and reassess what matters for justice and for healing (Daes 2008). To give us a starting point for different ways of thinking about justice and different ways of pursuing justice. To show that a relationship-based approach that includes all human beings (past, present, and future), non-human animals, and the natural world has the potential to differ in scope, content, and concern from most theories of justice. To put forward the view that we might get a very different way of framing justice if our starting point is relationships-based. To draw attention to the fact that we can obtain an approach that looks to have something different to say, and so an approach that could potentially reimagine, justice.

The second aim, and perhaps most important, is to demonstrate that further discussions that respectfully engage with indigenous perspectives of justice are possible. To explain that fuller and deeper conversations on the way that justice might be reconceived and just policies redesigned are viable. To make the point that cross-cultural engagement and discussion is needed because the pursuit and realisation of justice in our world today requires it. To encourage liberal philosophers concerned about justice to engage with, and to create space for, what indigenous peoples say about justice. Indeed, in many ways, the value of this chapter depends entirely on whether it can go some way to creating such a space.

CONCLUSION

This chapter brings to light some of the ways in which indigenous peoples feature in liberal theories of justice, and asks whether there is more that we ought to do to include the voices and perspectives of indigenous peoples. After a brief discussion of Will Kymlicka's liberal multiculturalism and

James Anaya's ideas about indigenous self-determination, I claim that both theorists fall short of fully grasping the implications of indigenous self-determination. Fully grasping indigenous self-determination requires that we engage with the perspectives of indigenous peoples, who remain on the outside of contemporary justice theorising.

The second part of the chapter begins to show what we might gain from engaging with indigenous perspectives. I do this by exploring justice as healing, and Māori creation narratives in order to provide a brief account of what justice looks like. I argue that justice from the perspective of indigenous peoples is grounded in the lives of people and communities, attached to what people are able to do and be, and based on the importance of relationships and connections for living well. Relationships and connections determine rights and obligations and extend to include all human beings, non-human animals, and the natural world. Such a perspective sets out from, and also deviates from, most liberal theories of justice in scope, content, and concern.

The questions considered here to a great extent remain (at best) underexplored in contemporary theories of justice. Until we can show how to bring indigenous perspectives to bear on questions about justice, our answers will remain incomplete, and indigenous peoples will remain marginalised. Problematically, liberal political philosophy will continue to speak on behalf of indigenous peoples. If we are serious about justice and self-determination, then we must be committed to opening up conversations about, and widening our perspectives of, justice. If we are serious about pursuing and realising justice in our world today, then we must accept that much more cross-cultural and intercultural conversations about justice are urgently required.

NOTES

The ideas in this chapter have benefitted from conversations with many people, including the research team at the James Henare Māori Research Centre, and the many wonderful people involved in the Ngāti Whātua Ōrākei Whānau Ora research project. This chapter has also been inspired by the work of many capability theorists who work with and for indigenous communities, especially Erika Bockstael and Mandy Yap, and the authors of a special issue of *Oxford Development Studies* on 'Indigenous peoples and the Capability Approach.

1. For an overview of the development of the declaration, see Errico (2007a, 2007b).

2. The right to self-government (article four), to participate in, and consent to, any decisions that affect them (articles nineteen and thirty-two), and to control (and have returned) traditionally owned lands and natural resources (article twenty-six) together form the basis of self-determination.

3. An important difference between Kymlicka and Anaya, concerns the issue of whether indigenous peoples ought to be differentiated from other (non-indigenous) national minorities in international law. The question of whether indigenous people's self-determination is fully captured by Kymlicka and Anaya (and liberal theory more generally) stands apart from whether indigenous and non-indigenous groups ought to be differentiated in international law. For this reason, I do not concern myself with this issue here.

4. It is important to say that Smith views 'celebrating survival' as a separate project among twenty-five projects for indigenous peoples (of which 'remembering' is also one), see Smith (2005, 145).

5. Here I focus on the capability approach as supplementing indigenous values. I have argued elsewhere that the foundations of Sen and Nussbaum's capability theories are unable to fully capture Māori values as they apply to the environment (Watene 2016).

6. It is important to acknowledge that there is no straightforward way to translate Māori into English—and that for the most part, any English translation of Māori concepts will not sufficiently capture all of what is meant in Māori. Wherever possible, I follow descriptions and translations from Māori Marsden.

7. Māori have developed a number of health models. The most widely used is Mason Durie's 'Whare Tapa Whā' which takes health to consist in emotional, whānau and spiritual concerns as well as physical pathologies (Durie 1998).

REFERENCES

Anaya, S. James. 2004. *Indigenous Peoples in International Law*. Oxford: Oxford University Press.

Australian Human Rights and Equal Opportunity Commission. 1997. *Bringing them Home: Report of the National Inquiry into the Separation of Aboriginal and Torres Strait Islander Children from Their Families*.

Awatere Donna. 1981. *Maori Sovereignty*. Auckland: Broadsheet.

Ballara, Angela. 2012. 'Ratana, Tahupotiki Wiremu', in *Te Ara: The Encyclopedia of New Zealand*. http://www.TeAra.govt.nz/en/biographies/3r4/ratana-tahupotiki-wiremu

Boxill, Bernard. 2015. 'Black Reparations', in Edward N. Zalta (ed.), *The Stanford Encyclopedia of Philosophy*. http://plato.stanford.edu/archives/win2015/entries/black-reparations.

Brave Heart, M., and L. DeBruyn. 1998. 'The American Indian Holocaust: Healing Historical Unresolved Grief'. American Indian and Alaska Native Mental Health Research 8(2): 56–78.

Daes, Erica-Irene A. 2008. *Indigenous Peoples: Keepers of Our Past, Custodians of our Future*. Conpenhagen: International Working Group for Indigenous Affairs.

Danieli, Y. (ed.). 1998. *International Handbook of Multigenerational Legacies of Trauma*. New York: Plenum Press.

Duran, E., & B. Durán. 1995. *Native American Postcolonial Psychology*. Albany: State University of New York Press.

Durie, M. 1998. *Whaiora: Maori Health Development. Second Edition*. Auckland: Oxford University Press.

Durie, M. 2003. *Nga Kahui Pou: Launching Maori Futures*. Wellington: Huia Publishers.

Errico, Stefania. 2007a. 'The Declaration on the Rights of Indigenous Peoples Is Adopted: An Overview', *Human Rights Law Review* 7(4): 756–59.

Errico, Stefania. 2007b. 'The Draft Declaration on the Rights of Indigenous Peoples: An Overview', *Human Rights Law Review*, 7(4): 741–55.

Hammond, John L. 2011. 'Indigenous Community Justice in the Bolivian Constitution of 2009', *Human Rights Quarterly* 33(3): 649–81.

Ivison, Duncan, Paul Patton, and Will Sanders. 2000. 'Introduction', in D. Ivison, P. Patton and W. Sanders (eds.), *Political Theory and the Rights of Indigenous Peoples*. Cambridge: Cambridge University Press, 1–22.

Kawharu, I. H. 1975. *Orakei: A Ngati Whatua Community*. Wellington: New Zealand Council for Educational Research.

Kawharu, I. H. 1977. *Māori Land Tenure: Studies of a Changing Institution*. Oxford: Oxford University Press.

Kawharu, M. (ed.). 2014. *Maranga Mai! Te Reo and Marae in Crisis?* Auckland: Auckland University Press.

Khader, Serene. 2011. *Adaptive Preferences and Woman's Empowerment*. New York: Oxford University Press.

Kymlicka, Will. 1995. *Multicultural Citizenship: A Liberal Theory of Minority Rights*. Oxford: Clarendon Press.
Kymlicka, Will. 2002. *Politics in the Vernacular: Nationalism, Multiculturalism and Citizenship*. Oxford: Oxford University Press.
Lane, Phil, Michael Bopp, Judie Bopp, and Julian Norris. 2005. 'Mapping the Healing Journey: First Nations Research Project on Healing in Canadian Aboriginal Communities', in Wanda D. McCaslin (ed.), *Justice as Healing*. Minneapolis: Living Justice Press, 369–408.
Leary, Degruy, L. 2005. *Post Traumatic Slave Syndrome: America's Legacy of Enduring Injury and Healing*. Portland, OR: Uptone Press.
Marsden, Rev. Māori. 2003b. 'The Natural World and Natural Resources: Māori Value Systems and Perspectives', in Charles Royal (ed.), *The Woven Universe: Selected Writings of Rev. Māori Marsden*. Ōtaki: The Estate of Rev. Māori Marsden, 24–53.
Marsden, Rev. Māori. 2003a. 'The Achievement of Authentic Being: God, Man and Universe, A Māori View', in Charles Royal (ed.), *The Woven Universe: Selected Writings of Rev. Māori Marsden*. Ōtaki: The Estate of Rev. Māori Marsden, 2–23.
Marsden, Rev. Māori, and Te Aroha Henare. 1992. 'Kaitiakitanga: A Definitive Introduction to the Holistic Worldview of the Maori'. Unpublished paper.
McCaslin, Wanda D. (ed.). 2005. *Justice as Healing: Indigenous Ways*. St. Paul, MN: Living Justice Press.
Mead, Hirini M. 2003. *Tikanga Māori: Living by Māori Values*. Wellington: Huia.
Metz, Thaddeus. 2007. 'Toward an African Moral Theory', *The Journal of Political Philosophy* (15:3): 321–41.
Mikkelsen, Cæcilie. 2014. *The Indigenous World 2014*. International Work Group for Indigenous Affairs.
Ministry of Health. 2015. *Tatau Kahukura: Māori Health Chart Book 2015*, 3rd ed. Wellington: Ministry of Health.
Mutu, Margaret, and Matiu McCully. 2003. *Te Whānau Moana i Nga Kaupapa me Nga Tikanga: Customs and Protocols*. Auckland: Reed.
Nussbaum, Martha. 2000. *Women and Human Development: The Capabilities Approach*. Cambridge: Cambridge University Press.
Nussbaum, Martha. 2006. *Frontiers of Justice: Disability, Nationality, Species Membership*. Cambridge, MA: Belknap Press.
Patterson, John. 1992. *Exploring Māori Values*. Palmerston North: Dunmore Press.
Patterson, John. 2000. *People of the Land: A Pacific Philosophy*. Palmerston North: Dunmore Press.
The Peoples Agreement. 2010. World Peoples Conference on Climate Change and the Rights of Mother Earth, Bolivia. http://pwccc.wordpress.com/support.
Qizilbash, Mozaffar. 2012. 'The Capability Approach: Its Interpretation and Limitations', in Francesca Panzironi and Katharine Gelber (eds.), *The Capability Approach: Practise and Publica Policy in the Asia-Pacific Region*. New York: Routledge.
Radzik, Linda, and Colleen Murphy. 2015. 'Reconciliation', in Edward N. Zalta (ed.), *The Stanford Encyclopedia of Philosophy*. http://plato.stanford.edu/archives/sum2015/entries/reconciliation.
Robeyns, Ingrid. 2005. 'The Capability Approach: A Theoretical Survey', *Journal of Human Development* (61): 93–114.
Robeyns, Ingrid. 2011. 'The Capability Approach', in Edward N. Zalta (ed.), *The Stanford Encyclopedia of Philosophy*. http://plato.stanford.edu/archives/sum2011/entries/capability-approach.
Robinson, Andrew, and Simon Tormey. 2009. 'Resisting Global Justice: Disrupting the Colonial "Emancipatory" logic of the West', *Third World Quarterly* 30(8): 1395–1409.
Royal, Te Ahukaramū Charles. 2012. 'Māori Creation Traditions', in *Te Ara: The Encyclopedia of New Zealand*. http://www.TeAra.govt.nz/en/maori-creation-traditions.
Sadler, Hone. 2007. 'Mātauranga Māori (Māori Epistemology)', *International Journal of the Humanities* 4(10): 1–16.
Sen, Amartya. 1988. *On Ethics and Economics*. Oxford: Blackwell Publishing.
Sen, Amartya. 1999. *Development as Freedom*. New York: Knopf Press.

Sen, Amartya. 2004. 'How Does Culture Matter?', in V. Rao and M. Walton (eds.), *Culture and Public Action*. Stanford: Stanford University Press.
Sen, Amartya. 2007. *Identity and Violence: The Illusion of Destiny*. London: Penguin Books Ltd.
Sen, Amartya. 2009. *The Idea of Justice*. London: Penguin Books.
Smith, Linda T. 2005. *Decolonizing Methodologies: Research and Indigenous Peoples*. London: Zed Books.
Smith, Linda T. 2006. 'Colonizing Knowledges', in R. Maaka and C. Andersen (eds.), *The Indigenous Experience: Global Perspectives*. Toronto: Canadian Scholars Press.
Song, Sarah. 2014. 'Multiculturalism', in Edward N. Zalta *The Stanford Encyclopedia of Philosophy*. http://plato.stanford.edu/archives/spr2014/entries/multiculturalism/.
Sotero, Michelle. 2006. 'A Conceptual Model of Historical Trauma: Implications for Public Health Practice and Research', *Journal of Health Disparities Research and Practice* 1(1): 93–108.
Stidsen, Sille. 2006. *The Indigenous World*. International Work Group for Indigenous Affairs.
Taskforce on Whānau Centred Initiatives. 2010. 'Whānau Ora: Report of the Taskforce on Whānau-Centred Initiatives'. Report Produced for Hon Tariana Turia, Minister for the Community and Voluntary Sector, Ministry of Social Development, Wellington.
Taylor, Charles. 1992. 'The Politics of Recognition', in A. Gutmann (ed.), Multiculturalism: Examining the Politics of Recognition. Princeton: Princeton University Press, 25–73.
Tomas, Nin. 2005. 'Maori Justice: The Marae as a Forum for Justice', in Wanda D. McCaslin, *Justice as Healing*. Minneapolis: Living Justice Press, 134–40.
Truth and Reconciliation Commission of Canada. 2012. *They Came for the Children*. Winnipeg: Truth and Reconciliation Commission of Canada.
Truth and Reconciliation Commission of Canada. 2015. *The Survivors Speak*. Winnipeg: Truth and Reconciliation Commission of Canada.
United Nations. 2009. 'State of the World's Indigenous Peoples'. Department of Economic and Social Affairs, Division for Social Policy and Development, Secretariat of the Permanent Forum on Indigenous Issues, New York.
United Nations Development Programme. 2004. *Human Development Report 2004*. New York: Oxford University Press.
United Nations Permanent Forum for Indigenous Issues. 2007. *United Nations Declaration on the Rights of Indigenous Peoples*. http://www.un.org/esa/socdev/unpfii/en/drip.html.
United Nations Permanent Forum for Indigenous Issues. 2008. *United Nations Development Group Guidelines on Indigenous Peoples Issues*. http://www2.ohchr.org/english/issues/indigenous/docs/guidelines.pdf.
Waikato-Tainui Te Kauhanganui Incorporated. 2013. 'Tai Tumu, Tai Pari, Tai Ao: Waikato-Tainui Environment Plan'. http://www.wrrt.co.nz/wp-content/uploads/EBook_FINAL_EP_Plan_sp.pdf.
Waitangi Tribunal. 2011a. *Ko Aotearoa Tenei: Te Taumata Tuatahi* (Wai 262), part 1. Wellington: Legislation Direct.
Waitangi Tribunal. 2011b. *Ko Aotearoa Tenei: Te Taumata Tuarua* (Wai 262), part 2. Wellington: Legislation Direct.
Walker, Ranginui. 1992. 'The Relevance of Maori Myth and Tradition', in Michael King (ed.), *Te Ao Hurihuri: Aspects of Maoritanga*. Auckland: Reed, 171–84.
Walker R. 2004. *Ka Whawhai Tonu Matou: Struggle without end*. Auckland: Penguin.
Watene, Krushil. 2016. 'Valuing Nature: Maori Philosophy and the Capability Approach'. Oxford Development Studies . http://dx.doi.org/10.1080/13600818.2015.1124077.
Watene, Krushil, and Mandy Yap. 2015. 'Culture and Sustainable Development: Indigenous Contributions', *Journal of Global Ethics* 11(1): 51–55.
Wessendorf, Kathrin (ed.). 2011. *IWGIA: The Indigenous World 2011*. Copenhagen: IWGIA.
Wessendorf, Kathrin, and lola Garcia-Alix. 2009. 'The Rights of Indigenous Peoples: An overview', in Diane Andrews Henningfeld (ed.), *Indigenous Peoples*. New York: Greenhaven Press.

Young, Iris Marion. 2005. 'Five Faces of Oppression', in Ann E. Cudd and Robin O. Andreasen, *Feminist Theory: A Philosophical Anthology.* Malden, MA: Blackwell Publishing, 91–104.

Youngblood Henderson, James 2000. 'The Context of the State of Nature', in Marie Battiste (ed.), *Reclaiming Indigenous Voice and Vision.* Vancouver: University of British Columbia Press, 1–38.

Youngblood Henderson, James, and Wanda McCaslin. 2005. 'Exploring Justice as Healing', in Wanda D McCaslin (ed.), *Justice as Healing.* MInneapolis: Living Justice Press, 3–12.

Chapter Nine

Justice in Regulation

Towards a Liberal Account

Rutger Claassen

In recent decades most Western states have privatized a range of public services and have increasingly chosen to focus on regulating markets instead of providing goods and services themselves. Some claim that Western states have deregulated the economy and increasingly withdrawn from economic life, marking an era of neoliberal governance. However, others claim that privatization has come with more and more intense forms of regulation. We would not be living in an era of 'less state', but of a different kind of state, a 'regulatory state' (Braithwaite 2008; Jordana and Levi-Faur 2005; Moran 2002). Regulation and deregulation are at the core of disputes about the role of the state in the economy. The 2008 experience of collapsing financial markets has only strengthened the sense of urgency surrounding questions of regulation.

This chapter is about the normative question *why and to what extent markets should be regulated.* While regulation has been discussed in law, public administration and economics, it has been relatively neglected in political philosophy. Given its growing importance, this neglect is untenable. A discipline with ambitions to grasp the nature and legitimacy of the state has to come to terms with the regulatory function of the modern state. More philosophical reflection may also be useful for these other disciplines (and ultimately regulatory practice) as well. For the way that standard handbooks of regulation deal with the problem, is rather pragmatic. A first overview of the prevailing legal and economic theories shows that there is a more or less consensus view that centres on a bifurcation of economic and social rationales for regulating markets, with the former having a higher status than the latter (section 1). This raises the question whether these two types of regulation stand in an unresolvable tension with each other or could be integrated into one normative framework. The main goal of this chapter will be to show that a philosophically integrated theory of regulation is possible, and to propose a way of doing so. This challenges the prevailing handbook orthodoxy which simply juxtaposes economic and social regulation without considering the tensions between them.

To work towards this goal, the middle parts of the chapter show why a philosophically integrated theory of regulation never came off the ground, but at the same time why there seem to be no principled impediments for developing such a theory. I will discuss the three most relevant subfields in political philosophy for the regulation question. The first one is that of *theories of justice*. In the second section I discuss Rawls's theory of justice and show how it relegates questions of market regulation to democratic practice. I argue this split renders Rawls's view inconsistent because it tacitly imports and accepts the utilitarian nature of economic theory that Rawls otherwise rejects. The second subfield is the discussion about the *moral limits of the market*. This field focuses on problematic markets that should be prohibited, but does not say much about regulating markets that should be allowed to exist. I will show, however, that when we apply an enlarged understanding of commodification, regulation of markets could also come into the picture (third section). In the fourth section, I address the final subfield: that of *liberal political theories about property*. The three most important currents in liberal theory (modern liberalism, classical liberalism, and libertarianism) do take a position about the legitimacy of regulation. Here we find in philosophical theorizing the same dichotomy between economic and social regulation that is expressed in handbooks of regulation. I argue this dichotomy renders liberal theorizing inconsistent because economic regulation is based on utilitarianism while social regulation relies on a non-utilitarian normative theory.

In the final section, I launch my constructive proposal for a philosophically integrated, liberal theory of regulation. The proposal builds around the liberal concept of autonomous agency. By giving centrality to this concept, I will suggest that we can understand economic and social regulation as emphasizing different aspects of a proper respect for autonomous agency and integrate both of them in a coherent liberal framework. This does require, however, abandoning the utilitarian version of economic regulation theory.

THE STATE OF REGULATION THEORY

There is a certain tendency in the literature to have an overly broad understanding of regulation according to which almost every state action could be classified as such. To avoid this, I adopt Arnold's definition, slightly simplified by me: regulation is best understood as a 'government-imposed limitation on O's freedom . . . with respect to the standard incidents of full, liberal ownership of φ by O' (Arnold 2009, 119).

This definition highlights three characteristics. First, regulation is confined to state or government interventions. (I refer to 'the state' as the regulating agent, even if transnational and supranational forms of regulation have become increasingly important. Most of the arguments can be applied *mutatis mutandis* to international regulation.) This excludes various forms of self-regulation: regulation refers to a public authority interfering with private exercises of ownership. A regulated market has a mixed private-public character, which makes it an intermediate between free (unregulated) private exercises of ownership and exercises of public ownership (public provision). Hence, I am interested here in the regulation of markets, not regulation in a wider sense (which might include regulation of public or quasi-public entities). Second, these interventions have as their object the ownership of an asset (φ) by a (natural/artificial) person. This excludes interventions to uphold that part of criminal law that aims to protect people's fundamental rights (to life and liberty) against assaults by others, since these are not based in property. Third, these interventions limit the freedom of owners. Some rules establish property rights, thus making a market possible in the first place, other rules restrain the use individuals can make of their property. Regulation only refers to the latter.

This definition distinguishes regulation also from the state's other economic functions; that is to provide economic goods and redistribute income or capital. The tripartite distinction of provision, regulation, and redistribution can most easily be explained using the contrasting concept of the market. When providing public goods, the state bypasses the market entirely and becomes itself an economic agent. When regulating, the state accepts the market as the main economic mechanism, but intervenes in order to limit free market activity. When redistributing, the state intervenes after markets have done work to transfer resources from one group to another. To a certain extent, these three roles can be alternatives for reaching the same publicly defined objectives ('the public interest'). The move from a provider state to a regulatory state can be understood as trying to achieve the same public goals through a different constitutive relationship between market and state.

What are the currently dominant normative theories of regulation? Handbooks in law and economics, such as Morgan and Yeung (2007), Ogus (2004), or Barr (2004) and overviews of regulatory principles such as those of Sunstein (1990) or Stiglitz (2009) converge on two central points: (i) they use a basic distinction between economic and social regulation; (ii) economic regulation receives more systematic attention as well as higher status than social regulation.

'Economic regulation' refers to regulation on the basis of the theory of market failure (Bator 1958; Hertog 1999; Cowen 1988). While obviously an umbrella term (there are several theories of market failure), they all start with the neoclassical idea of a perfectly competitive market. Such a market only comes into being when some highly restrictive assumptions are met: resources are privately held, and decisions about resources are up to their owners; there is no force or fraud; there is sufficient competition; consumption is private and does not affect others (non-tuism); transactions are costless; and utility functions are monotonic (Coleman 1985, 70; Gauthier 1986, 86–87). A market that satisfies these conditions is Pareto-optimal. No further transactions can be made without making at least one of the market participants worse off. Pareto-optimality is taken as a sign of *allocative efficiency*. Resources are used to maximally satisfy individual preferences of market agents. For these reasons the model of perfect competition is taken as a normative benchmark.

Deviations from this model are classified as a market failure. Since the assumptions are so restrictive, almost all authors recognize that deviations abound. There are no perfect markets in reality. These deviations are systematized into different categories, such as monopolistic competition, information asymmetries, public goods, and externalities. This gives rise to different forms of regulation. For example, monopolistic competition may give rise to anti-trust regulation, information asymmetry between producers and consumers to labelling requirements, non-excludability, and non-rivalness (the characteristics of public goods) to direct state provision, externalities to prohibitions, taxes, or subsidies. In all of these cases, markets do not function well on their own terms and regulation is expected to remedy this failure and restore Pareto-optimality.

These theories have been criticized on the grounds that often either voluntary solutions can remedy the market failure, so that government intervention is unnecessary, or government intervention gives rise to government failure, so that regulation is more costly than letting market failure persist. Both reasons (however legitimate) do not dispute the claim that the existence of a market failure is a *necessary*—albeit not sufficient—ground for government regulation.

Social regulation is distinguished from economic regulation because it refers to all grounds for regulating *other* than inefficiency. This is a merely negative definition; beyond this there is little agreement what should fall in this category. One common idea is that efficiency considerations are to be complemented with equity considerations. *Distributive justice* then becomes a second ground for regulating, in a dichotomous efficiency/equity theory.

Some would exclude redistributive measures from regulation, because it is done ex ante or ex ante/post to actual market processes. Their idea is that initial holdings are morally arbitrary; we may redistribute to bring about a more just initial allocation from which free exchanges can take place. This does not necessitate any regulation of the exchange relationship itself. However, this ignores the distributive impact of the exchange process (Dietsch 2010).

Another often-mentioned category is *paternalism*: human agents often act irrationally and therefore make decisions which go against their own best interest. To optimize welfare, governments in many situations could help individuals reach their preferred outcomes. No attempt is made to link these two additional grounds in a systemic fashion to the economic theory of market failure, or to integrate all three of them in a unifying framework. Some have urged an even more expansive understanding of social regulation. This has led to a variety of frameworks that go beyond economic regulation Stewart 1982; Sunstein 1990; Trebilcock 1993; Bozeman 2002; Soule 2003; Prosser 2006; Feintuck 2010). Each of these theories relies on different normative grounds and organizes the material in different ways. Nothing like a canonical theoretical framework has emerged, that is comparable to the theory of market failure for economic regulation.

Despite the fact that there is no accepted underlying unifying purpose, several categories of social regulation are fairly widely recognized (Arnold 2009, 132). Most theories recognize that the employment relation is a prominent item. Legislation about the terms of employment, minimum wages, anti-discrimination legislation, health and safety standards reflects our understanding that labour is more than a standard commodity (Radin 1996). Consumer protection is also an important component of social regulation. The sale of some (e.g., medical) products may be prohibited or subject to prior approval. This kind of regulation reflects a distrust of consumers and producers agreeing voluntarily about the riskiness of products. Third, environmental regulation is often included. Natural values are hard to quantify in an economic framework, but nonetheless they deserve state protection, according to proponents of social regulation.

Finally, note that economic and social reasons are most often presented as both distinct and complementary. They are *distinct* in that social reasons do not rely on an efficiency rationale while economic reasons do not rely on a social rationale (even though some economists do attempt to draw social regulations into an economic framework). They are *complementary* in that one can accept one and reject the other. Often, this means every sensible person is thought to accept economic regulation; some in addition will endorse some or all of what is in the 'social' category. Thus, Morgan and Yeung write in the context of social regulation: 'the task of prescribing substantive visions of values that regulation can legitimately pursue is controversial, given the pervasiveness of moral disagreement and value pluralism that characterizes modern societies' (Morgan and Yeung 2007, 36). The organizing idea of the handbooks seems to be that economic regulation is academically well-established and politically non-controversial whereas social regulation is controversial and should be left to politics. Later in this chapter I will show how this bifurcation can be overcome, by integrating economic and social regulation into a unified liberal framework. If my efforts there succeed, then the current inequality in status between economic and social regulation is itself a very controversial and ultimately untenable view.

Until now, there have been few attempts in political philosophy to develop a coherent normative regulation theory that could challenge this currently dominant mixture of a generally accepted economic theory supplemented with an underdeveloped theory of social regulation. In order to understand why, let's turn to our first subfield: theories of justice.

REGULATION BETWEEN JUSTICE AND DEMOCRACY

Since the publication of John Rawls's landmark *Theory of Justice* the standard move in this field has become to make a sharp split between principles of justice and their application in concrete contexts. Whereas the best definition of the principles was thought to be the work of philosophers, application should be left to others. These others can be academics from other disciplines (lawyers, economists, etc.), but the more principled view often found is that application is the work of democratic bodies, not of theorists. As a consequence, philosophers endlessly debated principles of justice, while leaving questions of application largely untouched. Meanwhile the others who were to complement their work were rarely familiar with philosophical work, so that this division of intellectual labour never happened. Admittedly this is a crude overview (e.g., there are notable exceptions of economists working on justice), but it does go a long way to explain why so few philosophers have reflected on regulating markets.

Rawls's own work pioneered this approach. Whereas the much-discussed first part of *Theory of Justice* set the standard for theorizing justice, the second part, where he present his views on economic systems, was often neglected. Here Rawls presents these views in a way which makes thinking about regulation essentially a non-philosophical task. At the start of part II, Rawls sets his economic reflections in the context of his famous 'four-stage sequence'. After having decided the principles of justice in the Original Position (first stage), the parties move to a constitutional stage, then to a legislative stage and finally to a phase in which rules are applied. Rawls then places social and economic policies in the legislative stage. He says:

> Now the question whether legislation is just or unjust, especially in connection with economic and social policies, is commonly subject to reasonable differences of opinion. In these cases judgment frequently depends upon speculative political and economic doctrines and upon social theory generally. Often the

> best that we can say of a law or a policy is that it is at least not clearly unjust. (Rawls 1999, 174)

Two pages later he draws the following conclusion from this indeterminacy of laws, from the point of view of justice:

> And similarly just laws and policies are those that would be enacted at the legislative stage. Of course, this test is often indeterminate: it is not always clear which of several constitutions, or economic and social arrangements, would be chosen. But when this is so, justice is to that extent likewise indeterminate. Institutions within the permitted range are equally just, meaning that they could be chosen; they are compatible with all the constraints of the theory. Thus *on many questions of social and economic policy we must fall back upon a notion of quasi-procedural justice*: laws and policies are just provided that they lie within the allowed range, and the legislature, in ways authorized by a just constitution, has in fact enacted them. (Rawls 1999, 176; emphasis added)

In this way, Rawls leaves a large space for democratic bodies to decide about specific regulations. If we follow this split between theorizing principles and applying them in a legislature, then regulatory theory cannot be an integral part of a theory of justice.

In the rest of part II, Rawls remains true to this division. He discusses which economic systems are in accord with his principles of justice, and approvingly presents a quite elaborate overview of conventional economic theory, discussing public goods, externalities and other market failures in some depth (Rawls 1999, 234–40). However, he makes it crystal clear from the start that this endorsement of economic theory is conditional and should in fact not even be considered a part of his theory at all:

> Certain elementary parts of economic theory are brought in solely to illustrate the content of the principles of justice. If economic theory is used incorrectly or if the received doctrine is itself mistaken, I hope that for the purposes of the theory of justice no harm is done. (Rawls 1999, 234)

Now, I think that Rawls's hope is misguided. The reason for this is *not* that we should completely reject the proposed division of labour between philosophical theorizing about justice and democratic decision-making. Philosophical theorizing, in the absence of empirical data, historical experiences with regulation, knowledge of human psychology, and so on can only bring us so far. Neither is the problem that, even with all this knowledge in hand, there may still be some under-determination of laws and policies measured against the requirements of a theory of justice. The latter theory, being more abstract, may reasonably allow for several just—or at least not unjust—applications and not point to a unique outcome.

Instead, I would propose that the problem is that Rawls puts the 'cut' between theorizing about justice and applying the theory too early. He thereby leaves out of philosophical scrutiny a theory (i.e., the economic theory of market failure) which itself is built on strong philosophical assumptions. The crux is that the theory of market failure is a utilitarian theory. It relies on maximising welfare in terms of individual preference satisfaction. Conventional economic theory takes individual preferences as the measure of what is normatively right in deciding which public goods should be provided by the state, which externalities require internalization, which corporate agreements are in breach of competition law, and so on. But utilitarianism is precisely the moral theory that Rawls has been at pains (correctly, in my opinion) to refute in his work. However, somehow he fails to realize that his endorsement of economic theory sits very uneasily with his rejection of utilitarianism.

Let us take as an example Rawls's views on public goods. On the one hand, he endorses an anti-perfectionism which makes it impossible for the state to deliver any public goods unless everyone in the polity assents to this. The 'exchange branch' in his theory can only work on the basis of unanimity. In any polity of some size, there will always be some people who will disagree and block agreement, so that no public goods will be delivered (Rawls 1999, 249–51). On the other hand, Rawls as we saw endorses the economic theory of public goods which does not require such unanimity if overall welfare is maximised by delivering the public good (Rawls 1999, 235–36). Finally, he endorses democratic decision-making as decisive, which entails commitment to a simple majority criterion as the hallmark of what a just society would do about public goods (Rawls 1999, 313–18). Thus Rawls is torn in different directions. He embraces three different positions, two substantive ones (anti-perfectionism and utilitarianism/welfarism) and one procedural position (democratic majoritarianism). It seems to me that Rawls, in the face of the deep disagreement between his anti-perfectionism and economic theory's utilitarianism, cannot retreat to proceduralism. His theory of justice must say more about the just criteria for providing public goods (for a more detailed analysis see Claassen 2013, 287). Similar conflicts can be shown, I believe, between the utilitarian assumptions underlying other categories of market failure and Rawls's (or indeed any non-utilitarian) theory of justice.

A theory of justice must say more about the principles for regulating markets and cannot leave this to democratic decision-making; at least, it cannot do so in the sense mentioned earlier, in which we strive for a reasonable demarcation of which parts of political decisions require fundamental reflection and can be meaningfully treated philosophically, and which parts rely so much on empirical detail that they must be left to more specifically located decision-makers. Theorizing the normative criteria for regulation should be part of theorizing justice. And given the influence of the theory of market failure, this is certainly the case for those who do not want to leave economic theorizing to utilitarians. Justice should not be narrowed down to 'distributive justice', if the latter is meant as only making pronouncements about the redistributive function of government (which corrects market-based income and wealth distributions ex post). The provider and the regulatory roles of government are just as much part of the basic structure. Justice should be about all of these roles of government.[1]

THE MARKET AND ITS LIMITS

One may have wondered whether, if we are looking for a philosophically substantiated regulation theory, we have been looking in the wrong place. After all there has been, over the last decades, a debate in moral philosophy about the market and the moral limits to commodification. This debate was sparked by Michael Walzer's seminal contribution in *Spheres of Justice* (Walzer 1983), arguing that some goods should not be bought and sold. For a variety of moral reasons, these should be 'blocked exchanges' (Andre 1995). For Walzer this was based on a differentiation of social spheres, each sphere characterized by its own appropriate distributive principle. Other philosophers have defended the same line of argument in more detail than Walzer did, each arguing that some things should be left out of the reach of the market. Thus Elizabeth Anderson argued for sphere differentiation on the basis of a theory about different proper modes of valuation for different goods (1993). Margaret Radin argued for a theory of market-inalienabilities for those items which are personal, non-fungible property (1996). Debra Satz proposed an egalitarian theory concerned with the harmful effects of markets on the equal standing of agents (2010). Michael Sandel defended a loosely civic republican view of putting limits to markets (Sandel 2012).

These theories are animated by a worry that markets will spread everywhere, invading domains of life where other than commercial values should reign. This kind of theorizing tends to promote a dichotomous scheme in which some goods are sheltered in non-market-domains while other goods are left completely to market forces. For those goods left to the market, these theories do not present normative concerns to limit the 'deepness' of marketization itself. Implicitly, this playing field is left to the existing economic theory of market failure. To be sure, this is *not* a necessary consequence of these theories. There is nothing incoherent about acknowledging *both* that some goods should be off the market *and* that other goods can be on the market but should be subject to further restrictions. Sometimes it has been explicitly acknowledged that commodification of a good itself can be incomplete (Radin 1996) and that spheres can overlap (Anderson 1999). However, this theoretical recognition never led to a theory of market regulation. I would like to suggest that this did not happen because the discussion is structured by a narrow definition of what 'commodification' (or marketization) is. To open up the possibility for a moral theory of market regulation requires a reconceptualization.

The institutional set-up of society as consisting of different social spheres, or as I would prefer to say, different socio-economic exchange mechanisms, suggests that a good can be commodified in three ways (Claassen 2009, 427–28). First, a good which has previously not been subject to the market can become marketized. Call this *market creation*. For example, a government can legalize a new market (say, for kidneys) which was previously prohibited, where the good was either not exchanged at all or subject to a different exchange mechanism (such as gift exchange). This is the traditional meaning of 'commodification'. However, there are two further meanings. Second, a good which is already subject to market exchange can become more fully commodified when restricting regulations are removed. This happens, for example, when governments lift constraints such as quota, restrictive opening hours, certification requirements, and so on. Call this *market deepening*. Finally, when a good has simultaneously been subject to both market mechanisms and one or more non-market mechanisms, the market may become relatively more dominant. This happens, for example, when more viewers start to watch commercial television and fewer of them watch publicly funded television (a different exchange mechanism), so that the latter loses audience share to the former. Call this *market enlargement*.

Using this tripartite scheme shows how worries about commodification might stretch beyond worries about the creation of new markets that should remain blocked. (In the legal regulation literature, prohibitions are one possible means [or technique] of regulation, thus the first category is subsumed under the second one.) If we accept this extension of the commodification concept the question of market regulation comes into the reach of moral theory just as much as the question of market blocking. Regulation may serve to prevent market deepening or market enlargement. This raises two follow-up questions.

First, which moral criteria are going to be proposed? One option is to use different criteria for judging cases of all three types, while the other option is to use the same criteria. I see no barriers to using the same criteria. In principle we could try to extend all the existing commodification theories to market regulation. This would parallel the move that has been made in economics with the rise of institutional economics, which uses the same utilitarian theory for questions of market regulation and for choices between market and non-market mechanisms (Williamson 1985).[2] Here I will not argue in favour of one specific commodification theory, but it seems to me essential, for whichever theory one is prepared to defend, that it is coherent over all three instances of commodification. For only then will such a theory be a serious contender against the economic theory of market failure.

Second, should such a theory start from a (non-utilitarian) theory of *market* failure? In a sense it is strange that the existing theories of regulation do so. For at first glance they present themselves as about the regulation of the private sphere as a whole. But the private sphere is much larger than the market; for example, it also includes regulation of what we do with our own bodies (Arnold 2009, 105–114). Even when we confine ourselves to external objects that can be owned and exchanged, we have seen that there are private non-market exchange mechanisms (such as voluntary gift exchanges). So it seems arbitrary for a theory of regulation to start from the market as a privileged social arrangement and then argue that regulation is justified only when the market fails. One could just as well wonder why we do not start from gift exchange as our favoured mechanism and build a theory of *gift failure* to demonstrate cases where markets might be preferable to gifts.

Ideally a theory of regulation applies its normative principles to two questions: (1) which exchange mechanism should be chosen for a given good in the first place as the best one; and (2) whether that exchange mechanism should be surrounded by additional restrictions (regulations). For such a theory there is no use in starting from the market as a favoured exchange mechanism. Moreover, these two tasks are interrelated. In decisions about privatization of public services, for example, it is very important how a service is privatized, in other words, to which regulations it will be subject when privatized. For many politicians and citizens, a decision to privatize (i.e., a transfer from the public to the market exchange mechanism) will itself be acceptable only when the right regulations are guaranteed. The acceptability of privatization thus is a package deal. The question of blocking or creating markets (the original commodification question) cannot even be answered without considering how markets would be regulated when created.

The best way of proceeding, then, seems to be with a comparative institutional analysis which 'starts from nowhere' in the sense that it does not have the market or any other exchange mechanism as a default. We simply consider which institutional arrangement (exchange mechanism-cum-regulation) would best satisfy the given set of normative principles. However, this exercise itself needs be decomposed into a separate consideration of how each exchange mechanism would perform, only then to compare the results for different mechanisms in a second step. A (non-utilitarian) theory of market failure is a necessary component of such an exercise. It teaches us what the potential of the market is to maximise a given set of normative criteria with respect to a specific good (see also section 5).

LIBERALISM AND REGULATION: THE QUESTION OF PROPERTY

Up to this point, I have not directly argued why we should want a *non-utilitarian* theory of regulation. I have used the authority of Rawls to suggest we might do so, but even if many political philosophers are non-utilitarian, this will not convince a single economist. Economists, like other citizens of Western societies, do have strong liberal commitments. Liberal political theory is a broad camp, ranging from left-wing to right-wing variations. Given that it encompasses so much of the political field, a consideration of what liberal political theory would say about regulation seems appropriate. Happily, liberal theorists have considered the regulation question, namely in the guise of their theorizing about the legitimacy of private property. Relying on work by others (Arnold 2009; Freeman 2011; Tomasi 2012), I will present an overview of the three main families of liberal theory on the regulation of property. This reconstruction serves to identify coherent positions on regulation, despite the fact that specific authors will not always fall neatly into one of these camps. I will use three levels of analysis, loosely paralleling Rawls's first three stages of his four-stage sequence (see table 9.1).

At the legislative level the three theories defend different attitudes towards the acceptability of regulation. Libertarians reject both economic and social regulation, because they believe in the market as a free and spontaneous order, where agents can act as they see fit. Classical liberals only defend economic regulation. While they share libertarians' positive evaluation of the market, they also acknowledge that freely acting individuals sometimes are unable or unwilling to guarantee a well-functioning market. Government intervention is then needed to help individuals to secure this goal. Modern liberals defend both economic and social regulation. In contrast to the other two, modern liberals do not start from an *a priori* positive evaluation of the market, but from certain social values. They recognize that a well-functioning market may contribute to these values (support for economic regulation)

Table 9.1.

	Modern liberals	Classical liberals	Libertarians
Market regulation (legislative level)	Social and economic regulation	Economic regulation	none
Basic rights (constitutional level)	Civil, political rights (or: and economic and social rights)	Civil, political, and economic rights	Economic rights
Moral theory (level of justification)	My proposal (section 5): autonomous agency	Natural rights theory, utilitarianism.	Natural rights theory (possibly others)

but when even a well-functioning market would offset these values they do not hesitate to intervene to adjust its outcomes (support for social regulation).

These positions can be related to different stances at the constitutional level. Liberalism is characterized by its commitment to individual freedom as a superior value and also by an institutional commitment to protect individual freedom through a constitutionally guaranteed set of individual basic rights against government that cannot easily be overridden by non-rights considerations. The basic status of any right is meant to protect some individual interest against a political majority's ideas about the common good. There are four possible categories of rights that could be basic: civil rights (like freedom of expression or religion), political rights (like right to vote and stand for office), economic rights, and social rights. Economic rights here refer to the bundle of rights that come with private property, which includes freedom of contract, that is the ability to alienate one's property.

Libertarians only recognize economic rights as basic. They give property an absolute status and subsume civil and political rights under private property rights (Narveson 2001: 66). This gives their position a special, some would even argue illiberal outlook (Freeman 2001, 114–15, 123–31). Libertarians cannot accept any form of regulation, as market agents' free decisions should be decisive over all market transactions. For example, they often do not accept anti-trust legislation, and this is consistent from their viewpoint. Respect for individual property rights implies respecting the exercise of these rights in Pareto-inferior ways. Libertarians choose to protect these rights and have to accept higher prices and lower output that are the typical result of cartels or monopoly (Freeman 2001, 137; Vanberg 1999, 232). The deeper reason for this, on a third and final level, seems to be that libertarians most often (but not always) rely on a natural rights justification to explain the absolute status they accord to property rights. Individuals in a state of nature are said to have property rights 'by nature' (Freeman 2001, 125; Nozick 1974, 118).

Classical and modern liberals differ from libertarians in treating individuals' civil and political rights as basic. In addition, classical liberals give economic rights the same basic status and endorse a freedom defence of markets similar to what one finds in libertarian authors. Because of their insistence on economic rights protecting core economic freedoms, they are (like libertarians) suspicious about social objectives overriding these rights. However, unlike libertarians, classical liberals do accept the economic theory of market failure. As Freeman put it:

> liberals generally, including classical liberals, maintain that, when markets break down due to monopolistic concentration of market power, or when markets are incapable of adequately supplying goods or services that are important to individuals' independence and well-being, it is government's role to

> intervene and address such 'externalities' or 'neighbourhood effects' by restoring competition and providing for these 'public goods'. (Freeman 2011, 23)

Thus, classical liberals are committed both to market-based freedoms (economic rights) and to welfare-maximising policies that can come into conflict with these freedoms.[3] The latter implies a commitment to utilitarianism, and this commitment also helps to explain classical liberals' rejection of social regulation. Markets are to function according to individual preferences. Social regulations substitute a collective judgment for these preferences and that makes them unacceptable to the (preference) utilitarian. While this rejection of social regulation is consistent with their acceptance of economic regulation (both can be explained by utilitarianism), the problem for classical liberals is how to reconcile their utilitarianism on these issues with their strong (libertarian-style) endorsement of economic freedoms.

Modern liberals are often presented as differing from classical liberals because they give economic rights a lower, non-basic status (Arnold 2009, 17; Freeman 2011, 19–20; Tomasi 2012, 67). Because they do not accord basic status to economic rights, they can defend interventions with these rights 'for the common good', both of an economic and of a social nature. However, this defence of economic and social regulation can also be construed (as it has, in many constitutional traditions) as based on an acceptance of *both* economic *and* social rights as basic rights. Social objectives then become themselves part of the basic rights package, so that trade-offs between economic and social goals become trade-offs between economic and social rights. Whichever of these two constructions one prefers, in essence for the modern liberal economic freedoms are as important as certain social objectives (like a basic right to an adequate standard of living, or health care and education) and certain economic objectives (welfare-maximising markets). Either this equivalence is expressed by treating both as basic rights or by treating neither as such.

There is no accepted normative theory backing up modern liberals' defense of economic and social regulation. Modern liberals do not have the same problem classical liberals have because, while they do accept economic regulation (i.e., utilitarianism), they do not accept economic rights (i.e., market freedom) as basic (or when they do, social rights have the same basic status). They do face an inconsistency, however, between their preference satisfaction utilitarianism and their defence of social regulation. This is so because social regulation is based on a critique of the unquestioning status of individual preferences in utilitarianism. We saw that there are broadly two categories of social regulation: paternalist and equity-based regulations. Paternalist regulations presuppose that individuals' own (deformed or misguided) preferences are not a reliable guide of what will bring them well-being. Equity-based regulations presuppose that one should not (always) aggregate utility across persons and maximise overall utility. So what can explain the modern liberal's simultaneous commitments to economic freedom, utility, and non-utility considerations?

In conclusion, both positions on regulation require a deeper explanation to make them consistent. The utilitarian character of the economic theory of market failure causes trouble for classical liberals, because it is in tension with unqualified economic freedoms (the libertarians' only commitment), and it causes trouble for modern liberals since it is in tension with socially motivated regulations. Is there an explanation that can resolve these tensions?

AUTONOMOUS AGENCY IN MARKETS

The explanation I will propose is that modern and classical liberals are both trying to do justice, in different ways, to the core liberal value of *autonomous agency*. Moreover, I will suggest that this has peculiar implication for modern liberals: they will have to abandon their utilitarian analysis of market failure and replace it with an agency-based analysis of market failure.

Take classical liberals first. Why are they committed to the economic theory of market failure and its underlying preference utilitarianism? My speculation is that this is because they think that the expression of individual preferences in a market context is worthy of respect. Subjective preferences have normative authority. Classical liberals do not value a utility-maximising overall state of affairs as intrinsically valuable. This would make a fetish of the value of states of affairs over the value of persons. Since only persons have value in themselves (as any liberal would claim), their voluntarily expressed preferences in a free market count for something. This is why classical liberals cannot embrace an objective-value variant of utilitarianism, where happiness or well-being (say, measured scientifically) instead of subjective preferences would be the basis for regulation. For this would quickly lead to paternalist legislation which claims to know better about citizens' well-being. The classical liberal cannot accept this critique of subjective preferences, because he takes the person expressing these preferences as having superior value.

This liberal defence of preference utilitarian considerations in a market context is consistent with the classical liberal's equally important commitment to economic freedoms. For these freedoms to hold and exchange private property at will are the legal guarantees that allow an autonomous agent to act upon his subjective preferences. Again, the authority of the individual person as he expresses his self-conception (in his preferences) is behind the defence of these basic economic freedoms. The difficulty, for the classical liberal, is that, in the market, the free expression of preferences of some will come into conflict with that of others. Thus, in the case of a cartel, the preferences of consumers cannot be satisfied because producers (who outsmart the consumers by colluding) win the conflict. The classical liberal must then decide whose preferences have *more* authority. Unlike the libertarian, a classical liberal cannot be satisfied by deciding this conflict *a priori* by declaring economic freedom sacrosanct. Instead, he decides to give everyone's preferences equal weight and see whether it is possible to have as much preference-satisfaction as possible. The machinery of the economic theory of market failure is brought into play as a way of solving conflicts between autonomous agents whose preferences deserve equal respect, that is, as a way of reconciling the negative freedom of one agent with that of others.

All of this presupposes, and this is the hallmark of the classical liberal's *way* of respecting autonomous agency, that all participants in the economy are already (sufficiently) respect-worthy persons. Autonomous agency, for the classical liberal, is a postulate, something that is assumed to be present in persons. The modern liberal, by contrast, sees autonomous agency as something that may or may not be present. Autonomous agency is something that needs to be achieved in a social context. This achievement requires hard work of the person and society surrounding her, to develop her rational and other capacities to make informed decisions and act upon them; hence the modern liberal's commitment to paternalist and equity-based regulations. To the extent that market participants are not automatically autonomous agents, (1) their preferences have no inherent authority, and (2) regulation is required to ensure that they become such agents whose preferences can come to have authority. Many paternalist regulations help them to acquire such skills or information, or redress imbalances in power in the market (e.g., bargaining between employees and employers) so that each can develop sufficient agency vis-à-vis others.

This different way of respecting autonomous agency also explains modern liberals' attachment to economic regulation and economic freedoms. For just like the classical liberal, the modern liberal believes that *to the extent* that persons have autonomous agency, their preferences should be respected. But in contrast to the classical liberal, I would argue that the modern liberal makes a mistake if she accepts the utilitarian analysis of market failure. For the classical liberal, as we saw, accepted market failure theory as part of his respect for (as his postulate goes) already well-formed agency and preferences. The modern liberal, however, should suspect that in many cases of market failure, what may be at stake is *lacking agency on the part of some participants, or lack of equality of agency between participants*. Thus, public goods cases for him are cases not where one seeks to use a government mechanism to satisfy preferences that the market cannot satisfy on its own. They are cases where government may deliver goods that are necessary conditions of autonomous agency, which the market cannot deliver (Claassen

2013). Negative externalities may be harms to others outside of the market which diminish the agency of those who are harmed (Claassen 2016). Collusive agreements between producers may serve not to maximise their profits to the detriment of consumer welfare, but to protect agency interests of third parties (Claassen and Gerbrandy 2016). Information asymmetries may be caused by insufficient agency of some market participants. In all such cases the modern liberal has to weigh agency interests, making trade-offs between different (groups of) persons, but these are now trade-offs in terms of agency development, not preference satisfaction.

As a consequence, social and economic regulation should merge. The traditional categories of market failure should only have a heuristic value for the modern liberal. They point to situations where government regulation may be necessary to *protect the equal agency-development of all participants*. The same thing is true for paternalist and equity-based regulations. Paternalism is better described as a concern for the constitution of an individual's future agency. Just as a liberal is prepared to prohibit voluntary enslavement because she cares for the person's freedom tomorrow (Freeman 2001, 110–13), so she is prepared to restrict her market-based freedom because she cares for her future agency. Similarly, distributive concerns are often concerns about the extent to which agents have effective agency vis-à-vis others within the market. Differences in wealth are not problematic per se, but they are judged problematic where they upset this equality of agency.

When social and economic regulation are unified on this basis (as a concern for agency-development), what remains is a conflict between this commitment to develop everyone's agency and the commitment to respect the exercise of agency once developed (economic freedoms). For the modern liberal does aim to respect the negative economic freedom of agents, if and where they are sufficiently autonomous. In this free space, agents can act as maximisers of their own preferences, if they so choose. Thus the modern liberal's principle of justice is double-edged: to *protect the equal agency-development and respect the equal agency-exercise of all participants*. The tension between these two parts is irreducible—it leads to a tension between demands for regulation in the name of agency-development and demands for deregulation in the name of respect for agency-exercise. The borderline is determined, amongst other things, by one's concrete view of agency (which capabilities does it include?) one's aspirations (how much agency-development is taken to be enough? Where does one put the threshold?) and one's judgments in applying these norms (how much agency have these participants developed?).

Answering these questions requires much more theoretical work. What I have attempted to show is that the standard juxtaposition of economic and social regulation in handbooks of regulation can be found back in modern liberal political theory. However, once we look at the liberal roots of accepting both economic freedoms and economic regulation and social regulation, the only way I can see of unifying this multiplicity of commitments is to construct it as being animated and justified in the end by a concern for the opportunities for citizens to exercise effective autonomous agency in the economic sphere. This is my first conclusion.

The second one is that this in turn requires us to reconceptualise the economic theory of market failure that underlies economic regulation; and see the traditional categories of market failure as instances in which what is at stake is not so much a government regulating to maximise subjective preferences where citizens cannot do so themselves, but a government regulating to protect and respect the equal agency of all parties involved. This requires a rethinking of each of these categories that is only in its infancy and should be the program of much more work.

NOTES

1. This increased space for theorizing does not take away the fact that in the end, *every* aspect of political decisions about regulation (theoretical and applied) should be left to democratic organs; or at least so a theory of justice would say which points to democracy as what justice requires in the area of decision-making. See Claassen 2011.

2. One can even extend this to a third question, about the moral evaluation of actions *within* the market. For example, Heath defends a market failure approach to business ethics (Heath 2014).

3. Maybe even libertarians cannot rely on freedom considerations alone, as (Cohen 1995) argued with respect to Nozick's reliance on utilitarian considerations. Freeman argues that 'neoliberals' such as Friedman and Hayek are predominantly utilitarians (Freeman 2011, 34–35).

REFERENCES

Anderson, Elizabeth. 1993. *Value in Ethics and Economics*. Cambridge Massachusetts: Harvard University Press.

———. 1999. "Contested Commodities (Book Review)." *Ethics* 109: 914–17.

Andre, Judith. 1995. "Blocked Exchanges: A Taxonomy." In *Pluralism, Justice and Equality*, edited by David Miller and Michael Walzer, 171–96. Oxford: Oxford University Press.

Arnold, N. Scott. 2009. *Imposing Values: An Essay on Liberalism and Regulation*. Oxford: Oxford University Press.

Barr, Nicholas. 2004. *Economics of the Welfare State*. Fourth edition. Oxford: Oxford University Press.

Bator, Francis M. 1958. "The Anatomy of Market Failure." *Quarterly Journal of Economics* 72 (3): 351–79.

Bozeman, Barry. 2002. "Public-Value Failure: When Efficient Markets May Not Do." *Public Administration Review* 62 (2): 145–61.

Braithwaite, John. 2008. *Regulatory Capitalism*. Cheltenham, UK: Edward Elgar.

Claassen, Rutger. 2009. "Institutional Pluralism and the Limits of the Market." *Politics, Philosophy, and Economics* 8 (4): 420–47.

———. 2011. "Making Capability Lists. Philosophy versus Democracy." *Political Studies* 59 (3): 491–508.

———. 2013. "Public Goods, Mutual Benefits, and Majority Rule." *Journal of Social Philosophy* 44 (3): 270–90.
———. 2016. "Externalities as a Basis for Regulation: A Philosophical View." *Journal of Institutional Economics*, forthcoming.
Claassen, Rutger, and Anna Gerbrandy. 2016. "Rethinking Competition Law: From a Consumer Welfare to a Capability Approach." *Utrecht Law Review* 12 (1): 1–15.
Cohen, G.A. 1995. *Self-Ownership, Freedom and Equality*. Cambridge: Cambridge University Press.
Coleman, Jules. 1985. "Market Contractarianism and the Unanimity Rule." *Social Philosophy and Policy* 2 (2): 69–114.
Cowen, Tyler. 1988. "Public Goods and Externalities: Old and New Perspectives." In *The Theory of Market Failure: A Critical Examination*, edited by Tylor Cowen, 1–26. Fairfax, VA: George Mason University Press.
Dietsch, Peter. 2010. "The Market, Competition, and Equality." *Philosophy, Politics, and Economics* 9 (2): 213–44.
Feintuck, Mike. 2010. "Regulatory Rationales beyond the Economic: In Search of the Public Interest." In *The Oxford Handbook of Regulation*, edited by Robert Baldwin, Martin Cave, and Martin Lodge, 39–63. Oxford: Oxford University Press.
Freeman, Samuel. 2001. "Illiberal Libertarians: Why Libertarianism Is Not a Liberal View." *Philosophy & Public Affairs* 30 (2): 105–51.
———. 2011. "Capitalism in the Classical and High Liberal Traditions." *Social Philosophy & Policy* 28 (2): 19–55.
Gauthier, David. 1986. *Morals by Agreement*. Oxford: Clarendon Press.
Heath, Joseph. 2014. *Morality, Competition and the Firm: The Market Failures Approach to Business Ethics*. Oxford: Oxford University Press.
Hertog, Johan Den. 1999. "General Theories of Regulation." *Encyclopedia of Law and Economics*, 223–70. Cheltenham: Edward Elgar.
Jordana, Jacint, and David Levi-Faur. 2005. *The Politics of Regulation: Institutions and Regulatory Reforms for the Age of Governance*. Cheltenham: Edward Elgar.
Moran, Michael. 2002. "Understanding the Regulatory State." *British Journal of Political Science* 32: 391–413.
Morgan, Brownen, and Karen Yeung. 2007. *An Introduction to Law and Regulation*. Cambridge: Cambridge University Press.
Narveson, Jan. 2001. *The Libertarian Idea*, Ontario: Broadview Press.
Nozick, Robert. 1974. *Anarchy, State, and Utopia*. Oxford: Blackwell Publishing.
Ogus, Anthony. 2004. *Regulation: Legal Form and Economic Theory*. Oxford: Hart Publishing.
Prosser, Tony. 2006. "Regulation and Social Solidarity." *Journal of Law and Society* 33 (3): 364–87.
Radin, Margaret. 1996. *Contested Commodities: The Trouble with Trade in Sex, Children, Body Parts, and Other Things*. Cambridge, MA: Harvard University Press.
Rawls, John. 1999. *A Theory of Justice*. Revised edition. Oxford: Oxford University Press.
Sandel, Michael. 2012. *What Money Can't Buy: The Moral Limits of Markets*. London: Allen Lane.
Satz, Debra. 2010. *Why Some Things Should Not Be for Sale: The Moral Limits of Markets*. New York: Oxford University Press.
Soule, Edward. 2003. *Morality & Markets: The Ethics of Government Regulation*. Lanham, MD: Rowman & Littlefield.
Stewart, Richard. 1982. "Regulation in a Liberal State." *Yale Law Journal* 92: 1537–90.
Stiglitz, Joseph. 2009. "Government Failure vs. Market Failure: Principles of Regulation." In *Government and Markets: Toward a New Theory of Regulation*, edited by Edward Balleisen and David Moss, 13–51. New York: Cambridge University Press.
Sunstein, Cass. 1990. *After the Rights Revolution: Reconceiving the Regulatory State*. Cambridge, MA: Harvard University Press.
Tomasi, John. 2012. *Free Market Fairness*. Princeton: Princeton University Press.

Trebilcock, Michael. 1993. *The Limits of Freedom of Contract*. London: Harvard University Press.

Vanberg, Viktor. 1999. "Markets and Regulation: On The Contrast between Free-Market Liberalism and Constitutional Liberalism." *Constitutional Political Economy* 10: 219–43.

Walzer, Michael. 1983. *Spheres of Justice: A Defense of Pluralism and Equality*. New York: Basic Books.

Williamson, Oliver. 1985. *The Economic Institutions of Capitalism*. New York: Free Press.

Chapter Ten

The Recognition Gap

Why Labels Matter in Human Rights Protection

Stacy J. Kosko

One way to understand human rights is as guarantors of certain broad principles of justice, principles that are then codified in specific norms and laws.[1] Much discussion about the protection of human rights centres on whether these laws are adequately specified and implemented to ensure that the principles of justice in question are enjoyed by all. When they are not, what is commonly called a 'protection gap' arises. A human rights 'protection gap' is a space in which protections for one or more human rights, or classes of rights, are absent, inadequate, inapplicable, or under-enforced, leaving the rights holder susceptible to the very sort of injuries against which human rights laws are meant to protect. To the extent that human rights laws are meant as expressions of our most fundamental principles of justice, we must be relentless in our efforts to identify and close this protection gap wherever possible. Doing so, however, requires a more nuanced understanding of the protection gap, one that breaks it down into its several constituent forms.

In this chapter, I will first address what are commonly called the 'implementation' and 'normative' gaps, the kinds of failures of justice that most have in mind when referring to a 'human rights protection gap'. Then, I will propose and explore what I call the 'recognition gap' by examining some particularities regarding the situation of ethnocultural minorities (including indigenous peoples) under international law, especially in Europe. I aim to demonstrate that the degree to which—and ways in which—different ethnic minority and indigenous groups are protected in international human rights law is not necessarily in direct response to their particular vulnerabilities, that is, to the challenges they face in enjoying the principles of justice that the international human rights system demands be upheld for every human being. Rather, their protection is heavily dependent upon the label that the government under which they live has applied to them. That is, certain specialised forms of protection are predicated upon the highly politicised practice of categorising different 'types' of minorities and applying those different protections accordingly, through recognition as, for example, national minorities or indigenous peoples. This practice gives rise to a sort of legal typology of minorities with the result that different groups with very similar vulnerabilities may be protected differently by the same law.

The failure of justice captured by the recognition gap is of an altogether different nature than the more commonly acknowledged gaps. It interposes the politics of recognition between the principles of justice in which human rights laws are grounded and the application of existing human rights laws to some of society's most vulnerable groups. The recognition gap is one problem of protection that has yet to be clearly articulated in the literature and yet, as I will aim to demonstrate, at risk of falling into it are many members of Europe's largest, poorest, and fastest-growing minority: the Roma. The 'Roma' are a diverse people. There is controversy over the term but I follow convention by including under this umbrella Roma, Sinti, Ashkali, and others. Most official estimates put Europe's Roma population at around ten to twelve million, but many estimates are much higher.

PROTECTION GAPS

The idea of a 'protection gap' has been with us for decades. It began to show up in the 1980s with respect to workers' rights to safe labour conditions (Kasperson and Lundblad 1982). Then following the massive humanitarian crises of the 1990s it took off in discussions of the particular vulnerabilities of displaced persons and persons affected by conflict (Clarance 1997; Guest and Bouchet-Saulnier 1997; Türk and Dowd 2014). It was not until well into the twenty-first century that we began to see the term applied to other areas of human rights. The idea has been much elaborated since, although the conversation in both the practice and scholarly communities remains largely focused on displaced and stateless persons and irregular migrants. While the term is used with some frequency in discussions of other sorts of human rights (for example see Haglund and Stryker [2015] and AWID [2015]), there is little emphasis on understanding the source and nature of the protection gap itself outside of its application to migrants' rights. But invoking the general idea of a protection gap is only helpful insofar as it alerts us to a problem. The diagnosis of a generic 'gap' does not help us to identify its sources or seek solutions. However, we can break the general idea down into several specific kinds of gaps. Scholars and practitioners have lately offered us at least a half a dozen terms in an effort to distinguish between them.

The most commonly discussed problem is what is often referred to as an 'implementation gap'. Michael Freeman argues that 'the dominant human-rights problem in the contemporary world is the gap between human-rights ideals and law, on the one hand, and the reality of gross human-rights violations, on the other' (Freeman 2011, 158). This kind of gap arises where international laws and norms exist to address the vulnerabilities of certain groups, but those laws are not enforced or the norms are not implemented in domestic policies and legislation. Some refer to this same problem as a 'compliance gap' (Hafner-Burton and Tsutsui 2005), while still others use descriptive phrases such as 'the gap between international human rights principles and practices' (Clark 2001, 4) or between 'de jure and de facto' protection (Landman 2005, 34). This appears to be the kind of gap that dominates the academic literature and many advocacy efforts and is the kind of failure of justice that most have in mind when referring to a 'human rights protection gap'. David P. Forsythe describes this as 'the enormous gap between legal theory and political behaviour, as public authorities both endorsed human rights standards and systematically violated—or failed to correct violations of—the newly emerging norms' (Forsythe 2012, 6). This type of gap is generated by lack of political will, inadequate resources for enforcement, poverty, and other forms of structural injustice. But some other types of protection gaps arise because of the way the human rights system itself is structured and has evolved.

The international human rights system rests on a complex and interlocking web of courts, supervisory bodies, and multilateral treaties going back to the League of Nations a century ago. This international legal framework complements legal protections at the national and sub-national level. A 'normative gap' arises as a result of this structure, dependent as it is at the international level on treaty making. It arises when no legal human rights standards exist to address the vulnerability or harmful practice in question. A 'normative gap exists where persistent acts and circumstances depriving a person or people of their dignity are not provided for in existing human rights law' (Murphy 2012, 2). To put this problem in another way, imagine a group with a certain set of vulnerabilities. In some cases, a variety of protections exist that pertain to this group, but they don't address some of their particular vulnerabilities. This gap arises because the broadly stated, highly inclusive nature of most human rights laws is not finely tuned enough to the *very* particular vulnerabilities that certain groups might face. This is so even if the threats they confront are common, serious, and remediable (in Henry Shue's terms). Examples include persons with disabilities; older persons; and lesbian, gay, bisexual, transgender, and intersex (LGBTI) persons.

Another problem of protection, one that is even less acknowledged, is what I call the 'recognition gap'. We might again imagine a group with this same set of vulnerabilities. Imagine now that protections (legal norms) *do* exist to address this set of vulnerabilities, but they do not apply to this group. This can happen either 1) when a group (especially a large and diverse one comprised of many sub-groups: 'national minorities', for example, or 'indigenous peoples') that is the target of a particular set of protections is defined by the state in a way that excludes certain groups that share those same vulnerabilities, or 2) when a group seems to fall well within the commonly understood definition of the target population, but the government under which the group lives does not recognise it as part of this target population. It is as if the international human rights system (in the first case), or government body (in the second), is saying: 'You experience these vulnerabilities, and we have a list of rules here that is supposed to help reduce those vulnerabilities and protect your dignity, but we do not think that the label fits you quite right, so these laws do not apply to you'. This amounts to a denial of what Hannah Arendt famously calls 'the right to have rights'. This is fundamentally a structural (legal) problem, although sometimes it is one of *interpretation* of the law.

The only reference I have found in the literature to anything like the recognition gap is in a 2006 report by the International Council on Human Rights Policy. The authors call it an 'application gap', a term that is helpful in understanding the critical idea that norms exist but are not *applied* to particular, similar cases. 'An "application gap" exists when an international instrument applies to a specific situation or a category of people, but does not apply to similar cases"' (International Council on Human Rights Policy 2006, 8). The authors go on to illustrate this gap with respect to the problem of forced disappearance, but the report says little more about the origin or nature of this particular type of gap. The problem, however, is considerably more complex—and political—than the term 'application' suggests. The recognition gap, at least with respect to minority groups, arises in part from the current system of categorising different 'types' of minorities, formally *recognising* certain groups as falling within the specified category (sometimes irrespective of what the group members themselves might think), and applying different protections accordingly. It receives considerably less attention than the implementation gap, or even than the normative gap.

The recognition gap, however, is different in important ways from both the implementation and normative gaps. Here is an example: a group very much in today's media is the Rohingya of Burma (Myanmar), a Muslim minority rendered officially stateless by government decree, whom Amnesty International has called 'the most persecuted refugees in the word' (Hamling 2014). With no official recognition as an ethnic group, and a 1982 'Citizenship Law' that rendered them stateless, 'their rights to study, work, travel, marry, practise their religion and access health services are severely restricted' (Amnesty International 2015). However, having been officially denied citizenship of their home country (and all others), the Rohingya *do* fall under the 1954 UN Convention on the Reduction of Statelessness. And when they flee Burma and find their way to their neighbours' shores, they fall under the 1951 Refugee Convention. The countries to which they are fleeing have been reluctant to honour their obligations under international law (an implementation gap), but the laws are there (there is no normative gap) and there is little disagreement about whether the Rohingya count as stateless persons and/or refugees (there is no recognition gap).

This example is complicated by the fact that Thailand and Malaysia, two major destination countries for the Rohingya, are not signatories to the Refugee Convention, which some would say make this a case of a normative gap. But Türk and Dowd point out that much of the contents of the Convention including, crucially for the Rohingya, the principle of *non-refoulement*, have gained the status of international customary law. They instead call this an 'application gap', in reference to the 'less than universal application' of the Convention (Türk and Dowd 2014).

There is a larger nether-category of individuals, however, who share many of the same vulnerabilities as the Rohingya, but do not fall neatly under the either of these Conventions. As Carol A. Batchelor points out, there are some who can technically be classified neither as a refugee nor as a stateless person, and thus fall into a gap between the international standards targeting both of these, but nevertheless be without 'the usual attributes of an effective nationality' (Batchelor 1995, 12). What she is describing is, precisely, the recognition gap. Her examples include the Jews under the laws of the Third Reich and 'boat people' in transit through Hong Kong (Batchelor 1995, 232–33). But the reach of the recognition gap goes far beyond the effectively stateless. The recognition gap can affect groups of people who are very similar to, but lack recognition as, nationals (citizens) of a particular state, or national minorities, or indigenous persons, or refugees, thus falling outside the international standards relevant for these groups. In section 3 I will discuss the distinction between several types of minorities and the implications of this system of classification for the protection and promotion of human rights.

Before I move to this legal typology of minorities, however, let me return to the question of distinguishing between the recognition gap and other types of gaps. First, the recognition gap is not just another expression of the implementation gap. The duty-bearer in question will point out that the seemingly relevant existing norms do not apply to the group in question, thus no derogation of duty has occurred; there is nothing to implement. So is the recognition gap not then just another form of the normative gap? Is it not the case that if a group is lacking protection in the form of international human rights treaties, then we can say that that lack of relevant (or sufficient) norms is enough to diagnose a normative gap and get on with agitating to draft one? No. It *is* true that normative and recognition gaps often come together, as in the example of lesbian, gay, bisexual, transgender, and intersex (LGBTI) persons in many countries. There is currently no international convention on the rights of LGBTI persons (a normative gap), but there are also many states that deny the existence of such persons on their territories in the first place. Mayor Anatoly Pakhomov of Sochi, Russia, home to the 2014 Winter Olympics, famously told the BBC's Panorama program: 'We do not have [LGBTI persons] in our city' (CBS/Reuters 2014). In September 2007, Iranian president Mahmoud Ahmadinejad was met with a mix of laughter and scorn when he told a crowd at Columbia University: 'In Iran we don't have homosexuals like in your country' (DailyMail.com 2007). This statement is at odds, of course, with the Iranian penal code, under which homosexuality between men is punishable with death.

Not *recognising* the existence of LGBTI persons means not *recognising* their vulnerability as a minority or crimes against them as hate crimes, for example. It often means not taking a stand when their rights are violated. No official recognition as a minority with 'particular disadvantages' (to borrow Kymlicka's term for ethnocultural groups) means no legal recourse when those vulnerabilities are exploited, even if norms already exist to protect those same vulnerabilities (for example, discrimination in employment) in others (Kymlicka 1992, 141). This is a recognition gap. As Navi Pillay, the former UN High Commissioner for Human Rights, makes explicit in her 2011 annual report, recognition is important, *inter alia*, in order for states to enact comprehensive anti-discrimination laws, to investigate all killings or violent crimes against sexual or gender minorities and prosecute such targeted crimes, to update asylum laws to accept sexual orientation and gender identity as targets of persecution, and to prevent the *refoulement* of LGBTI persons fleeing such persecution (Office of the High Commissioner for Human Rights 2011). In addition to opening the door for the drafting of new laws (and thus closing important normative gaps), such recognition will allow LGBTI persons to bring claims under *existing* anti-discrimination and anti-hate laws. Political recognition is powerful.

Such considerations apply also to other groups in need of political recognition, such as ethnocultural minorities, many of whom also suffer at the intersection of a normative gap and a recognition gap (to say nothing of egregious implementation failures). The European Roma are one such group. There is no International Convention on the Rights of Roma, Gypsies, and Travellers, nor are they *recognised* as 'national minorities' by some of the states in which they live, complicating their access to protection under the European Framework Convention for National Minorities (FCNM), an important international standard that offers some much needed protections but that remains out of reach for Roma individuals and groups in some states. It is to the case of European minorities that I now turn.

A 'TYPOLOGY' OF MINORITIES

'Minorities' in Europe are typically divided into one of two large, politically charged categories: immigrants and long-standing 'homeland minorities' (Kymlicka 2007). The degree to which—and ways in which—different minority groups are protected is heavily dependent upon the label that the government under which they live has applied to them. This fact is one reason why indigenous status is often sought by minority groups and sometimes denied by governments. European governments are in varying stages of experimenting with multicultural policies, that is, policies 'designed to provide some level of public recognition, support or accommodation to non-dominant ethnocultural groups' (Kymlicka 2007, 16). But as these are applied to different 'types' of minorities, some are protected differently than others by the same laws and policies.

European governments and human rights organizations have largely concentrated their protection efforts on non-immigrant groups sometimes referred to as 'homeland minorities', 'groups that have been historically settled within a particular part of a country for a long period of time, and as a result of that historic settlement have come to see that part of the country as their historic "homeland"' (Kymlicka 2007, 176). Accommodations for these homeland minorities fall into two legal-political trends: policies aimed at 'indigenous peoples' (who are generally agreed to not exist in most European states under the common understanding of the term but whose protections are the most robust under international law) and 'national minorities'.

The 'homeland minorities' commonly called 'indigenous' or 'first nation' peoples are typically characterised by a distinctive cultural heritage and language; deep, historic, and sometimes spiritual attachment to land (often but not always on which they are currently residing); small numbers relative to the dominant cultural group; self-identification as an indigenous people; and frequently also the experience of marginalization and extreme vulnerability, including agency vulnerability (Cultural Survival 2015; Kosko 2013). These groups are usually understood to be those who were the subjects of colonization, especially in the New World from the fifteenth to the early twentieth centuries. As such, their claims in the international system are framed as ones of justice, identity, territory, and self-determination and the rights they have won carry the strongest forms of protection. This has led some states to resist recognising their indigenous peoples as such, or at least as indigenous in the sense intended by the two main international standards, the 2007 United Nations Declaration on the Rights of Indigenous Peoples and the earlier International Labour Organization Convention concerning Indigenous and Tribal Peoples in Independent Countries (commonly, 'ILO 169'). Russia and Indonesia are just two of the many countries whose policies of recognition (which groups, if any, the state deems 'indigenous') come into direct conflict with indigenous advocacy groups within the state (International Working Group for Indigenous Affairs [IWGIA] 2015). In Russia, for example, of the more than 180 'peoples', only 40 are legally recognised as 'indigenous, small-numbered peoples of the North, Siberia and the Far East'. The 'small-number' limit is 50,000 or fewer members, and Russian law has no word for 'indigenous' without the numerical qualification. Larger, and presumably stronger or more politically powerful, groups such as the Buryat, Komi, and Khakass are too large to 'count' as indigenous peoples. An example of a recognised indigenous people in Russia is the Sámi, who also reside in Scandinavia.

The category of 'national minorities', the other common 'homeland minority' classification besides 'indigenous peoples', encompasses Europe's territorially concentrated national sub-groups and cross-border irredentist groups. These have received weaker forms of minority rights protection than the first group (Kymlicka 2007, 2011). They often frame their claims as ones of identity and nationhood and, sometimes (though rarely accepted), self-determination. To complicate matters, it is ultimately up to governments to decide whether or not a given ethnocultural group constitutes a 'national minority'. This decision has very real consequences for social policy. Examples of recognised national minorities in Europe are the Frisians in Kingdom of the Netherlands, all of the Celtic peoples of the United Kingdom (but not the arguably pre-Celtic Irish Travellers), and Albanians in the Republic of Macedonia.

The third recognised, but most weakly protected, category of minorities is immigrants. Though internationally accepted definitions are few and vague, immigrants are generally understood to be foreign-born individuals residing (legally or not) within a 'host' state, not 'national minorities', whose protections are much more clear, having been codified for specific historical reasons. This group is typically sub-divided into refugees and those economic, social, and otherwise non-asylum-seeking migrants we typically refer to simply as 'immigrants'. The former is a very limited category, the membership in which is defined clearly by law and determined by asylum officers in host countries. The immigrant minority group is relevant to a discussion of multiculturalism and minority rights insofar as they might constitute a large ethnocultural sub-group within a state, but as noted there are few and weak international standards for protecting them *as such* (unless, as stated, they are legal refugees, but then the applicable law is a reflection of their vulnerability as displaced persons and not of their status as a distinct cultural group). Here, I do not engage the question of migrants (or their children, born elsewhere or in the destination country), as they are generally recognised as requiring very different sorts of protections—and for different reasons—than the other two 'homeland minority' groups named above. (Nevertheless, as communities of migrants establish themselves in number and longevity, distinctions—and rights claims—will increasingly blur). Already the current refugee crisis in Europe is playing a profound role in challenging the presumed firewall between these two types of immigrants, with possibly game-changing consequences for both.

Distinguishing between indigenous peoples and national minorities is confusing, highly political, and complicated by a perverse incentive structure that encourages any minority group seeking stronger cultural protections to recast itself as indigenous. Governments, by contrast, have an incentive to limit the class of 'indigenous peoples' as much as possible, lest they have to accept greater autonomy, more substantial subsidies, and more stringent restrictions on land and resource use in areas occupied by the group. Thus, there is a danger that the category to which a given group belongs—and thus the cultural, security, and subsistence protections it receives—are often decided as much by political considerations as by actual vulnerabilities. This is the crux of the problem, and a chief source of the recognition gap. According to Kymlicka:

> International law treats the distinction between indigenous peoples and national minorities as a categorical one, with enormous implications for the legal rights each type of group can claim. In the post-colonial world, however, any attempt to distinguish indigenous people from national minorities on the basis of their relative levels of vulnerability or exclusion can only track differences of degree, not the difference in kind implied by international law. The attempt to preserve such a sharp distinction is not only morally and conceptually unstable, it is also, I suspect, politically unstable. (Kymlicka 2007, 283–84)

For example, the Sámi, an Arctic people who traditionally made their livelihoods through reindeer herding, have been recognised by the Russian Federation as among the 'numerically small' groups subject to special protections (never mind whether these are enforced in practice, an implementation gap), but the Izhma Komi, or Izvatas, another fairly small Arctic group that has traditionally survived through reindeer herding, has received no such recognition and are considered, generically, an ethnic group. In another example, the Irish Travellers are legally recognised by the government of the United Kingdom as an 'ethnic minority', something akin to a national minority, but not territorially concentrated and without the clear protections as would be found in the Framework Convention for the Protection of National Minorities, leaving it up to the UK government to decide what rights such a status confers, while the Irish, Scots, Welsh, and now also Cornish are recognised 'national minorities'. In a third example, the Roma, also not territorially concentrated, are nevertheless explicitly recognised as 'national minorities' by some European governments (Sweden and Macedonia) but not by others, meaning that the Framework Convention may protect the Roma in only some countries, an issue on which I elaborate below.

Despite these broad categories of 'minorities'—or more likely as a result of their vagueness—a substantial protection gap remains. This gap is manifested in all three of the forms I identify above. First, existing laws frequently go ignored, and violations unpunished, an implementation gap. Second, there remain gaps in the international legal norms: treaties not yet drafted or specific rights not yet promulgated, a normative gap. And third, there remain some groups whose particular vulnerabilities make them candidates for certain kinds of protections, but the rights are formulated in such a way—or the target groups defined in such a way—that the rights do not explicitly 'apply' to those groups, thus leaving them unprotected by those laws and policies. Put another way, the governments under which they reside fail to *recognise* them as the 'type' of minority that would warrant protection under a particular protection regime. This is a recognition gap. A highly visible case, the position of the Roma in international law offers a useful illustration of this problem of protection.

THE CASE OF THE EUROPEAN ROMA

Falling into a nether-category in the minority typology is Europe's largest and poorest minority: the Roma, more commonly (and pejoratively) known as 'Gypsies'. The Roma are the most visible case of a group that does not seem to fall neatly into any one category, though 'ethnic minority' seems to be the best fit. International law has not clearly weighed in on this topic and it has been left to states to determine the applicability of various treaties to their different minority groups, with the result that Roma are treated differently (with regard to the scope of the law) in different states. There are about ten to twelve million Roma in Europe alone, at a minimum equal to the population of Hungary. By most accounts, they began arriving in Europe from India in large numbers as early as a millennium ago, and have been present nearly everywhere in Europe for centuries. Many Roma have immigrated in recent years as part of the wave of Eastern Europeans heading to Western Europe, but the vast majority have not. Yet, they are frequently considered foreigners in their own countries, that is, where they live and enjoy citizenship, often with terrible implications for their well-being and freedom. Immigrants, in any standard sense of the term, they are not.

Are they indigenous, then? Kymlicka (2007, 2011) argues that the UN has singled out indigenous peoples—for whom a clear definition is not given in any treaty or legal document (see Office of the High Commissioner for Human Rights 2010, section I)—as separate from other minorities in part because of their extraordinary vulnerability and powerlessness, and the general urgency of their situation. The Roma clearly fit these criteria, and some have argued that the best way to protect the cultural autonomy and reduce the vulnerability of Roma individuals might be through a recognition of indigenous status akin to the one accorded the Sámi people in Finland's constitution. Indeed, Kymlicka (2011) notes that some Roma leaders, as well as some leaders of Afro-Latino, Palestinian, Chechen, Kurdish, Dalit, and Tibetan rights movements, have begun to consider recasting their claims as ones of embattled indigenous peoples rather than oppressed minorities. They would be following the lead of the Ahwaz, an Arabic-speaking minority in Iran, who have stopped sending their leaders to the UN Working Group on Minorities in favour of the UN Working Group on Indigenous People. But the term 'indigenous people', as used by the UN, also implies that they have been colonised in their homeland—until recently almost always understood as in the 'New World'—by distant peoples; the Roma obviously have not been. In any case, it would be an uphill battle to gain acceptance for the idea that Roma in, say, Ukraine or France are 'indigenous' as the term is popularly understood, especially given the xenophobic perception of Roma as 'foreigners' in many countries.

This leaves the other 'homeland minority' candidate group: national minorities. Are Roma candidates for recognition as national minorities in Europe? Coming back to the problem that got us on this taxonomic journey in the first place, the European Framework Convention for the Protection of National Minorities does not define 'national minority', leaving it to the states themselves to determine the scope of the relevant law. Many states included their own definitions in their reservations upon accession to the treaty. For example:

> The Republic of Estonia understands the term 'national minorities', which is not defined in the Framework Convention for the Protection of National Minorities, as follows: [they] are considered as 'national minority' those citizens of Estonia who reside on the territory of Estonia; maintain longstanding, firm and lasting ties with Estonia; are distinct from Estonians on the basis of their ethnic, cultural, religious or linguistic characteristics; are motivated by a concern to preserve together their cultural traditions, their religion or their language, which constitute the basis of their common identity. (Council of Europe 1995)

Such a definition seems to include Romani citizens, and Estonia's reservation does not explicitly exclude them or name only a few groups to which the treaty does apply, although it has been criticised for restricting FCNM protections to *citizens*. As it turns out, though, the Roma do not fit the definition of 'national minorities' applied by certain other states, since they are not residing on an historical 'home' territory nor are they territorially concentrated or bound. Austria, for example, applies the FCNM to those groups that 'live and traditionally have had their home in parts of the territory of the Republic of Austria' (Council of Europe 1995). Other states do not offer a definition, or they refer to a domestic legal code, leaving it up to internal and often ad hoc policy decisions to determine whether the state's treaty obligations pertain to the Roma. No states *explicitly* exclude Roma, but some seem to exclude members of this group by way of specifying which *other* groups the Convention will apply to. For example, The Kingdom of the Netherlands says only that it 'will apply the Framework Convention to the Frisians' (and it is probably not a coincidence that The Netherlands explicitly labelled them as national minorities at a time when some Frisian activists have begun to refer to themselves as indigenous) (Onsman 2004). Other states go out of their way to include the Roma; still others deny the existence of any 'national minorities' whatsoever on their territory and assert that their ratification of the Framework Convention is meant as an act of solidarity with other, more diverse, states.

Then where does that leave the Roma? The existing typology for ethnocultural groups—established as the Council of Europe, the EU, and other international bodies attempted to formulate standards for their protection and on which domestic governments rely in their own policy-making—seems to need refining (or abandoning). That the world's only legally binding human rights treaty aimed explicitly at protecting ethnic minorities should allow states to circumscribe the target population in a way that can leave out Europe's largest single ethnic minority group is a serious lacuna, not only because this group suffers from the worst forms of human rights abuses Europe has seen since the Balkan Wars and the most degrading poverty on the continent, but also because it is such a clear example of the pressing need for governments to recognise the link between human development and human rights (including the contested categories of 'minority' and 'group rights'), a link whose importance supposedly played a key role in instigating the development of existing indigenous and minority protection regimes and domestic multiculturalist policies in the first place. There is some progress where the Roma are concerned, as more and more their exclusion from the historical and diplomatic use of the term 'national minorities' (as sub-state groups) is being contested (Kymlicka 2007, 203), but the recognition gap they face in many states remains a troubling example of the inadequacy of the current European system that puts classification before protection rather than treating classification and protection simultaneously or dialectically, with each being relevant for the other.

While the Roma may be the largest and most visible case, other European groups also fall into the recognition gap. The Pomak (a Bulgarian-speaking Muslim minority) and longstanding ethnic Macedonians in Bulgaria are two examples. Although both groups consider themselves a distinct people, the Bulgarian government claims that they are in fact ethnic Bulgarians, stripping them of the recognition necessary for them to claim minority protections under domestic law or through the FCNM. (Human Rights Council

2011). In many places, linguistic minorities are denied language protections and are subject to cultural and linguistic assimilation because their governments do not recognise them as an ethic minority. For example, it was not until 2014, nearly a decade after the entry into force of the European Framework Convention, that the government of the United Kingdom recognised the Cornish people as a national minority, affording them the protections already enjoyed by other UK Celtic peoples: the Scots, Welsh, and Irish (Milmo 2014). In these cases, as with the Roma in certain places, groups that need and would otherwise be covered by existing (binding) treaties such as the European Framework Convention for the Protection of National Minorities are denied certain rights because, it is argued, those laws don't apply to them. They are not *recognised* as legitimate rights-holders within the context of that particular treaty. Labels matter.

While determining which category various ethnocultural groups in Europe and elsewhere belong to is difficult, it is necessary so long as different categories of peoples are understood to possess different rights and be in need of different protections for their cultures as well as their individual members. This reality illuminates a discrepancy between how lists of human rights have evolved and how those rights might be justified. On the one hand, the international human rights protection regime is structured to protect minorities that fall into certain categories. Groups get different kinds of protection depending on the group into which they fall. These categories, as we have seen, are ill-defined and left to considerable interpretation on the part of states (sometimes, it is fair to say, for good reason). Moreover, the specific rights to which members of different categories can lay claim differ. These differences, however, have more to do with the political evolution of the regime than the particular vulnerabilities of the groups (Kymlicka 2007). It is not obvious, for example, that the Navajo in the United States are more culturally vulnerable than the Cornish in the UK (though in human development terms their needs are undeniably greater). However the rights that the Navajo are understood to possess are far more powerful than those the Cornish are understood to possess. I am not denying that indigenous groups have unique vulnerabilities and therefore have unique claims: they undoubtedly do. My point here is simply that the dividing line between different types of minorities is vague and often highly politicized, and the *recognised* claims of each group (which may or may not map precisely onto their justifiable claims) are even more so. This problem is exacerbated for groups that, unlike the Navajo (an indigenous people), or the Cornish (a national minority), do not seem to fall neatly into *any* established, legally recognised category (the Roma, for example), or *do* seem to fall into one of these categories but are not so *recognised* by their government (for example the Pomak in Bulgaria).

Thus, I argue that the international (minority) human rights protection regime is out of step with an understanding of human rights as responses to historic and contemporary vulnerabilities, aimed at protecting the dignity of all, an understanding like the one James W. Nickel proposes. Nickel (2007) makes a compelling case for both minority and group rights that rests not on one's identification with a certain category of minority group but rather on the existence of a certain need that is not met or cannot be met by existing rights. He makes a case for protections against *non-standard* (but still common, serious, and remediable) threats, a significant re-thinking of the kinds of rights that make good candidates for legal protection. A typology of rights that responds to vulnerability and need as well as to historical protection gaps—as Nickel (2007), Shue (1996), and others persuasively argue human rights should do—does not correspond neatly to the international typology of vulnerable ethnocultural groups as it is currently divided (with respect to indigenous peoples and national minorities, with significant overlaps and gaps). The result is a protection gap that is manifested in several forms. Many human rights scholars, including Nickel and Shue, make strong cases for basing protection upon lived vulnerabilities and suffering. Sometimes this means elaborating new norms targeted at under-protected groups. But such an approach tends towards elaborate, top-down typologising of human beings and of the human experience, an exercise that Nickel and others recognise will never result in perfect coverage. Yet the type of protection gap that results most directly from this slippery system of classification is also the one that has not been clearly articulated and explored: the recognition gap.

CONCLUSIONS

Once the United Nations, the Council of Europe, the African Union, and other international and multilateral organizations chose to move beyond their core 'universal' human rights declarations and treaties, they did so—perhaps quite naturally—by focusing their instruments of protection on particular groups of people: minorities of varying kinds, indigenous peoples, women, children, persons with disabilities, and so on. That is, the international community has in many cases tried to close the protection gap by identifying more kinds of minorities with more specific vulnerabilities, and writing up more declarations and treaties. But perhaps the process, if not the approach itself, needs to be re-thought. Despite these advancements, acute vulnerabilities remain as these regimes, while specialised, still fail to account for the particular disadvantages of certain groups. Moreover, and crucially, for a person to claim such protections, she must be *recognised* by her state authorities as the appropriate 'type' of minority. Otherwise, the rules will not apply to her. In all of these cases, labels matter.

The existence of the recognition gap points to a need to refine, or perhaps retire, the existing typology of ethnocultural groups. At the same time, there is a clear tension between the need to reduce as much as possible all forms of serious vulnerability, while not allowing the human rights system to become overly fragmented and unwieldy. Indeterminate proliferation, generating 'an impractically and implausibly long list' (Shue 1996, 29), does not really seem to be the answer. Already, '[p]erhaps lists of human rights have gotten too long' (Nickel 2007, 96). Even those theorists who do not advocate for an ultra-minimalist handful of legal rights stop well short of calling for open-ended treaty proliferation.[2] Drawing up of new international standards is no small task. It is complicated, expensive, and extremely time consuming. And there is no guarantee that the time, money, and effort invested will be rewarded with a new treaty. Furthermore, while more nimbly targeted, fine-grained international human rights instruments offer the promise of pulling many groups from the normative gap, they also come with the risk of widening the recognition gap. The more narrowly drawn the target population, the easier it is for authorities to pick and choose who will be recognised as rights-holders under the new treaty.

Perhaps a bottom-up exploration of the recognition gap, conducted through case studies and with the involvement of groups such as the Roma and Pomak peoples in Europe, or other groups elsewhere, can help identify needed protections in terms broad enough to encompass more groups but without losing the specificity necessary to ensure that the protections do their job. But how do we reach a balance between the universality to which the human rights system aspires and the specificity that it requires? Is there a 'sweet spot' in which a working typology of minority groups is no longer grossly inadequate and increasingly unstable? Is such a typology necessary, or even desirable, for human rights law and policy to function properly? Can revising or abolishing it help address the politics of recognition that have generated such a legal typology in the first place?

Beginning to answer these questions will take us far beyond the space I have here, but unpacking the protection gap from which they spring is crucial for anyone seeking to reduce and eliminate the vulnerabilities that threaten so many ethnocultural minorities (and others). Many parts of this general protection gap have been identified elsewhere, and one of these, the implementation gap, plays a significant role in the continued marginalization, suffering, and disempowerment of many. Another, the normative gap, receives justified attention for calling out the ways in which existing human rights norms remain blind to many threats. But a third, which I am calling the 'recognition gap', also traps individuals and groups for whom protections *do* in fact exist, but either (1) their lack of recognition by their own governments precludes them from benefiting from those protections or accessing those recourses to justice, or (2) the target group recognised by the existing norms is so narrowly drawn as to miss covering analogous groups that share these vulnerabilities. As long as it is left to states to confer political recognition based on top-down labeling decisions, rather than on bottom-up self-identification and acknowledgment of specific lived vulnerabilities, then even our existing international human rights norms will offer uneven protection at best to society's most vulnerable ethnocultural groups.

NOTES

1. This chapter is about legal human rights and leaves aside the broader categories of 'moral' or 'natural' rights. Here and elsewhere I use the term 'law' broadly, to refer to international conventions, treaties, covenants, and, in some cases, declarations or articles therein that have attained the force of law as a result of having been interpreted as expressions of international customary law. These are the instruments that are meant to be the impetus, and set standards, for domestic human rights legislation.

2. See Kymlicka (2011) for a helpful discussion with respect to the indigenous-minority divide; see Nickel (2007, chapter 6), for a broader treatment of 'The List Question;' see also International Council on Human Rights Policy 2006 for a discussion of pros and cons of resolving protection gaps through hard law (i.e., norm proliferation) versus other, soft law mechanisms. See Rawls (1999) for an example of an ultra-minimalist view (and list) of human rights.

REFERENCES

Amnesty International. 2015. "Why Are the Rohingya Fleeing Myanmar?" *Amnesty International.* May 28. Accessed June 22, 2015. https://www.amnesty.org/en/latest/news/2015/05/why-are-the-rohingya-fleeing-myanmar/.

AWID. 2015. *Protection Gaps for Sexual Rights: Side Event at the 30th Session of the Human Rights Council.* September 25. Accessed October 29, 2015. http://www.awid.org/news-and-analysis/protection-gaps-sexual-rights-side-event-30th-session-human-rights-council.

Batchelor, Carol A. 1995. "Stateless Persons: Some Gaps in International Protection." *International Journal of Refugee Law* 7: 232–59.

CBS/Reuters. 2014. "Sochi Mayor: There Are No Gays Here." CBSNews.com. January 28. Accessed June 23, 2015. http://www.cbsnews.com/news/sochi-mayor-there-are-no-gays-here/.

Clarance, William. 1997. "Field Strategy for the Protection of Human Rights." *International Journal of Refugee Law* 9 (2): 229–54.

Clark, Ann Marie. 2001. *Diplomacy of Conscience: Amnesty International and Changing Human Rights Norms.* Princeton: Princeton University Press.

Council of Europe. 1995. *Framework Convention for the Protection of National Minorities.* Strasbourg: Council of Europe, February 1. Accessed March 5, 2009. http://conventions.coe.int/Treaty/EN/Treaties/Html/157.htm.

Cultural Survival. 2015. *Who Are Indigenous Peoples?* Accessed October 30, 2015. http://www.culturalsurvival.org/who-are-indigenous-peoples.

DailyMail.com. 2007. "'We don't have any gays in Iran,' Iranian President Tells Ivy League Audience." September 25. Accessed June 22, 2015. http://www.dailymail.co.uk/news/article-483746/We-dont-gays-Iran-Iranian-president-tells-Ivy-League-audience.html.

Forsythe, David P. 2012. *Human Rights in International Relations* 3rd edition. Cambridge: Cambridge University Press.

Freeman, Michael A. 2011. *Human Rights: An Interdisciplinary Approach.* 2nd ed. Cambridge: Polity Press.

Guest, Iain, and Francoise Bouchet-Saulnier. 1997. "International Law and Reality: The Protection Gap." In *World in Crisis: Populations in Danger at the End of the 20th Century*, by

Médicins Sans Frontières/Doctors Without Borders, edited by Julia Groenewold and Eve Porte. London: Routledge.

Hafner-Burton, Emilie M., and Kiyoteru Tsutsui. 2005. "Human Rights in a Globalizing World: The Paradox of Empty Promises." *American Journal of Sociology* 110 (5): 1373–411.

Haglund, LaDawn, and Robin Stryker. 2015. *Closing the Rights Gap: From Human Rights to Social Transformation.* Oakland: University of California Press.

Hamling, Amie. 2014. "Rohingya: the most persecuted refugees in the world." Amnesty International. August 13. Accessed June 22, 2015. http://www.amnesty.org.au/refugees/comments/35290/.

Human Rights Council. 2011. "Report of the Independent Expert on Minority Issues: Addendum, Mission to Bulgaria." January 3. Accessed June 24, 2015. http://www.ohchr.org/Documents/HRBodies/HRCouncil/RegularSession/Session19/A-HRC-19-56-Add2_en.pdf.

International Council on Human Rights Policy. 2006. "Human Rights Standards: Learning from Experience." Relief Web, September 1. Accessed June 22, 2015. http://reliefweb.int/report/world/human-rights-standards-learning-experience.

International Working Group for Indigenous Affairs. 2015. *The Indigenous World.* Accessed June 22, 2015. http://www.iwgia.org/regions/.

Kasperson, Roger E., and John Lundblad. 1982. "Closing the Protection Gap: Setting Health Standards for Nuclear Power Workers." *Environment: Science and Policy for Sustainable Development* 24 (10): 14–38.

Kosko, Stacy J. 2013. "Agency Vulnerability, Participation, and the Self-Determination of Indigenous Peoples." *Journal of Global Ethics* 9 (3): 293–310.

Kymlicka, Will. 1992. "The Rights of Minority Cultures: Reply to Kukathas." *Political Theory* 20 (1): 140–46.

Kymlicka, Will. 2007. *Multicultural Odysseys: Navigating the New International Politics of Diversity.* New York: Oxford University Press.

Kymlicka, Will. 2011. "Beyond the Indigenous/Minority Dichotomy?" In *Reflections on the UN Declaration on the Rights of Indigenous Peoples*, edited by Stephen Allen and Alexandra Xanthaki, 183–208. Oxford: Hart Publishing.

Landman, Tood. 2005. *Protecting Human Rights: A Comparative Study.* Washington, DC: Georgetown University Press.

Milmo, Cahal. 2014. "Cornish People Formally Declared a National Minority along with Scots, Welsh and Irish." *Independent,* April 23. Accessed June 22, 2015. http://www.independent.co.uk/news/uk/politics/cornish-people-formally-declared-a-national-minority-along-with-scots-welsh-and-irish-9278725.html.

Murphy, Maggie. 2012. "International Human Rights Law and Older People: Gaps, Fragments and Loopholes." OHCHR Open-Ended Working Group on Ageing, HelpAge International, August. Accessed June 29, 2013. http://social.un.org/ageing-working-group/documents/GapsinprotectionofolderpeoplesrightsAugust2012.pdf.

Nickel, James W. 2007. *Making Sense of Human Rights.* 2nd ed. Malden, MA: Blackwell.

Office of the High Commissioner for Human Rights. 2011. *Discriminatory Laws and Practices and Acts of Violence against Individuals Based on Their Sexual Orientation.* Geneva, Switzerland: United Nations. Accessed June 29, 2013. www2.ohchr.org/english/bodies/hrcouncil/docs/19session/A.HRC.19.41_English.pdf.

Onsman, Andrys. 2004. *Defining Indigeneity in the Twenty-First Century:-A Case Study of the Frisians.* Lewiston: Edwin Mellen Press.

Rawls, John. 1999. *The Law of Peoples.* Cambridge, MA: Harvard University Press.

Shue, Henry. 1996. *Basic Rights: Subsistence, Affluence, and U.S. Foreign Policy.* Princeton University Press.

Türk, Volker, and Rebecca Dowd. 2014. "Protection Gaps." In *The Oxford Handbook of Refugee and Forced Migration Studies*, edited by Elena Fiddian-Qasmiyeh, Gil Loescher, Katy Long, and Nando Sigona. Oxford: Oxford University Press. Accessed October 29, 2015. http://www.oxfordhandbooks.com/view/10.1093/oxfordhb/9780199652433.001.0001/oxfordhb-9780199652433-e-024#.

UNHCR. 1951. "Convention and Protocol Relating to the Status of Refugees." Accessed June 22, 2015. http://www.unhcr.org/3b66c2aa10.html.

Index

Anaya, James, 134. *See also* indigenous peoples
Annas, Julia, 101
Aristotle, 43–44, 67, 87, 101, 103. *See also* virtue ethics

Bentham, Jeremy, 75, 76–77. *See also* utilitarianism, Hedonic Utopia
broken world, 6, 30; affluent philosophy, 32n2; Rawlsian Favourable conditions, 16; survival lottery, 16, 30, 32n1. *See also* communitarianism; Hobbes, Thomas; Locke, John; Nozick, Robert; utilitarianism, human utilitarian; utilitarianism, hedonic utopia;

capability approach, 8, 76, 82–84, 85, 141; capabilities as metric, 57, 125–126; John Rawls, 125–127; Nussbaum versus Sen, 86–89, 110–111; public reason, 110–111; stakeholding, 125–129. *See also* indigenous peoples; Nussbaum, Martha; Sen, Amartya
classical liberalism, 8
communitarianism, 28; broken world, 28–30; loyalty, 29; transgenerational community, 28
cosmopolitanism, 3, 66

De-Shalit, Avner, 28–30. *See also* communitarianism

egalitarianism, 8

future ethics, 31; importance of history, 31; moral imagination, 31

Habermas, Jürgen, x
Hobbes, Thomas, 54; and broken world, 20–22
Honneth, Axel, x
Hooker, Brad, 82
Hursthouse, Rosalind, 101

indigenous peoples, 7, 138, 176, 179, 181, 183, 186; capability approach, 134; explained, 133; first nations residential schools, 138; healing, 138, 139–142; international law, 136–137; liberal multiculturalism, 134–135; liberal theory, 134–137; national minorities, 181, 182; rights, 1, 143, 181; stolen generations, 138; Sami, 181; trauma, 138–139. *See also* Maori

justice and alliances, 95, 98–99, 100, 101–102; ad hoc collaboration, 99–100; character, 95; collective actors, 106; collective identity, 107; comparative versus categorical, 101, 103
justice as comparative, 4, 6, 37, 54, 55, 57, 59–61, 85, 103, 112; open-endedness, 84; utilitarianism, 76, 83–84

justice as healing, 138–142; comparative, 140; distribution, 141; historical trauma theory, 139; remembering, 140; resilience, 140; rights, 141
justice as stakeholding, 7; capability approach ; Green, T. H., 119–121; Hegel, G. W. F., 118; political liberalism, 123–124; political stability, 122–123; principle of justice, 115, 117; reciprocity, 123–124; stakeholder economy, 116–117. *See also* capability approach; public reason
justice as a virtue, 7, 95, 101; motivation, 106–108; multidimensionality, 37, 103, 109
justice in regulation, 153; autonomous agency, 167–170; classical liberalism, 165–166; economic regulation, 153–154, 155–156, 165, 166, 167, 169–170; environmental regulation, 157; libertarianism, 164–165, 165; market limits, 161–163; modern liberalism, 166–167; paternalism, 154, 167; property, 164–167; Rawls, John, 158–161; regulation theory, 154–158; rights, 165–167; social regulation, 155–158, 169, 170; utilitarianism, 161–167, 167

Kymlicka, Will, 134–136, 180, 183

libertarianism, 8
Locke, John, 15; and broken world, 17, 22–24

Maori, 7, 138, 142; colonisation, 138, 143; creation narratives, 142, 144; reciprocity, 143, 144–145; rights and obligations, 143, 144; whakapapa (genealogical layering, relationships), 142–143; whanau ora policy, 145
Mill, John Stuart, 25–26, 27, 27–28, 76, 76–77, 121. *See also* utilitarianism, human utilitarian

Nozick, Robert, 17–19; *Anarchy, State, and Utopia*, 17–19; Lockean proviso, 17; principled anarchist, 18; property rights, 15
Nussbaum, Martha, 3–4, 6, 75, 80, 82, 141; Aristotle, 86; emotions, 107; frontiers of justice, 3, 3–4, 87–88; list of capabilities, 111; overlapping consensus, 88–89, 126–127; Rawls, John, 88–89, 126–127

Plato, 67
Pettit, Philip, 82
pluralism : worldviews, x
public reason, x–xi, 53–54, 104, 109–110, 110–111, 121–122, 123; framework, 63–64, 69; open partiality, xi; utilitarianism, 90, 160

Rawls, John, 79; criticisms of, 122; favourable conditions, 2, 6, 16; justice as fairness, 54, 65, 78, 79; *Law of Peoples*, 2, 62–63; overlapping consensus, 80, 121, 124; political liberalism, x, 7, 53, 80, 121, 126; realistic utopia, 81. *See also* theory of justice

Sen, Amartya, 75, 80, 81–86, 87–89; approach versus theory, 75, 85–86; flute example, 61; idea of justice, 4, 86, 100, 101, 103; incompleteness, 60–61, 61, 70, 70–71, 76, 78, 83–84, 84–85; Rawls, John, 125–126
Sidgwick, Henry, 75, 77, 79
Singer, Peter: 'Famine, Affluence, and Morality', ix
Smith, Adam, 64, 69; impartial spectator, 65, 66–67, 69; original position, 65; theory of moral sentiments, 67, 78
Smith, Linda. *See* indigenous peoples, remembering

theory of justice, ix, 1–2, 5, 76, 112, 121, 122, 124–125; criticisms of, 3; extensions of, 3; incompleteness, 78; just savings, 30; original position, 1–3, 54, 61, 63, 64, 66, 67, 76, 82; primary goods, 2, 44, 57, 80, 82, 84, 124–126; principles of justice, 2, 43, 54, 57, 62–63, 80, 82, 159, 173–174; utilitarianism, 77, 79

Thomson, Judith Jarvis : 'A Defense of Abortion', ix
transitional justice, 6; accountability, 37; compromise views, 38–41; criminal justice, 36–38; defined, 35; democracy, 35, 48–49; forgiveness, 45; justice gap, 43; moral judgment, 35; recognition, 47–48; restorative justice, 44–46

utilitarianism, 6, 24, 75, 81–86; hedonic utopia, 24–25, 26, 27; human Utilitarian, 25–26, 26–27, 27, 28; sum-ranking, 81, 95, 98, 100–101; welfarism, 81

Van Parijs, Philippe, 82
virtue ethics, 7, 100, 106, 112–113; dilemmas, 104–105; flourishing, 108, 145; motivation, 106–107; practical reason, 102, 106, 109–111; relationships, 101

Walzer, Michael, 161
Williams, Bernard, 76

Contributors

Thom Brooks is Professor of Law and Government at Durham University. He is the author of *Punishment* (Routledge, 2012), *Hegel's Political Philosophy: A Systematic Reading of the Philosophy of Right* (2013), and *Becoming British: UK Citizenship Examined* (2016), and coeditor with Martha C. Nussbaum of *Rawl's Political Liberalism* (2015). He has held visiting positions at the universities of Oxford, St Andrews, Uppsala, and Yale.

Rutger Claassen is Associate Professor of Ethics & Political Philosophy in the Department of Philosophy at Utrecht University. He holds MA degrees in Law and Philosophy, and obtained his PhD in 2008 for a dissertation about the moral limits of markets. He has published in journals such as *Economic & Philosophy, Inquiry, Law & Philosophy, Journal of Social Philosophy and Politics*, and *Philosophy & Economics*. He also regularly publishes articles and books in Dutch, to bring philosophy to a broader audience.

Jay Drydyk is Professor of Philosophy at Carleton University, a former president of the International Development Ethics Association, and a Fellow of the Human Development and Capability Association. He is the co-author of *Displacement by Development* (2011).

Stacy J. Kosko is Research Professor in the Department of Government and Politics and Assistant Director of the minor in International Development and Conflict Management at the University of Maryland, and an Academy of Innovation and Entrepreneurship Distinguished Fellow. She has consulted for the World Bank on human rights and social inclusion and for Romanian NGO Ovidiu Rom on minority education. Before joining the University of

Maryland, she was the Deputy Director of The Advocacy Project, a Washington, DC–based human rights organization.

Tim Mulgan is Professor of Philosophy at the University of Auckland, and Professor of Moral and Political Philosophy at the University of St Andrews. He is the author of *The Demands of Consequentialism* (2001), *Future People* (Oxford University Press, 2006), *Understanding Utilitarianism* (2007), *Ethics for a Broken World* (2011), and *Purpose in the Universe: The Moral and Metaphysical Case for Ananthropocentric Purposivism* (2015).

Colleen Murphy is Associate Professor in the College of Law and the Departments of Philosophy and Political Science at the University of Illinois at Urbana-Champaign. Prior to joining the Illinois faculty, she was an Associate Professor of Philosophy at Texas A&M University. During 2010–2011, she was a Laurence S. Rockefeller Visiting Faculty Fellow at the University Center for Human Values at Princeton University. She is the author of *A Moral Theory of Political Reconciliation* (2010), and *The Conceptual Foundations of Transitional Justice* (forthcoming).

Mozaffar Qizilbash is Professor of Politics, Economics and Philosophy at the University of York. He has held previous positions at the Universities of Southampton and East Anglia. He is a former vice president of the Human Development and Capabilities Association. His work falls at the intersection of economics and philosophy and his publications have focussed on topics relating to well-being, incommensurability, capability, and utilitarianism among other areas.

Amartya Sen is Thomas W. Lamont University Professor, and Professor of Economics and Philosophy, at Harvard University and was until 2004 the Master of Trinity College, Cambridge. His research has ranged over social choice theory, economic theory, ethics and political philosophy, welfare economics, theory of measurement, decision theory, development economics, public health, and gender studies. His books have been translated into more than thirty languages, and his awards include Bharat Ratna (India), Commandeur de la Legion d'Honneur (France), the National Humanities Medal (United States), Ordem do Merito Cientifico (Brazil), Honorary Companion of Honour (UK), Aztec Eagle (Mexico), Edinburgh Medal (UK), the George Marshall Award (United States), the Eisenhauer Medal (United States), and the Nobel Prize in Economics.

Krushil Watene is Lecturer in Philosophy at Massey University, New Zealand. She currently serves on the International Development Ethics Association and is a member of the Australasian Association of Philosophy diversity committee. Previously she was post-doctoral research fellow in the James Henare Māori Research Centre, at the University of Auckland. Krushil belongs to the Ngāti Manu, Te Hikutu, Ngāti Whātua Ōrākei (Māori), and Tongan (Pacific) communities.

www.ingramcontent.com/pod-product-compliance
Lightning Source LLC
LaVergne TN
LVHW100022220926
848483LV00001BA/79
9781783484041